I'LL BE SEEING YOU

K FRENCH

ISBN: 978-1-3999-5214-9

For my mum

Chapter One

JUNE 1939

Mauve hills with their rich soil dwarfed him, while shards of grit and limestone rubbed against the soles of his worn shoes. Somewhere on the outskirts of Castleton, in the heart of the Peak District, Henry Shepherd had taken a wrong turn – now he was far from where he wanted to be.

Sweat trickled between his shoulder blades. He pulled down the peak of his cap to shield his eyes from the brightness of the summer sun and scanned the rocky landscape. He saw a tall, slender spire in the distance. With his spirits lifted, Henry stepped out onto a small country road when, out of nowhere, a blue Sunbeam came speeding past, causing him to lose his balance.

'Bloody idiot! Watch thee sen!' he shouted, raising his fist. He half expected the car to stop, so he readied himself for a fight, but it sped on down the lane leaving a cloud of dust in its wake.

Henry did not care much for their sort – the ones with money. He hated how they tended to look down their noses at the working classes, having never done a decent day's work and with no regard for anyone but themselves.

With his hands trembling, he took a cigarette from his jacket pocket, lit it, then drew on it heavily, sucking in his cheeks before slowly releasing the smoke. A tiny bit of tobacco stuck to his tongue, so he spat it to the ground.

As he navigated his way towards the village, through fields of sheep, his mind wandered to home. He was tired of the grey stifling city with its sulphurous smog. Of late, he was tired of listening to the constant talk of war. Not that it came as a surprise to anyone. The government had already built air-raid shelters and handed out gas masks. Of course, nobody wanted it to happen; everyone was still hoping for a peaceful solution, particularly as the previous war was still fresh in the minds of the nation. Still, 'thanks to bloody Hitler, it is certain to happen,' his dad had said. Eager for adventure and excitement, Henry and his brother had replied with, 'we're ready to fight for King and country.' His mum had given her opinion on the matter with a quick slap to the back of their heads. Henry rubbed a sweaty palm over his neck and smiled to himself. He didn't know who was worse, Hitler or his mum.

As Henry neared the village, he took in the view, unspoilt apart from the Sunbeam that had nearly run him down half a mile back. It had come off the road and was now stationary in front of a tree. Steam escaped from the engine. But from what Henry could see, the car wasn't too damaged.

'Serves 'em reight,' he said to himself. He had half a mind to have it out with the driver for being reckless, but he thought better of it. He was too tired to argue. Instead, he felt the urge to gloat. He took his time walking over to the car. As he neared, he could hear raised voices.

'Ey up!' shouted Henry. 'What 'ave we 'ere, then?' He leaned forward and looked inside with a faint grin, half mocking, half smiling, but his smile soon dropped when he saw who was inside. He took off his cap and used it to wipe the sweat from his eyes. He wanted to walk away, but his mum would never forgive him if he didn't behave chivalrously.

'Want some help?' he asked, patting the car's bonnet. Henry could tell, from their appearance, and the way they looked back at him that these were not the type of girls he was used to meeting.

'What do you think?' replied the driver tilting her head back and lowering her eyelids. 'We don't plan on staying here all day.' She wrinkled her freckled nose. Henry's jaw tensed.

'Excuse my friend. She appears to have left her manners at home. Let me express our gratitude on her behalf,' replied a second girl. Henry watched as she opened the rear car door to step out. 'Maybe I can be of assistance?'

'No...no,' he stammered. Henry felt his cheeks redden as he glanced at the prettiest girl he'd ever seen or was ever likely to see again, with her striking green eyes, honey-coloured hair and warm smile. 'You stay in the car, miss. I can manage,' he said, his eyes crinkling at the corners.

'Are you sure?'

Henry nodded before putting his cap back on.

'What's your name?' she asked.

'Henry, miss. Henry Shepherd.'

'Well, Henry Shepherd, it's a good job you came along

when you did, otherwise we'd have been stuck here all day. I am Frances, Frances Eton.' She offered him her gloved hand. Henry wiped his hand on the back of his trousers before gently shaking hers. Frances smiled. She looked at her friends who were gawking at her. 'This is Alice, and the crazy redhead who got us into this mess is Harriette.'

Henry nodded to them both. Harriette looked affronted, and the girl Alice began sobbing into her handkerchief; strands of dark hair had fallen loose onto her face.

'I don't care much for cars, but I know enough to recognise this is an expensive one,' said Henry, looking at the undercarriage. 'Shame you almost buggered it up.'

'I beg your pardon!' said Harriette.

'Well, just because it's fast, doesn't mean you should drive like you're in the Grand Prix.'

Harriette glared at him, but Henry ignored her. 'Reight, what you need to do is—'

'Are you sure you know what you're doing. You don't look the sort to have ever owned a car,' said Harriette.

'Harriette!' said Frances.

'Do you want my help or not?' replied Henry. Harriette shrugged.

'Of course we do. Don't we, Harriette?' said Frances. She turned to Henry. 'I'm sorry, she doesn't mean to...'

'Don't fret,' winked Henry. 'I've got thick skin.' He walked around to the front of the car. 'Reight, milady,' he shouted to Harriette. 'You need to put the car in reverse and lightly put your foot on the pedal. I'll push. Ready?' Harriette did as he instructed. 'Easy does it!' shouted Henry. 'I don't want to fall flat on me face.' He pushed the car back onto the road, almost tearing his trousers.

'I do hope my father's car is alright. He is not going to be happy to hear I drove it into a tree,' said Harriette.

'There's just a small dent at the front, nothing you can't fix,' said Henry. ''Appen you'll be more careful next time. You could have done some serious damage or, worse, killed someone.' Henry looked at Frances; he noticed she had a mark on her head. He wanted to shake Harriette by the shoulders to knock some sense into her for all the good it would do.

'Yes, well,' said Harriette. 'You can spare me the lecture.'

'I did warn her to slow down,' said Frances. 'She never listens.'

'Are you alright, miss?' he asked.

'Me? I'm perfectly fine. Why?'

'It looks like you hit your head.' He raised his hand to her face as though to touch her forehead, then, in one swift movement, pulled back. Frances took out a little compact mirror from her clutch and checked her appearance.

'Oh,' she said. There was no blood, but a small lump had appeared.

'It looks sore, Frances,' said her friend, Alice, wiping away tears. 'Are you sure you're alright?'

'I'll live.'

'Maybe you should see a doctor,' said Henry. Frances giggled.

'What's so funny?' asked Henry.

'Her father is a doctor,' said Harriette, drumming her fingers on the steering wheel. Henry looked away. 'I think he likes you, Frances.'

'Shush, Harriette!' said Frances. 'I'm sorry if my friend—'

'No need to apologise,' replied Henry. He picked up his

jacket and satchel; then he looked around and tried to figure out which way he needed to go to get home.

'Are you lost?' asked Frances.

'Aye,' he replied, smiling.

'Where are you going?' asked Alice.

'Sheffield.'

'That's where we live,' Frances said.

'Is it now?' A teasing smile curled his lips.

'Maybe we could give him a lift, Harriette?' whispered Frances. 'He did just save our bacon.' Harriette glared at her.

Henry's smile broadened. 'Don't fret thee sen. I'll find me own way back. I always do.'

'See,' said Harriette. 'He'll be fine.' Henry noticed the look of relief on her face.

'Don't you have a compass?' asked Alice.

'Aye, but it's brock.'

'Brock?' questioned Alice.

'Broken,' whispered Frances.

'Oh, I see,' said Alice.

'I'll be off then.' His attention fixed on Frances. He didn't care too much for the other two.

'Goodbye,' replied Frances. 'And thank you once again.' She smiled at him.

A warm feeling spread through him as she held his gaze.

'Yes, thank you,' said Alice, still dabbing her eyes. Frances scowled at Harriette.

'Thank you,' said Harriette.

'I'll be seeing you, Frances Eton,' said Henry. 'And if tha wants to make it home in one piece,' he said to Harriette, 'slow bloody down!'

Harriette saluted.

He took one last look at Frances, trying to memorise every inch of her beautiful face. He watched as they drove away. The corners of his lips rose, and his cheeks dimpled. He was smitten, but then he looked down at his grubby fingernails and was reminded of who he was. Frances belonged to a different class, one he had no understanding of. Not that he was ashamed of where he came from, only he couldn't picture her hanging out with him and his friends on a Saturday night or coming to his house for tea. Her delicate nature didn't belong in the grey harshness of his world.

Henry rested his back against a dry-stone wall overlooking a stream and stretched out all six feet of his tired body. He pulled out his compass from his trouser pocket. 'Some bloody use this is.' He rubbed his thumb over the glass and held it up to the light to examine its intricacies. He watched as the light bounced off its smooth metal surface. The words on the back had faded over time, but Henry had committed to memory what remained of the worn inscription.

Now and forever yours, Ivy.

The compass had once belonged to his grandfather. It had been a gift from his wife, Henry's paternal grandmother, then given to Henry after his grandfather had passed. It was the only thing of value Henry possessed. He placed a grateful kiss on the glass. 'My lucky charm,' he whispered. Although broken, it had led him to Frances Eton. He would never let it out of his sight. He held it tight and hoped it would lead him to her again.

He finished off the last of his sandwich, then closed his eyes and listened to the birds and the occasional buzzing insect. Soon he began to daydream about what it would be like to live in such an idyllic setting, away from all the pollution, to wake every morning and be greeted by rolling hills of vast green, and blue skies.

Henry Shepherd had always felt different from his brothers, who seemed content and accepting of the path their lives were taking. He never heard them talk about leaving Sheffield. His eldest brother Harold had a job and a wife, and Arthur was a law unto himself and content to live at home. Only Henry dared to dream of something different – a life away from the city.

Harold worked for English Steel; he had worked for them from an early age. Now he held a good position, which had not always been the case. He and countless others had had to work hard to prove themselves. During the Depression, it had been a struggle for many to hold on to their jobs. Henry remembered the strains those times put on his family, especially his dad. It was commonplace to see unemployed men walking down the street, feeling like failures due to their inability to provide for their families. Times had been hard, but with increasing tensions in Europe and the all too real threat of war, the factories were alive again making weapons and ammunition.

It was Harold who had found Henry work at the factory. Henry had been grateful, but it was not what he had in mind when he finished school. Mr Green, Henry's teacher, often remarked that Henry was intelligent enough to get his higher school certificate. Henry had wanted to see more of the world. But for generations, his family had either worked in the factories or down the pits. Now, all Henry saw was the inside of a hot factory full of molten iron and heavy, dangerous machinery. He worked long hours and was often physically and emotionally exhausted. Although only twenty-one, at times, his body felt like a man twice his age. He had seen how factories had consumed the lives of hard-working men. Henry didn't want to die young, so when the weather was fine and when he wasn't too tired, he would take himself off for some respite in the Peak District. Out here he could breathe; he could forget, if only for a brief time, that he was a steelworker from Sheffield.

Having momentarily forgotten where he was, Henry pushed himself up. From the position of the sun, he knew if he was going to find his way back before dark, he needed to leave soon.

As he set out on the long journey home, he kicked the dirt and cursed. He looked at his hands. He'd never paid attention to them before, but now he resented their calloused roughness, like fine sandpaper. He would have liked to have studied further, maybe then his hands would be smooth, like the ones he imagined Frances was accustomed to seeing. But folks in his neighbourhood thought you were 'getting above thee sen' if you talked about going to university. Working with their hands was all they understood. Steel ran through their veins; it was in their blood.

He wondered if Frances had made it back safely. If he hadn't got lost, he would have made the train back from Hope station and would, right now, be home seated by the fire eating his supper. His stomach growled at the thought of food. But − he pulled out his compass from his pocket and smiled − if he had not taken a wrong turn, he would never have met Frances Eton.

Chapter Two

Frances slumped back in her seat. 'I don't know why you always have to be so rude, Harriette. What was wrong with giving him a lift?'

'Do you have to ask, Frances? He was so uncouth. Father wouldn't approve of allowing his sort in his car.'

'Yes, and he sounded like he had a mouth full of York-shire pudding,' said Alice. Harriette burst into laughter.

Frances loved her friends dearly, but sometimes she thought them a bit too stuck up. Harriette had always been the same; even though she was the eldest of the three, she infuriated Frances sometimes. At school she was constantly getting into mischief and blaming it on others. Not that Harriette ever cared. Yet she had been kind enough to drive them in her dad's car, so they could enjoy the countryside, even if Harriette's driving scared Frances out of her wits most of the time and had almost got them all killed.

The heat and sweet smell of summer filled the small

space of the car. Frances pushed her hair behind her ear and slid her fingers inside the collar on her dress to touch her skin as she recalled how Henry had looked at her, like they were old friends. She wondered if he would make it home before nightfall.

Of course, her mother wouldn't approve of him, but she didn't approve of many things these days, like Frances trying out the latest fashions for one. When Frances was growing up, she had always thought her mother to be stylish, but now she seemed out of touch. Frances didn't dare tell her she wanted to colour her hair platinum blonde like Jean Harlow's.

'Please can we go back for him?' asked Frances. She felt guilty for not insisting on giving him a lift. She'd never encountered someone like Henry before, self-possessed and eyes so full of life. He was unlike any of the boys she knew back home. 'He must be exhausted after helping us, and now he has to walk miles home.'

'He's as strong as an ox,' commented Harriette. 'His *kind* are built for hard work.'

'What do you mean, 'his kind'?'

'Why do you care so much?' said Alice. 'I thought you didn't have time for boys.'

'I don't.'

'Pull the other one,' said Harriette. 'You can admit it to us, Frances; after all, we are your friends.'

'Just because I wanted to give him a lift home, it doesn't mean anything.'

'Be that as it may, it's too late now,' said Harriette. 'Besides, it's not like you're ever going to see him again.' Harriette glanced at the other two girls before turning her eyes back to the road. 'Shame he was so grubby though because he was rather dishy. A bit of a rough diamond.'

Frances didn't comment.

'Did you see his blue eyes?' replied Alice. 'He looked just like Gary Cooper.' She fanned her face. 'And he was so strong. The way he effortlessly pushed the car back onto the road.'

'Yes, but did you see his worn shoes and tired-looking shirt,' said Harriette.

Frances hadn't noticed his clothing; she had been too busy admiring his face, with his hair the colour of Whitby jet, and his angular, squared jaw. She thought him devilishly handsome, all dark and mysterious, like a character from the movies.

'What did you think, Frances?' asked Harriette. Frances turned her head.

'I suppose he was good-looking,' she said quietly.

'Suppose?' Alice squealed. 'You've never been a good liar, Frances Eton.'

'Who says I'm lying?' replied Frances, her voice high pitched. Her friends knew her too well. Unlike them, his slightly dishevelled appearance didn't bother her. It fuelled her imagination and added to his mystique. She recalled his shirt sleeves rolled up past his elbows to reveal muscular arms. She couldn't stop herself from thinking about the fine dark hairs on his forearms or his big strong hands. Her cheeks flushed as she pictured him holding her tightly at the waist and gazing into her eyes before kissing her passionately like all the Hollywood men kissed their leading ladies. It was Frances' dream to be one of those leading ladies.

When she was fifteen, she had plucked up the courage to

audition for an operatic society. She told no one, not even her best friend, Agnes, for fear of her mother finding out and putting a stop to her plans. But when they offered her a place, she came clean to her father. Luckily for Frances, he didn't oppose the idea. The company wasn't anything fancy, but the shows were well attended, and Frances loved being on stage. She was never cast as the leading lady but one night the lead, Betty Smith, fell ill and Frances had to step in.

Unfortunately, after this performance, Frances was forced to quit when the producer, Miss Simmons, gave her a sharp telling-off for kissing the leading man too passionately. It wasn't Frances' fault. It had been Richard's, or tricky Dickie as Frances nicknamed him, who had got carried away – and not for the first time. He was always making suggestive comments, but Frances, being so young and inexperienced, never knew what to say back. She tried her best to avoid him; she didn't like the fact his clothes always reeked of tobacco. Later, she discovered that Miss Simmons had declared her love for Richard, but Richard had run off with one of the chorus girls. It had caused quite the scandal.

As soon as she was able to, Frances planned to travel to London. Her singing voice was better than average, and she was a good dancer – she was certain she would find work in one of the many theatres in the capital. Hopefully, a big movie producer would discover her and whisk her off to America. Then she would show Miss Simmons.

'Frances is in love,' teased Alice.

'I hope not,' said Harriette. 'I don't think Charles would approve. He's been trying to court you for months.'

'*Charles*,' repeated Frances; she'd forgotten all about him. Charles was Harriette's cousin. His family were rich, so this made him potential husband material in her mother's eyes. Her mother had gone on and on about him for days after she had discovered he'd bought Frances a bottle of expensive French perfume. Frances didn't like the smell of it, but she didn't have the heart to tell Charles.

'You know he's not going to give up. He's simply mad about you.'

Frances crossed her arms and sighed. It's not that she didn't think Charles was a nice person; it was more she didn't find him attractive. For one, he was too short, and his skin was too pink. He was kind and attentive – a bit too attentive for her liking.

'Just think,' said Harriette, 'if you did marry him, we would be related.'

'We could be your bridesmaids,' giggled Alice turning fully to face her.

Frances stuck her tongue out at her. 'I've told you before, I am not getting married!'

'Why not? Don't you want a big white wedding, a husband, and children?'

'No, I do not!' groaned Frances. 'I want adventure! To go to Hollywood and become a movie star.' She gestured with her arms spread out wide.

'I don't think your mother would approve,' said Harriette. 'Besides, you're not old enough to go on your own.'

'It's my eighteenth birthday soon.'

'You are silly,' said Alice.

'What's so silly about that?' huffed Frances.

'Because America is miles away, and besides, you've never had any real acting lessons. Remember when we performed 'A Midsummer Night's Dream'?' said Harriette.

'I played an amazing Titania, didn't I?'

'Yes, and Alice was a fantastic Bottom!' said Harriette laughing.

Frances put her hand to her mouth to stop herself from laughing.

'It's not funny,' snapped Alice. 'I didn't have a choice. Mrs Broughton didn't like me. She was never going to give me a female part. She cast me as Bottom out of spite.'

'Poor Alice,' said Frances.

'What time is it?' asked Alice.

Frances looked at the wristwatch her parents had bought her for her birthday last year. 'It's almost five o'clock,' she replied.

'My goodness,' cried Alice. 'I have to get home. My parents have friends coming round for dinner. They're expecting me to be there. I need to change my dress.'

'Don't worry!' said Harriette. 'We'll be home before you can say God save the King! We'll sing a song to pass the time. Frances, you start us off! Sing that one, you know the one, "Sing as We Go".'

'No, not that one,' said Alice. 'Sing "Love is the Sweetest Thing"...please!'

'How about "Jeepers Creepers" then?' said Harriette.

'Yes, sing that one!' said Alice.

Chapter Three

An exhausted, hungry Henry walked through the front door and his mum rushed to greet him.

'Where've you been? We were about to put out a chuffing search party?' She smoothed down her pinafore.

'I got lost.'

His dad was sitting in his favourite armchair by the fireplace with his eyes closed, listening to the latest news on the wireless, a folded newspaper on his lap.

'Lost?' He scratched the bristles on his chin.

'I'll tell you all about it, but first I need to spend a penny.'

He ran into the yard, wincing as his shoes rubbed against the blisters on his feet. He lived in a courtyard made up of seven more houses. They shared the two toilets that were in the yard. It wasn't pleasant, especially in the winter months when the pipes froze, but it was all Henry had ever known.

Back inside, he fell into a heap at the small kitchen table.

Potatoes, a mutton chop, and a couple of slices of bread and margarine were waiting for him.

'Do you want a cup of tea, love?' asked his mum.

'That'll be smashing,' he replied. "You're a lifesaver. Has our Harold been?'

'Aye, 'bout an hour ago,' said his dad.

'You're lucky,' said his mum. 'He nearly finished off thee supper.' She placed a hot tea in front of him and seated herself down opposite. She pushed her spectacles up her nose and watched him as he ate. Henry pictured Frances' face and her warm smile.

'What you grinning at, you daft bugger?' she asked.

'Nowt,' said Henry. He dropped a couple of sugar lumps into his tea.

'Come on, what's gone on?' she asked.

'I met a girl today,' he said, finding it hard to suppress his smile.

'A girl?' said his dad. He switched off the wireless and came to stand in the doorway.

'Aye and she was the prettiest girl I've ever seen,' said Henry.

'Take that silly look off your face and eat thee supper.' His mum tutted.

'What's her name?' asked his dad.

'Frances Eton. She's not like rest around here.' He took a bite of his bread.

'And what's wrong with the girls round here?' snapped his mum.

'Nowt.'

'Where's she from?' asked his dad.

'Sheffield,' replied Henry.

'Oh, aye, whereabouts?' asked his dad.

'I don't know. I didn't get a chance to ask.'

'It's like that chuffing fairy tale,' laughed his dad. 'You know which one I mean.'

'Fairy tale? I've heard it all now,' said his mum, shaking her head.

'I suppose it is, in a way,' said Henry.

'Stuff and nonsense! And don't you go encouraging him!' She pointed her finger at her husband. 'He's soppy enough! He hasn't got time to be chasing girls all over Sheffield. He works every chuffing day.'

'Leave him be,' remarked his dad, placing his thumbs under the straps of his trouser braces. 'It's only a bit of fun.'

'Aye well. He ought not to be getting any ideas,' said his mum.

'She's too good for the likes of me anyway but, if things were different, she'd be the one, Mum.'

'What are you going on about, "the one"? You've only just met her, and you don't even know where she lives.' His mum tutted again. 'And I'll have none of that! Nobody is too good for my boys.'

'If I had money... who knows, maybe.' Henry had finished eating. He put his plate in the sink. 'I'm going up. It's been a long day. Night, Dad, night, Mum.'

Henry entered the attic room he shared with his brother Arthur. Arthur wasn't home yet. Henry had not expected him to be; he was always out late. Henry stripped down to his vest and underpants and climbed into bed, his legs aching, and pulled the sheets up to his neck. He knew he wouldn't sleep much because he couldn't get Frances out of his mind. He didn't care what his mum thought. He had felt a connection to Frances, and he sensed she had felt it too, despite their differences. God willing, he would meet her again one day.

The tapping of the knocker-upper's pole against his neighbour's window woke Henry. It was still dark outside. He dressed quickly, shivering in the cold. As he did, he glanced over at Arthur's bed. His brother was lying on his back, snoring lightly.

Henry shook his head when he noticed Arthur's black eye. It was the third one this month. He just hoped the other bloke had come off worse. If is mum really knew what Arthur got up to, there would be hell to pay. He made his way down the stairs that led into the living room. He felt well rested, despite thinking about Frances.

His parents were already sitting around the kitchen table having breakfast. Pouring himself a cup of tea, he glanced at his mum.

'What time did our Arthur get in?' he asked.

'Bout midnight,' she replied. 'No idea what he gets up to.'

Henry looked at her and shifted in his seat before taking a sip of his tea.

'He's probably got a lass somewhere.' His dad winked at Henry.

'Well, if he's got a girl,' said his mum, 'appen she's a fighter, cos he came home with another belter.' She started to clear away the breakfast things.

Henry and his dad grinned. She scowled at them both.

'Reight, I'm off. I've got to drop off two frocks at Mrs Martin's house.' She pulled on her coat and fastened it. Checking her reflection in the mirror above the fireplace, she brushed her hair away from her eyes, positioned her hat on her head, and then secured it with a decorative pin.

'Hang on,' said his dad. 'I'll walk with thee t' tram stop. Then I'll head off to work.' He got up, dragged on his steel-capped boots and work jacket, and put on his cap before taking a last gulp of tea.

'Put the rest of the things in the pantry, Henry love,' said his mum. 'I don't want to be late. Mrs Martin is a good customer.'

'No problem, Mum. I'll see you both tonight.'

'See you tonight, love.'

Henry watched them leave. He thought how much older and tired they looked these days. He often wished his mum would make herself some new clothes, instead of pandering to the needs of all those snobs who didn't appreciate what they had.

After having her children, instead of going out to work, his mum had stayed at home to raise them. She'd worked from home doing alterations and repairs, and sometimes even other people's laundry. Their home might have been small, but it was spotless; with other people's clothes hanging about, it had to be.

During the 1920s and the Depression, only a select few could afford to buy new clothes. This meant Mary, his mum, was often busy making copies of the latest styles seen in the

French magazines for her more well-off customers. Over the years she had built a reputation for herself as a dressmaker. Although it wasn't regular work, it paid well when it came in. Like the one she had been working on recently. Mrs Martin lived in one of the more affluent parts of Sheffield and his mum was heading there that morning.

'Any tea left in pot?' Henry turned to see his dishevelled brother, Arthur, standing in the doorway dressed in just his trousers and vest.

'Aye but it's cold.' He watched as his brother put the kettle under the tap and filled it.

'What happened to you?' asked Henry. 'We won't be allowed in the City Hall with you looking like a lout.' Henry was looking forward to the dance. It promised to be a good night, if Arthur could make it through the evening without getting into trouble.

'It was just a scuffle. I earned a few bob too, and we'll be reight; I know someone on the door. Now, pass us the jam!'

'I'm off to work. Make sure you tidy up after thissen.'

'Will do, Mother.'

As Henry closed the front door and set off walking, his thoughts drifted once more to Frances. He wondered if she was awake. He sighed at the image of her lying in her bed, her soft hair caressing her pillow. He wondered if she was dreaming about him as he had dreamed about her. His heart sank. She won't even remember me when she wakes, he thought. Why would she? I'm nobody to her. I'm just kidding missen if I think I am ever going to see her again.

Henry decided to put her to the back of his mind, at least until he finished work. He couldn't afford a distraction.

Overseeing hot iron and molten metal, gigantic hammers and huge rollers, daydreaming could cost him his life if anything went wrong. He decided it was safer to concentrate on the machinery and not on the girl of his dreams.

Chapter Four

Agnes had been ill with a fever. She was still in her bed when Frances and her father arrived that morning, her brown hair pinned away from her pale face. After Frances' father had finished examining her, he went to speak with Agnes' mother and left the two of them alone to talk. Although Agnes was getting better, she was still fragile, so Frances did most of the talking. She told her all about her day trip to the Peak District.

'Sounds like you had fun,' said Agnes smiling. 'You were lucky that boy was walking past.'

Frances returned her smile. 'Unquestionably.' She looked down at her painted nails. 'Although, I doubt I'll ever see him again. Besides, can you imagine what mother would say? You know she's trying to marry me off? I mean... me... married... ha! Ridiculous!'

After Frances had left school, she first noticed her mother appeared to change towards her. In her mother's eyes

Frances was no longer a little girl. From the moment Frances turned sixteen, her mother was always dropping hints about taking Frances with her to London to meet her friends – in particular, her friends' sons. But the pressure had cranked up a gear on the lead-up to Frances' eighteenth birthday. Arguments broke out when her mother realised that Frances was not willing to go along with her mother's plan. This had caused a rift between them.

'It wouldn't be so bad,' said Agnes.

'Agnes Shaw, you wash your mouth out!' Frances put her hand over her heart and pretended to be hurt.

'I'm sorry, Frances, but you act like it's the end of the world and, well, I don't. I think I'd like to get married and have children one day.'

'One day, maybe, but I want to live a little first. There's a big world out there and I for one intend on seeing it; I thought you wanted to experience all it had to offer too. I thought you were going to come with me. I thought you wanted all the glitz and the glamour. What about those wild parties where we would drink champagne cocktails and stay out until morning? What's changed?'

'I do want all those things... but being stuck here, lying in this bed has given me time to think' – she sighed and looked around – 'about my life.' Agnes started coughing.

Frances passed her the glass of water that was sitting on a bedside cabinet. Frances didn't speak for a moment; she just looked at her friend. She noticed again how different she looked; she was a lot thinner and had dark shadows beneath her eyes.

'I should go now and let you get some rest. You look tired. Hurry and get better soon. I'm so bored without you.'

Frances reached for her friend's hand and patted it gently. She took the glass from her and placed it back down on the cabinet. 'I do hope you will be well enough to go to the dance with me this Saturday like we planned. We haven't been out together in such a long time.'

'I'm really sorry, Frances, but I don't think I will feel up to it.'

'What shall I do? I can't go on my own?'

'I really am sorry; I know you had your heart set on going but I'm only just starting to feel myself again.'

'Things never work out for me,' said Frances, more to herself. A frown line appeared between her brows but then she remembered her manners. 'Never mind, I'm sure there will be other dances. You just concentrate on getting well again.'

'Goodbye, Frances. Do visit again soon.' Agnes laid her head back down on her pillow and watched as Frances walked towards the door.

'Goodbye, Agnes.'

Her father was still talking to Agnes' mother; she was paying him a half crown for his visit when Frances came down the stairs. She adored her father. He was a gentle, kind man, who never spoke ill of anyone.

'Are you ready to leave, Frances?' asked her father. Frances nodded.

They left Agnes' house and climbed into the car. Frances rested her head on the car window and sighed. She started to bite her nails – a bad habit she had developed when she was worried.

'I have a few more calls to make before we head for home. Cheer up, dear! Agnes will be well again in no time.'

As the city came into view, Frances' heart sank even further at the sight of grey hopelessness. Vast plumes of smoke and vapour rose from large chimneys behind blackened buildings. Whistles screamed from the steelworks and iron clanked. She caught glimpses inside cellars where men were gathered around small hot furnaces, making knives. The streets were busy with shoppers. Enviously, Frances watched them go about their business. They drove past a cinema and Frances' heart soared as she read the latest film posters. There was a new George Formby film being advertised. Agnes liked him: maybe they could go together. Before she could ask her father when he thought Agnes would be well enough to go out again, she was forced forward in her seat. The car had come to an abrupt halt behind a stationary tram. Straightening herself, she noticed a crowd had gathered, causing all traffic to come to a standstill. Frances' father beeped the car horn, but nobody moved.

'I'd better take a look,' he said. He turned off the car engine and opened his door.

'Be careful!' said Frances, putting her hand on his arm.

'I always am,' he said. He smiled and left her sitting in the car.

Frances watched as he made his way to where the crowd had gathered and politely pushed himself to the front. Deciding to see for herself what all the commotion was, she stepped out of the car and headed towards the crowd. But she didn't get far before her father reappeared and stopped her in her tracks.

'Fetch me my bag, Frances, please!' he shouted.

'What is it, Father?' asked Frances.

'No time to explain – hurry!'

Sensing the urgency of the situation, Frances ran back to the car and reached inside for his black bag. She handed it to her father and then followed closely behind him as he made his way back through the crowd. She gasped as she took in the scene before her. A man lay on the ground, his face contorted with pain. His right leg was twisted at an impossible angle; blood pooled around his head. Frances guessed he must have been hit by the tram and come off his bicycle when she spotted it crushed under the tram's wheels. Her stomach muscles tensed. An overwhelming sensation to vomit consumed her.

'Frances, hold this while I...' said her father, but she couldn't move. 'Frances! Don't just stand there; I need your help!'

'Father,' she replied. She wiped tears from her eyes. 'I...I...'

'Pull yourself together! Now hold the man's hand! Talk to him! If not, go and wait for me in the car because you're no use to me here!'

Standing there forced to watch this man suffer, she managed to get a grip on her emotions. As though another person had taken over her body, she found herself kneeling beside the man and holding his hand as her father tried to stop the bleeding.

'Hello, my name's Frances; what's yours?' she said softly.

'Stanley, miss,' he cried.

'It's nice to meet you, Stanley. Now, Stanley, I know you must be in terrible pain right now, but you mustn't worry. My father is an excellent doctor, and he will take exceptional care of you. Try to relax.' She gently squeezed his hand to comfort him. 'There, there Stanley.' She looked over at her father who encouraged her to keep talking. 'Tell me about your family Stanley; are you married?'

'I am, miss. My wife, Audrey has just had a baby... It's our first.' He tried to smile at Frances. 'I was on my way to the hospital after I received the news. I was so excited I didn't see the tram.' Frances had to pinch a little bit of skin between her thumb and finger to stop herself from crying. 'Is it bad? Am I going to die?' he asked. Sweat trickled down his forehead and he had turned deathly pale.

'No, no, you're going to be fine, Stanley, just fine. I promise.'

When the police arrived, they cleared away the crowd and spoke at length to the visibly shaken tram driver. Frances' father did all he could for the young man at the scene before he was taken by ambulance to the nearby hospital.

Frances desperately wanted to get home, to rid herself of her dirty clothes and take a hot bath. She was exhausted. She didn't understand how her father could handle so much illness and suffering daily, when all Frances had felt like doing was bursting into tears at the sight of the young man's mangled leg. But she was glad she had been there to help. She just prayed Stanley would be all right.

'You're late. Edna is not happy. She's had dinner waiting,' said her mother, her posture rigid. Frances inwardly groaned. She could tell when her mother was in one of her moods.

'Good, I'm famished,' replied Frances' father.

'I'm not hungry. I just want to go to my room,' replied

Frances. From the look on her mother's face, this wasn't going to be a pleasant family dinner.

'We need to talk,' said her mother. Her bobbed, wavy hair was immaculate, and her steely blue eyes were fixed on Frances.

'Do we have to?' said Frances. Her mother opened her mouth to speak, but then closed it again when Frances' brother Thomas entered the room. Frances edged towards the door. Her mother shot her a look.

'Good evening, Mother, Father,' said Thomas. He kissed his mother's cheek.

'Good evening, Thomas,' replied Frances' mother, her earlier frostiness disappearing. 'How was your day?'

'You know, can't complain. I was with some friends in Endcliffe Park. We were having a game of cricket.'

'Why weren't you studying like the good boy you are?' said Frances.

'Don't be so churlish!' replied her mother.

'It's alright, Mother,' said Thomas. He turned to Frances. 'It's the holidays or have you forgotten?'

'Have the trenches been roofed over yet, Thomas?' asked Frances' father.

'The shelters are all finished now,' replied Thomas. Thomas looked at Frances. 'So why the long face?'

'I've been trying to discuss my trip to London, Thomas. Frances doesn't want to go, heaven knows why. You'd think she would jump at the chance, instead of being cooped up here all the time,' said Frances' mother.

'It has been a trying day,' said Frances' father. 'Maybe you should leave it, Clarissa.'

'Why? What happened?' asked Thomas.

'There was an accident. Frances is a little shook up.'

'Bad was it, Father?'

'Let's just say the young man will be lucky if he keeps his leg.' Frances gasped.

'It was awful. I can't stop thinking about it,' said Frances.

'You always have been squeamish,' said Thomas.

'Well, we can't all go through life unaffected by everything,' retorted Frances.

'Now, now you two,' said Frances' father.

'If you had listened to me in the first place, and not given in like you always do. Did I not say it was a bad idea for Frances to visit Agnes?'

'And I told you, Clarissa, Agnes is no longer contagious.'

'Yes, but... oh never mind.'

'Well, Mother, you know Frances. She's as stubborn as a mule. You can't have two perfect children,' teased Thomas.

'Indeed,' said Frances' mother.

'I just want to have a bath,' said Frances.

'Can we please get back to the subject of London? I don't see what all the fuss is about, Frances. We could see a show or visit the sights. You know how much you love doing that.' Her mother had tried tirelessly over the past week to convince Frances to accompany her to London but to no avail.

'I'll go with you, Mother,' said Thomas. Frances' eyes widened. Frances hated the way Thomas behaved obsequiously towards their mother. Anyone would have thought he was the youngest child.

'That's sweet of you, Thomas,' said Frances' mother, patting Thomas' hand. 'But I think Frances should come with me.'

'I'm not interested, Mother. I know you have an 'ulterior' motive for asking me to join you. It is more than just the Tower of London you want me to see.'

'Are you going to allow her to speak to me that way, Edward?'

'Well, it's true, Father! Mother has hinted I should be 'seen' more, go out in 'certain circles' as she puts it. I know she thinks I should be trying to attract a suitor and preparing for a husband. It's Mother's wish that I should attend one of the many parties which are taking place, now I'm turning eighteen.'

'Is that so wrong of me?' asked her mother. 'I am only thinking of our daughter's future, Edward.'

'But I don't want a husband! I want to be an actress and have adventures!' declared Frances. 'I'm not like you, Mother!' She glared as Thomas started laughing. 'What's so funny?'

'You. Isn't it about time you let go of this idea of being an actress and grew up? I mean, seriously, you can't even act, and I've heard you singing in your room.'

'Thomas, don't be so unkind to your sister.'

'Sorry, Father. But you cannot honestly think it is a good idea,' said Thomas.

'Two of your old school friends are travelling to London with their mother this week. I ran into Mrs Martin at a local horticultural show. You remember Mrs Martin, Edward?' said Clarissa. He nodded and picked up the newspaper. 'She delighted in telling me about the dresses she was having made just for the occasion.'

Although Frances' mother never raised her voice, Frances could tell she was annoyed. 'Mrs Martin asked after you. She was keen to know what you're doing now.'

'And what did you say?' asked Frances.

'Not a lot,' replied her mother. 'What could I say? She also asked after your brother. She asked if he was married yet. I told her 'No'. I said he was too focused on studying to be a doctor, like his father. You ought to have seen the expression on her face,' tutted her mother. 'Her eyes lit up, and I could see the cogs turning.'

'I know the girls you speak of and no thank you. I have some living to do first before I settle down. It's a big world,' said Thomas.

Frances' mother nodded in agreement. Frances stared at Thomas and then at her mother.

'I see. It's perfectly fine for Thomas to do what he wants, but not me. How is that fair?' She looked to her father for support.

'I said you might visit Mrs Martin,' continued her mother. Frances groaned loudly. 'Maybe her daughters will be a positive influence on you. Then you might stop daydreaming about going to America and focus more on your future here, in England.' She pursed her lips. This was one argument Frances was not going to win.

Edna entered with the dinner tray. Her rotund stature made it difficult to manoeuvre through the doorway.

'Ah, Edna!' said Frances' father. 'Just in time. It smells delicious as always.'

'It's your favourite, Dr Eton, steak and kidney pudding,' said Edna. She placed the serving dishes on the table. 'I'll be off now, good night.'

'Yes, good night, Edna,' replied Frances' mother.

'Good night, Edna,' smiled Frances. 'I'll look forward to

seeing you tomorrow. Maybe you could help me with my knitting again.'

'Knitting, really,' tutted her mother.

'Good night, Frances love. I'd be happy to if I have the time.' She winked at Frances.

Frances liked Edna. She had worked for Frances' parents since they had first arrived in Sheffield. Edna's husband had passed away, and her only son had married and left home. Edna had needed to fill the hole her late husband had left behind. She was a warm lady, unlike her own mother. She looked upon Edna like a grandmother she never had, although she couldn't have been much older than her mother, and Edna doted on Frances.

As Frances lay in her bed later that night, her eyes studying the flower pattern on her curtains, she reflected on her day. Sighing heavily and rolling over onto her stomach, she pushed her face into her pillow and groaned. 'Maybe my plan to go to America is a foolish one! But it's not any more foolish than getting married.'

Chapter Five

By the time Saturday arrived, Frances had managed to put the horrors she had witnessed to the back of her mind, for the time being at least. A big band from London was playing at the City Hall. It was going to be a special night, and Frances was determined not to miss it. She was so preoccupied with deciding on what to wear that she no longer cared about what her mother would have to say when she returned from London. Agnes was feeling a lot better, but she was still too weak to go dancing. Frances had called Harriette and Alice, who were sitting on Frances' bed, helping her choose the right accessories to match her champagne-coloured dress.

'Harriette, what are you doing? Thomas has left already,' Frances teased.

'Will he be there on his own?' asked Harriette.

'If you mean, is he meeting a girl, then I'm afraid I don't know.'

'Do you think tonight might be my chance with him, Frances?'

'With your hair like that, maybe. But I don't think you should get your hopes up.'

Harriette had agreed to let Frances curl and pin her hair on the top of her head. 'Does it really look all right?' Harriette asked.

'Of course, it looks sophisticated.'

Harriette watched as Frances pulled on her stockings and put the final touches to her hair and make-up. 'You're so lucky, Frances. Clothes always hang well on you.'

'You look pretty tonight, Frances,' said Alice. 'I wish I could get my hair to fall like that. It looks like Hedy Lamarr's.'

Alice looked at her reflection in Frances' dressing table mirror and screwed up her face. She should have listened to her mother and not eaten so many sugary treats; her blue flowered dress was a little too snug.

'Thank you,' replied Frances. 'You both look lovely too.' She grabbed her bag from the dressing table and did a little twirl in front of her full-length mirror. She was so excited. Tonight would be her first real dance. 'Are we ready ladies? I'm so nervous,' she declared.

'You? Nervous?' said Harriette. 'What do you possibly have to be nervous about; you look fabulous as always.'

'I don't know. I just have butterflies in my stomach.'

'Seriously?' chuckled Alice. 'You'll soon relax once all the boys start asking you to dance. Boys always fancy you. It's Harriette and I who ought to be nervous—'

'Speak for yourself!' interrupted Harriette. 'I intend to wear holes in my shoes tonight!'

'Are you ready?' called Frances' father from downstairs.

'Coming!' shouted Frances. 'You girls go on; I just need to get one thing.'

Harriette and Alice headed to the hallway. Frances ran into her mother's bedroom, picked up her mother's expensive perfume from the dressing table and dabbed some of it behind her ears before rejoining them.

'Right, do you have your tickets, girls?' asked Frances' father. They all nodded.

He drove them to town and dropped them off outside the City Hall, close to the main entrance. 'Right, stay together girls and remember Thomas will be there to look after you if you require assistance.'

'We will, Father,' said Frances. She leaned in through the open car window and kissed his cheek.

'I'll be outside later to collect you so look for me around here,' he said, waving his finger randomly. 'Have fun, girls.'

'Thank you, Dr Eton,' said Alice.

'Night, Father,' said Frances. She waved him off and turned to her friends.

There was a sizeable queue already forming outside the main doors, but Harriette's father knew the manager, so she led them to the side door.

'Come on, ladies, get a move on!' squealed Harriette. She handed the tickets to the man at the door, and they walked inside together.

Cream columns with red and gold detail bordered the dance floor. The band, dressed in black tie, played on a raised platform at the back of the hall. A woman dressed in an elegant full-length evening gown was standing on the platform, singing into a free-standing microphone. Her voice was low and velvety.

'This is so exciting!' said Alice, jumping up and down.

'Try and act less like a child, Alice, please!' scorned Harriette. 'No boy is going to look at us twice with you behaving as if you've never left the house before.' Harriette turned and walked towards a table at the edge of the dancefloor that was empty. Alice stuck her tongue out at the back of her head.

'Frances!' came a familiar voice. Frances turned her head. Heading towards her, with his blonde hair greased back and his baby face already dripping with perspiration, was Charles. Frances closed her eyes and breathed out slowly before opening them.

'Charles!' she said through clenched teeth.

He took her hand and kissed the back of it. She gently pulled it away, trying hard to hide her disappointment. Why couldn't it be a handsome tall dark stranger, instead of a boy in an expensive suit? she thought.

'You look beautiful, Frances, as always,' he said, smiling. 'Simply radiant and you smell divine.'

'Charles, you mustn't—'

'Charles!' said Harriette. 'Who are you with?'

'Tom and George. Would you girls care for a drink?' he asked, unable to stop staring at Frances.

'Yes please,' said Harriette. 'Ginger beer.'

He looked at Frances and Alice. 'Do you ladies want the same?' he asked. They nodded. 'Right, I'll be back in a jiffy.'

'That's all I need,' declared Frances once he was out of earshot. 'Charles hanging around me all evening.'

'He's harmless,' said Harriette.

'Be that as it may, I won't get rid of him now,' she huffed.

'Just dance with him and then maybe he'll go,' said Alice. Frances raised her eyebrows.

'I love this song!' declared Harriette as the woman began singing a rendition of 'Begin the Beguine'. 'I've heard it a few times on the wireless.'

'Me too,' said Alice. Both started to move in their seat, tapping their feet inconspicuously under the table.

'Look, there's Thomas!' said Harriette.

'Where?' asked Frances. Harriette waved at him and then stopped moving as he started to walk towards them.

'Do I look alright?'

'You look lovely,' said Alice.

'Sis!' said Thomas. 'Ladies.' He nodded to Harriette and Alice, who both fanned their faces and moved to stand next to him. 'What do you think? Not bad, eh?' He looked around the hall completely unaffected by the attention he was getting from Harriette and Alice.

'It's excellent,' replied Frances. She was about to say something else but then Charles returned.

'Thomas,' nodded Charles as he handed the girls their drinks.

'Charlie boy! How are you?' asked Thomas, slapping him on the back.

'I'm well, thank you,' replied Charles.

'You asked my sister to dance yet?'

Frances glared at him.

'Not yet.' He blushed.

'Better get on with it then before some other fellow does. Right, I'm off. If you need me, I'll be just over there.' He pointed to where his friends were all standing talking to some girls. 'Catch you later.'

'Bye,' enthused Harriette, gazing after him liking an adoring puppy.

'Would you care to dance, Frances?' asked Charles.

The band had started to play another song, making it difficult to hear over the music. It was one of Frances' favourites, 'Dancing in the Dark,' so she would have been lying if she had said no. She loved to dance. It was just disheartening it was Charles asking her. She placed her drink down on the table and allowed him to take her hand. He led her to the middle of the dance floor. Once there, he placed one hand softly at the base of her spine and held her hand with his other. She tentatively placed her free hand on his shoulder, and they started to dance slowly. They moved quite well together and, to anybody watching, they would have appeared to be a couple, but his sickly sweet scent and the heat from his hand against the fabric of her dress made her feel uncomfortable. As a distraction, Frances focused on the hundreds of mesmerising lights coming from the giant glitter ball overhead, shining on the couples and on the surrounding surfaces in the hall, making everything look magical.

'Did you know?' said Charles close to her ear. 'That two ounces of gold leaf were used to decorate each of the sixteen pillars.'

'No, I didn't.'

He was about to say something else when they spotted Thomas dancing with a girl. Frances inwardly cursed as he winked over at Charles.

The music then changed to a quickstep. Charles held her tighter, but he was struggling to keep up with the rhythm.

'Do you mind if we sit this one out,' he asked breathlessly.

Frances breathed a sign of relief. She wanted nothing more than to go back to her friends, but she hadn't had the heart to tell him.

'I'm afraid the quickstep isn't my thing,' he said.

'That's alright. I'm feeling quite out of breath myself.' Usually, she loved being on the dancefloor. She envied all the girls that looked like they were having the time of their lives. He held her hand and led her through the sways of people back towards her friends.

When they drew nearer to Harriette and Alice, Frances noticed a young man towering over them. He was handsome but not classically. His hair was thick and dark, and his clothes looked like they struggled to fit over his muscular build. His blue eyes had a sort of murderous intensity about them. Harriette and Alice seemed to squirm in their seats. Frances offered them a calming smile.

'How do,' said the man.

'Hello,' said Alice weakly. Harriette pulled at her arm.

'Don't speak to him, Alice, we don't know who he is.'

'Sorry, me name's Arthur,' he said.

Charles had noticed the young man too. He let go of Frances' hand and puffed up his chest.

'Is he bothering you?' asked Charles, ignoring Arthur. He looked at their worried expressions and chivalrously pushed himself in between them so Arthur couldn't get any closer.

'No, pal,' said Arthur. 'I was just going to ask them to dance.'

'Well, I don't think they want to, so on your way,' instructed Charles.

Arthur turned red in the face. Slightly drunk, he raised his arm as though he was about to punch Charles. Frances tried to move to stop him but, when his arm went back, he almost knocked her over. Harriette jumped up out of her seat and grabbed Charles quickly before he realised what was going on and led him to the dance floor. Alice ran to Frances' aid.

'Are you hurt, Frances?' she asked.

Frances straightened her dress and smoothed a hand over her hair.

'I'm so... so... sorry, miss,' Arthur spluttered.

'That's alright,' she replied. 'No harm is done.'

For an uncomfortably long time, Arthur stared down at her. Frances didn't know where to look. His stare was unnerving. Alice signalled to Frances that maybe they should go to the ladies' room together. Frances took a step towards her.

'Do you want to dance?' asked Arthur.

'Maybe later,' she said politely. Alice grabbed her hand and pulled her away. As Frances looked over her shoulder, he was still standing in the same spot watching her.

'He was strange,' declared Alice when they were safe inside the ladies'. 'Do you think he'll still be waiting when we go back?' Frances said nothing. She checked her appearance in the mirror and applied more lipstick. 'Maybe we should find Thomas and stay with him for the rest of the night,' added Alice.

Harriette was still dancing with Charles when they neared the dance floor. Frances scanned the area for the strange man, but she couldn't spot him anywhere. Alice led her through the crowds of people dancing to the back of the room where Thomas said he would be, but he wasn't there either. They finally spotted him on the dance floor with a different girl from the one earlier, so they waited for him to finish dancing.

Frances was feeling weary, and the music was starting to give her a headache. They had managed to get Harriette's attention, who was walking towards them with Charles close behind.

'There you are!' came a voice behind her, making her jump. 'I've been looking for you all over. How about that dance now?'

She turned around; her eyes came level with a broad chest and, as she lifted her eyes slowly to his face, she swallowed hard. An overconfident smile, which spread across a strong jawline, greeted her.

'I'm sorry, but I'm feeling awfully tired,' she said. 'Do you mind if we don't?'

'Just one dance and then I'll leave you alone. I can't leave tonight without dancing with the most beautiful girl here, now, can I? My name's Arthur; what's yours?'

'Frances,' she replied, and for a second, she thought maybe he wasn't that scary. He put his hand on her waist gently.

'Frances, what are you doing?' whispered Alice.

'Where's the harm in one dance?' she whispered and shrugged. They were about to walk off together when Charles appeared, frowning and red in the face at the sight of this guy having his hands on the girl he considered to be his!

'You again!' he spat. 'Take your hands off her!'

'Walk away now, little man, before I do something I might regret,' said Arthur.

'Little? Who are you calling little?' Charles lifted his fists as though ready for a fight. Arthur looked at him sardonically, which only egged Charles on further.

'Charles, it's fine,' said Frances, coming between them. 'I'm just having one dance with him.'

Arthur took her hand and tried to push his way past Charles, but Charles outstretched his arms to prevent them from moving. Arthur grabbed his shirt and forced him to the ground.

'If you know what's good for thee, you'll stay down,' ordered Arthur. Everyone around them stopped dancing and stared. Charles grew redder in the face.

'Look, maybe it isn't such a good idea,' said Frances to Arthur. She went to walk off, but Arthur grabbed her by the wrist.

'Ouch, you're hurting me. Let me go!'

Thomas came running over with some friends.

'Let her go!' shouted Thomas.

'What's it to thee?' said Arthur. 'I'm not hurting her. We're just going for a dance.'

A crowd had gathered around them. Frances hated that everyone was staring at her. She just wanted to go home. She tried to wriggle free but his hold on her was too tight.

Just then Frances thought she heard someone call Arthur's name. Momentarily distracted, Arthur loosened his grip. Seizing the opportunity, Charles jumped up and punched Arthur in the neck causing Arthur to drop Frances' arm. She rubbed the spot he had held her. Harriette and Alice rushed to her side.

'Come on!' said Harriette. 'Let's leave, the whole place is going to erupt.'

The three headed for the exit as Arthur retaliated and knocked Charles back to the floor with one punch. Frances glanced over her shoulder and saw Thomas and his friends join the fight. She could have sworn she saw someone who resembled the boy from the Peak District grab one of Thomas' friends and fling him off Arthur's back, but she shook it off – it had to be her mind playing tricks on her.

As they neared the door, Frances heard someone yell that the police were on their way. The band had stopped playing and the lights went on; it was suddenly silent, apart from the grunts and groans of the boys fighting. Revellers, scared things were getting out of control, flocked to the doors and out of the building, pushing Frances with them.

The cause of the commotion, Arthur, came running past and almost knocked Frances flying. His shirt was ripped, and his nose was bloody. She heard him shout to someone behind him.

'Come on, Henry, we need to keep moving! The Black Marias will be here soon.'

Frances turned her head. As she did, a cool evening breeze made her shiver. She swallowed hard as her eyes locked with a face – one she never thought she would see again.

Chapter Six

Henry's skin tingled like he had seen a ghost. Standing just outside the door, her honey-coloured hair shimmering in the moonlight, was Frances. She was standing next to the same two girls from the Peak District.

'Come on!' shouted Arthur again.

'You go on!' he called back. 'I'll catch thee up.'

'Please thissen,' said Arthur, and he ran down the road towards the direction of their home.

Henry looked down at his torn jacket and cursed. His mum had permitted him to borrow it on the proviso that he returned it as he found it because it belonged to one of her customers. Henry knew she would throttle him when she discovered its ruined state.

Looking the way he did, Henry was unsure if he should go over to Frances. He wanted to impress her, not scare her away. But he knew, if he didn't, he might never see her again.

Screwing up his courage, he strode purposefully over to where she was standing, the muscles in his stomach tightening. The pavement was filling up with people leaving the dance and, to his relief, her friends hadn't noticed him approach. He took a tentative step closer so there was only a small space between them.

'It's you,' she said.

That familiar warm feeling flowed through Henry's body as his eyes held hers. There was so much he wanted to say to her, but he was rendered mute. Henry couldn't stop staring. He noticed a few tiny freckles on her perfect nose, which sent his pulse racing. He wanted so much to tell her that he hadn't stopped thinking about her; but, hearing the police approach, he sensed precious time slipping away. He knew that if he didn't speak soon, he would never get the opportunity again. He was about to open his mouth to break the silence when a car approached. Henry heard one of Frances' friends call her name from near the car and he knew his time was up. He watched as she bit her bottom lip and mouthed, 'I have to go.'

'Come on, Frances!'

'Can we meet?' Henry blurted out as she turned to walk away.

'Please,' he begged. 'I have to see you again.'

Frances turned quickly back around and whispered, 'I'm not sure. After all, you're a stranger.'

'I'm a harmless stranger,' he teased.

'I must be crazy.' She gave him a playful smile. 'Do you know the Botanical Gardens?' Henry nodded. 'Well, I'll try to be there tomorrow after church.' Then she ran towards the waiting car.

'What time?' called Henry, but it was too late; the car was already driving away.

Henry jumped up into the air; he felt like he was floating. He couldn't stop smiling. People gave him a wide berth as they walked past him on the pavement but he paid no attention to the strange looks they gave him – he was happy and nothing was going to change that. It didn't matter that she hadn't told him what time to be there because, even if he had to wait there all day, he would. He would do anything to see her again.

'What's got into you?' came a voice. The police had cleared the building, and the dance was officially over. 'I thought you'd be long gone by now.'

Rose. In all the excitement he had forgotten about her. Henry had run into her a few times at other dances. He'd kissed her on a couple of occasions, too, but it was nothing serious. Tonight, he had been dancing with Rose before the fight broke out. He liked her because she wasn't complicated like the other girls he knew. She was fun and, more importantly, a great dancer. He knew she fancied him, but he wasn't interested. She was pretty and had a fine figure but, unlike Frances, she didn't fill him with a warm feeling. Without thinking, Henry picked her up and spun her around, making her squeal.

'This is the best day ever!' he said. He put her down and kissed her cheek.

'Henry Shepherd, are you feeling alright?'

'Never better, Rose,' he said. 'Let me walk thee home.'

Chapter Seven

'Not going out today, son?' asked Henry's dad as he listened to the wireless.

'Yes,' replied Henry. He was seated in the chair opposite his dad, reading the newspaper. His mum was in the kitchen cooking. Margaret, Harold's wife was giving her a hand.

'Is our Arthur not up yet?' asked Harold. He was shorter than his two younger brothers and his hair was a light brown, but he was considered just as handsome. He was standing in the doorway of the living room smoking a cigarette.

'He's just nipped out to fetch us some coal. He said he'll be back in a bit,' replied their dad.

'Give us a cig,' said Henry.

'Buy your own,' teased Harold.

'Clear the table!' ordered Margaret.

'Come on, you two!' said their dad. 'Quick, get that table-cloth out of the drawer and put out the knives and forks!'

Henry's mum walked in carrying a plate with bacon and sausages on. His dad started to slice the bread, while his mum fetched the eggs from the range. Henry gave everyone a plate and Margaret collected the pot of tea from the stove.

'Smells lovely, Mum,' said Henry.

Just as everyone was seated around the kitchen table, elbows rubbing elbows, in walked Arthur with a bucket of coal in one hand and a brown paper parcel tucked under his arm.

"Ow do, Harold, Margaret,' nodded Arthur.

'Ow do thissen,' replied Harold. 'Where's tha been?'

'Bit a business,' replied Arthur. Henry looked at him.

'What's thee got under thee arm,' asked his mum.

'Rabbits,' said Arthur.

'Rabbits? Where's thee chuffing got them from?' asked his dad.

'Fell off back of a lorry,' said Arthur. Henry laughed.

'Put em on t' side and come eat thee breakfast before it gets cold,' said his mum.

'Hurry,' said Margaret, smiling. 'Harold and I have got an announcement.'

Henry's mum was silent. She looked from Margaret to Harold. 'You're not, are you?' she whispered, her fork held in mid-air.

Margaret couldn't contain herself any longer. Henry watched on confused. 'Well, I'll go t'foot of our stairs.' Henry's mum couldn't stop smiling and clapping her hands together.

'What did I miss?' asked Henry.

'You're going to be an uncle,' said his mum.

'You dirty beggar!' said Arthur.

'Never mind him,' said Henry to Harold. 'Congratulations, to you both. He's just jealous.' He looked at Arthur. 'Cause he's an ugly chuff.'

'Who thee calling ugly? I'll knock that smug look off that pretty face of yours,' replied Arthur, laughing and pointing his fist at Henry.

Ignoring Arthur, their dad shook Harold's hand vigorously. Margaret and his mum were whispering and laughing about something.

'Only kidding, Harold, me old mucker!' said Arthur. 'Bout time we had some good news for a change.' Arthur slapped Harold on the back as he squeezed himself in around the table.

'A baby,' declared his mum. 'I'd better start knitting. When's it due?'

'Bout February,' said Margaret.

'It's wonderful news,' added his dad. 'Better than what I was listening to on wireless; that Hitler's not chuffing stopping.'

'We'll have no talk of that,' warned their mum. 'Today's a good day.'

'I hope there's not gonna be a war,' said Margaret, looking at Harold, her hand placed protectively over her stomach.

'If there is, we'll beat them bloody Jerries, won't we? We've done it before,' added Arthur.

'I hope it'll sort its sen out. I don't think I could shoot someone,' said Henry.

'Not even a bloody German?' asked Arthur.

'Enough!' said his mum. She glared at Henry's dad. Everyone went silent. Henry carried on eating. 'Reight, have you thought of any names yet?'

'Not yet,' said Margaret.

'I bet your mam and dad are excited,' said their mum. Margaret nodded. 'It's there first grandchild, isn't it?'

'No, second. Remember our Betty has a little one, Edith.'

'That's reight. I completely forgot. I'd forget me head if it weren't screwed on.'

'Reight, I'm off,' said Henry.

'Where to?' asked his mum.

'Nowhere in particular.' Henry looked at his empty plate. 'I just...' He was desperate to get to the Botanical Gardens, but he wasn't going to tell his mum that; he would never hear the end of it. 'I might go and see me mates.'

'What? Dressed in your best shirt?' said his mum.

'I bet he's meeting a lass,' said Harold.

'I'm not.'

'Bit defensive, aren't we?' replied Harold. He looked at Arthur and the two of them started laughing.

'Leave him be,' said Margaret. 'Stop teasing.'

Henry kissed Margaret's cheek. 'Thanks,' he said.

'Well, take your plate to the kitchen,' said his dad.

He cleared his plate and left them all talking about babies. He put his jacket on and headed out the front door. Arthur caught him up.

'Where you really off to?' he asked.

'Just out for a walk,' replied Henry. 'Nowt better to do.'

'It was a good night last night,' said Arthur. He jabbed Henry on the arm playfully.

'It was alright until you got the place shut down,' replied Henry.

'Saw you dancing with that Rose. She's a bit of all right. You seeing her again?'

'No. Rose is a nice girl, but there's someone else,' he said, jabbing Arthur back.

'Who?' asked Arthur.

'Just some girl.'

'Met the girl of my dreams last night too,' he joked. 'A beauty.'

'Is that who the fight was over?'

'Aye, 'appen it were,' replied Arthur.

'Well, I hope she was worth it.'

'Most definitely,' he said, punching Henry on his arm again. 'Although she was a bit posh for my liking. Reight, I'm off. Can you lend me ten bob? Someone owes me money, so I'll give it thee back.' Henry put his hand in his pocket and pulled out some coins.

'I've only got half a crown.'

'Cheers, our kid, I'll catch thee later.'

Henry waited for his brother to disappear before walking to the tram stop. He didn't want anyone to know where he was going. He knew they'd only tease him and say he was being stupid. But ever since bumping into Frances last night, he hadn't quite been himself. All Henry could think about was seeing her again. He guessed that, because she had suggested she would be at the Botanical Gardens, she might live close by. It was a stupid idea; deep down he knew that. She was too good for him, but he couldn't stop thinking about her, and even if she didn't show, he had to try and find her.

Chapter Eight

Frances was seated next to her father in church. He'd never given her the silent treatment before. Thomas had returned home the night before with a swollen eye, so they'd both had to explain to their father what had happened. Frances had tried to tell him it wasn't her fault, but her father refused to listen. He had told her how disappointed he was putting herself and her brother in danger. Frances felt dreadful. Her father had never yelled at her before either. Truth be told, Frances knew her father feared more what her mother would say about the situation when she returned. Although angry at Thomas for fighting, he was grateful to him for protecting his sister's honour.

Thomas was quite proud of his black eye. He said that Charles had come off worse. Frances couldn't help feeling sorry for poor Charles. Her father said that it wouldn't hurt for her to call on the young man and thank him for his efforts.

When they arrived home from church, Edna had cooked them a delicious full breakfast, but Frances had lost her appetite. Instead, she languidly ate her bowl of cereal. Her mother had telephoned to say she would be arriving home that evening with a visitor. Frances dreaded to think whom she had dragged up north with her.

She left her father and her brother reading the Sunday papers and went to her room. She lay on her bed and wrote in her diary. It may not have been a perfect morning, but she didn't allow it to dishearten her. Frances thought about Henry and wondered if he was already waiting in the park. She wasn't sure why she had suggested they meet, but he'd looked so desperate standing there with his jacket torn. She imagined the meeting unfolding in her mind like a classic romantic film. She played it repeatedly, each time delivering her lines differently. Of course, in her mind, she was wonderful like Claudette Colbert in *It Happened One Night*. She knew her decision had been a little rash. What did she know about this Henry? But still, she was glad she had told him to meet her – life was unexciting most days. It was about time she had some fun. Now all she had to do was to talk her father around.

Frances made her way back down the stairs in search of her father. She found him reading a book in his study and smoking his pipe. His room smelled of leather and tobacco.

'Hello, Father.'

He looked up at her from his book, his pipe still held between his teeth. 'Frances,' he replied.

She breathed a sigh of relief that he was no longer giving her the silent treatment. 'I was thinking that...' She ran her fingers along the edge of his beautifully polished walnut writing desk.

'Yes,' inquired her father.

'Well, as it's such a lovely day. I thought I might go for a walk.'

He placed down his book and looked out of the large bay window that overlooked their front lawn. Frances held her breath and waited for him to respond, fearful that he wouldn't allow her to go out.

'Yes, it is rather, isn't it?' said her father.

'It is what?' she asked, confused.

'A lovely day and I think I would like to go for a stroll too.' He rose from his chair and stretched out his arms, his pipe still rigidly fixed in his mouth. He grabbed his jacket from the back of his chair and headed towards the door. Frances waited in his study, unsure of what to do next. She hadn't expected him to let her go so easily and she certainly didn't anticipate him joining her. What if Henry was there already? How would she explain the situation to her father? Why she had suggested a meeting place so close to her home was beyond her. He probably won't even turn up, she mused. After all, she hadn't given him a time. What person in their right mind would hang around a park all day? But what if he did turn up? Panic gripped her heart; she had no idea what she would say to him. He was, after all, a stranger – albeit a handsome one – and she'd be with her father.

'Come on then, Frances. What are you waiting for?' called her father. He wore a brown suit and tie, looking as handsome as ever. He always looked suave and sophisticated, like David Niven, one of her favourite actors. She watched as he headed towards the front door. He was fit and healthy despite his leg, which affected the way he walked. It caused him discomfort, but he never complained about it. He had been badly injured in the war but would always refer to himself as 'one of the lucky ones'.

'Coming!' she replied, grimacing at now having an unwanted chaperone.

They walked side by side in the Botanical Gardens, stopping to admire the flowers. Many of the people out strolling knew her father and so stopped to say hello to him. At one stage, Frances left her father talking to a rather tedious and pompous old man and went for a wander around the old bear pit. She imagined herself walking along the same path with Henry, and a tickling, fluttering sensation erupted in her stomach. She glanced around in case she could see him. Nothing! Her mind was in a whirl; she needed a distraction. Looking for butterflies was usually a good distraction. She headed back towards the flowers. When she grew tired of looking for butterflies, she found her favourite spot underneath the old oak tree.

'I've been looking for you. Are you ready to go home?' asked her father. Frances nodded. She had discreetly placed one of her gloves behind the tree; she planned to make her excuses to go back for it later. They set off walking back up the hill towards the splendid glass pavilion.

'Have you thought about what you're going to do with yourself after your eighteenth birthday? You can't mope around the house all day.'

'No, I haven't, Father,' she replied. 'And I don't mope.'

'Well, maybe you should give nursing some considera- tion.' They had almost reached the main gates when the sun disappeared behind a large black cloud. 'The way you spoke to that young man and kept him calm throughout; I was impressed.'

'I don't think nursing is for me. I would like to take more acting lessons,' replied Frances. She pulled her coat tightly around her as her father held the gate open. It was getting chilly. Most people had begun to leave the park.

'I daresay your mother won't like that. Young ladies don't do that sort of thing. As far as your mother is concerned, young ladies stay at home. But I don't think she could object to nursing. I have friends who work at the hospital up the road. I could have a word with them, if you like, maybe make some enquiries.'

'I suppose it would be better than getting married.'

'Well, with all the trouble in Europe, we may need more nurses soon,' said her father. 'Just think about it; that's all I ask.'

'Do you think it will come to war, Father?' asked Frances. She hadn't given much thought to it; yes, she'd seen the newsreels at the cinema, but Germany was miles away. It seemed unreal to her, all that was happening in Europe. It didn't affect her daily life; for her, life just continued as normal.

'The clouds of war have been gathering for some time now. We thought that Mr Chamberlain waving his bit of paper was the end of it, but Hitler could not be trusted. His increasing brinkmanship has proven that. I am an optimist, Frances; I hope it won't come to war. Nobody wants another one, but I feel we must prepare ourselves for the worst.

Right, we need to hurry before it starts to rain.'

'You go ahead, Father; it appears I've misplaced one of my gloves. I must have left it back where I was sitting.'

'I can wait.'

'No, Father, you'll get wet. I'll see you at the house. Go on ahead. I won't take long.' She forced a smile, her jaw slightly tense. A drop of rain landed on his shoulder. He pulled down the brim of his hat.

'Alright.' He kissed her cheek and headed towards their home.

Frances ran quickly back through the park gates. She collected her glove and then found some shelter to wait out the rain as the clouds darkened overhead.

'Maybe this isn't a good idea after all,' she mumbled to herself.

Chapter Nine

Henry reached the gardens just as the heavens opened. He ran as fast as he could to the large glass pavilion and waited out the downpour with the other Sunday strollers caught in the rain. His heart sank and felt weighty against his ribcage. It had been a wasted journey, a fool's errand; there was no way Frances would be out on a day like this.

Just then, he spotted a familiar face. His spirits lifted slightly. It was one of the girls Frances had been out with when he had first met her. He couldn't remember her name. All he could remember was that she had been sobbing and was quiet, unlike the snooty redhead. Henry was relieved it hadn't been her in the pavilion. Frances' friend was with an elderly lady in a wheelchair, who, although wizened and with thin white hair, looked at tough as old boots, like an old battle-axe. As he glanced over, it was clear the old lady was deaf because he could hear her high-pitched cackle of a voice.

'Do you know that young gentleman, Alice dear?' asked the old lady.

'Who grandmother?' she replied.

'The one there, staring directly at you.' The old woman unabashedly pointed her wooden walking stick with its steel head towards Henry. He looked at Alice, who had followed the direction of the stick. She was looking directly at him and had turned crimson. He felt sorry for her having to put up with the old lady.

He began to walk towards them, past the numerous green plants. It was how Henry imagined the jungle to be. The humidity inside the glasshouse was beginning to make him feel uncomfortable.

Henry waved at Alice, who quickly turned her head and stared outside at the rain trickling down the glass; it was clear to Henry that she was pretending she hadn't noticed him.

'Well?' shouted her grandmother. Several people turned and glanced curiously at the old lady.

'I have no idea who he is,' shouted Alice. Henry thought she resembled a frightened mouse, upset by the undue attention she was receiving by onlookers.

'He's walking over here,' declared her grandmother.

'Excuse me,' said Henry as he politely pushed past an elderly old man and made his way towards Alice. She took a step back as Henry drew closer. Her face flushed.

'Hello again,' said Henry. He stretched out his hand in greeting. She did not reciprocate. Smiling, he dropped his hand to his side. 'You probably don't remember me,' he continued, rubbing his nose. There was no escaping the smell of the old woman's clothes, like mothballs, the kind of smell you got in a museum.

Henry watched as Alice fidgeted with the collar on her coat as though she was struggling to breathe.

'Are you alright?' asked Henry.

'I'm fine,' she replied. 'It's far too hot inside this place all of a sudden.' The old lady fixed her beady eyes on her as though she was waiting for an explanation that failed to arrive.

'We met briefly last Sunday... Peak District. Your friend's car—'

'Alice, who is this man? Tell him to go away,' snapped the old lady. 'I don't like strangers.'

'Yes... I remember now,' Alice murmured, wringing her gloved fingers. She looked as though she desperately wanted this conversation to be over.

Henry didn't care if the old lady wanted him gone. He was determined not to make today a complete waste of time.

'Your friend, Frances, does she live round 'ere?'

'Why yes, she lives just over...' She pointed over her shoulder and then stopped herself from continuing.

'Why is he still here?' said the old lady.

'I don't know, Grandmother,' said Alice. She turned her attention back to Henry. 'Why are you here? And why do you want to know where Frances lives?" she asked.

'Don't fret thissen. I won't be bothering you anymore. It's stopped raining now so I'll be on my way,' he said, still smiling.

The sun had reappeared, lighting up the grey sky. Henry left them and walked outside. He inhaled, smelling the sweet perfume from the rose bushes that filled the air, when he felt a pull on his jacket. Henry turned around. He couldn't believe his eyes. Standing before him was Frances, as beautiful as a rainbow after a storm. Her eyes sparkled through long lashes and her face glistened with droplets of rain.

'Why are you looking at me like that?' Frances placed a strand of hair behind her ear.

'Nowt, it's just you look so... so...'

'What?'

'Beautiful.'

'I doubt that. I probably look more like a drowned rat, but thank you,' she said smiling.

'I didn't think you'd be out in this weather.'

'I almost wasn't.'

'Shall we go for a walk?'

'That would be nice, but just once around the park; my father will wonder where I've got to.'

'Aren't you allowed out?' asked Henry.

'Yes, of course. I'm almost eighteen I'll have you know. Father just worries about me.'

'Why's that?'

'You know.' Henry shook his head. 'Well, because he doesn't want me to get into trouble with... *boys*.' Henry laughed.

'What's so funny?'

'Nowt. Meet a lot of boys then do you?' He grinned.

'I most certainly do not!' Frances folded her arms. 'What are you implying?'

'I'm only teasing,' said Henry hurriedly. 'I can see you're going to be easy to wind up. Come on, let's walk.' He hadn't intended on upsetting her. Having never spoken to a 'proper' young lady before, he sensed he would need to be on his best behaviour if he stood any chance of impressing her.

'So, your dad's protective. I suppose it's only natural. I think I would be if I had a daughter.' Frances looked at him and unfolded her arms.

'Well, he's happy for me to meet with my friends, some of whom are boys, just not *other* boys.'

'And especially boys like me.' Henry smiled broadly.

'Have you travelled far?' she asked.

'Not too far,' he replied. 'I live down t'cliffe. It's not far.'

'Where?' she asked.

'Attercliffe,' he repeated slowly and more pronounced.

'Oh,' she said.

'What's that mean?' he asked.

'Nothing. I didn't mean to sound rude, only I heard that it was, or rather used to be, a rough place.'

'It's not as posh as round 'ere, that's for sure. It's not a bad place though. Folk are decent enough. We take care of our own.'

Henry wasn't offended. He knew it would be hard for her to understand. Where he came from was rough to her, and who could blame her when she lived in such an affluent part of the city. He just hoped she would look beyond where he came from and like him for who he was.

They walked side by side around the flower gardens, their fingers within touching distance. Each took turns listening, while the other talked. Henry soon forgot about time; he was lost in the moment. It was the perfect after-noon. He could not think about anyone or anything else, only Frances. They wandered over to the bear pit that was shaded by the trees. There they rested against the cold stone wall. Their arms gently touched, transmitting warmth. Henry turned. His shoulder pressed into the wall. He watched her as she relaxed her head back, her eyes closed, allowing the small bit of sunlight to warm her face. He was captivated by a tiny pulse that flickered above her collar bone. He longed to touch her, but he didn't want to scare her away.

'When can I see you again?' he asked. Frances opened her eyes and turned her head slightly so she could meet his gaze.

'I'm not sure,' she replied.

'You do want to see me again?' he asked.

'I do, but I don't think we should.' Henry could feel her warm breath on his skin. She smelled heavenly.

'Why?' he asked. Henry usually acted cool around girls; he couldn't care less if he saw them again, but there was nothing usual about this situation. For the first time, Henry felt that he didn't need to put on an act. He wanted to see Frances again and he didn't care who knew it.

'I like you, but it's...' She touched his arm, then quickly pulled away.

'What? Are you worried what people will think?'

'No! Not at all.'

'Then what? I like you and you've just admitted you like me too.'

He reached forward so that the tips of his fingers were softly touching her hand. Slowly, he moved closer. He watched as Frances' eyes flickered from his mouth to his eyes and back to his mouth. She gently bit her bottom lip, causing Henry to swallow hard. His hand now tenderly gripped her upper arm. He lowered his head. Her sweet scent filled his nostrils as he breathed in and parted his lips; he could almost taste her. Frances breathed in deeply and the muscles in Henry's stomach tightened.

Children's voices grew louder as they neared the bear pit and Henry and Frances quickly moved away from each other. Frances blushed as the children and their parents entered the pit.

'I-I must be going now,' she stammered, and dashed for the exit.

'Hang on! I'll walk thee back,' said Henry. He kicked the ground and inwardly cursed. He knew he needed to take things slowly with Frances. She wasn't like the other girls he'd encountered before. The last thing he wanted was to frighten her away – if he hadn't done so already.

Outside the bear pit, Frances hurried on ahead. 'There's no need, honestly. I don't live far,' she said over her shoulder.

'Slow down, Frances, please,' said Henry. He caught up with her and held her arm to bring her to a stop. 'I'd like to walk you back,' he added. He tried to reassure her with his smile, feeling terrible that she was embarrassed. He'd never wanted to upset her. He had just got caught up in the moment.

'I think you should stay here.'

'Why? I can behave missen in public, Scout's honour.' He raised his hands in surrender. 'Me mam brought me up reight, I'll have you know,' he teased.

'Alright, you can walk me to the main gates. I'll be fine from there,' she said. Her flushed cheeks had returned to normal.

'As you wish,' he replied. He gave a gentleman's bow.

At the main gate, they moved to one side to let people pass.

'Shall we meet here again next Saturday?' asked Henry. 'If you don't mind roughing it, and if you're not too busy giving orders to your servants.'

'Don't tease! And no, I'm not too busy. I suppose it would be alright,' replied Frances. 'But don't go getting any ideas.'

'It's a date then,' he chuckled.

'I hope I don't live to regret this.'

'I promise you won't.'

Frances returned his smile and then walked away.

'Until next week,' Henry shouted after her as he watched her leave.

As she reached the other side of the road, she turned and waved. He waved back, and his heart swelled in his chest. He had never felt this way before. He waited until she disappeared around the corner before he headed for home, feeling on top of the world.

Chapter Ten

After she returned home, Frances dashed into the lounge and telephoned Agnes straight away. She urgently wanted to tell her about her meeting with Henry. As usual, Agnes' father answered before passing the telephone to Agnes.

'You won't believe the afternoon I've had,' she whispered into the receiver. 'You'd be proud of me Agnes.' Frances stiffened as the door opened and in walked her father. He looked over at her, before sitting in an armchair and picking up the newspaper. Frances quickly changed the subject. 'I'm so happy you're feeling better, Agnes... yes, of course... yes, Father is here. Indeed, sitting right next to me.' She put her hand over the receiver. 'Agnes says hello.' Agnes giggled on the other end. Then Frances had an idea.

'I would love to, Agnes,' she said. Her father looked at her. 'Next Saturday? Why of course... I'll ask my father.' Frances put her hand over the receiver again. 'Father, Agnes has asked if I could meet her next Saturday afternoon. She's feeling much better now and thinks it would be nice to go for a walk or maybe see a film. Is that alright?'

'Of course,' nodded her father. 'Only if Agnes is feeling up to it, though. Tell her I wouldn't want her to overexert herself.'

'Did you hear that, Agnes?' She turned to her father. 'She said she won't.'

She then continued her conversation with Agnes. 'Splendid, I'll see you then.'

'You are terrible, Frances Eton,' said Agnes. 'Don't go getting me into trouble. I don't know what you're up to. But you must be careful! You know what happens to people who play with fire.'

'Yes, yes, I know. I'll explain everything when I see you.' Frances smiled into the receiver. 'Cheerio, Agnes.' They both hung up.

Frances put her hand to her chest and felt her heart, which was beating amazingly fast.

'Are you alright?' asked her father.

'Yes, of course.'

'It's just that you look a little flustered.'

'Mmm, sorry, Father, what did you say?' mumbled Frances. She couldn't believe how daring she was acting. It was all so exciting. She walked over to her mother's old gramophone. There she pulled out a disc and placed it on the turntable. She lowered the needle carefully onto the record. It crackled slightly because of the static and then out came the soothing voice of Al Jolson, full of warmth and intimacy – 'April Showers'.

'My favourite,' declared her father. 'Care to dance?' He offered Frances his hand.

They danced slowly around the room, both laughing. It reminded Frances of when she was a little girl standing on top of his shoes; he'd moved her about effortlessly back then. My father must have been quite the dancer before his accident, she mused.

'I need to sit down; that's enough excitement for one day,' said her father as the song came to an end. 'Thank you for making an old man happy. I miss dancing.' He kissed her cheek. 'Now I must rest. I have to collect your mother from the station later. Did I tell you that she is bringing someone back with her?'

'Yes, you did, Father. Do we know who it is?'

'She didn't give me many details. Some cousin or other. You know your mother, likes to keep her cards close to her chest.'

'Indeed. Right, I'm going upstairs to have a lie down before tea,' said Frances.

Once upstairs, Frances looked out through her bedroom window and softly ran her fingertips over her lips. In the distance, she could see the Botanical Gardens. Foolishly, she thought that if she spotted Henry she would rush outside and put her arms around him, maybe even let him kiss her. Earlier it had been a close call. She had wanted Henry to kiss her, but she had never kissed a boy before. 'What if I make a mess of it?' Frances turned and caught her reflection in the mirror. 'Henry must never see me like this again,' she said.

She sighed heavily, sat at her dressing table, picked up her hairbrush and began brushing her untidy hair. She hoped it wouldn't rain next Saturday. She also hoped they could spend longer together. A smile spread across her face as she thought about their next meeting and what she might wear. 'I wonder how his lips would feel against mine?' She touched her lips again. 'He has such wonderful lips, such a beautiful smile. Far better than any Hollywood film star.' She giggled. She darted to her wardrobe and started pulling out her dresses. 'I wonder what his favourite colour is. Maybe I should wear my blue dress. The one Agnes likes. It will match his eyes.' There was a gentle tap on her bedroom door.

'Dinner's ready, Frances,' came her father's voice.

'Coming,' replied Frances.

Frances pushed her plate away, having hardly touched her dinner; she was too distracted to eat. She couldn't understand why her stomach felt full of butterflies, making her feel queasy. She patiently waited for her father and Thomas to finish theirs too so she could leave the table. She wanted to go back to her room to be alone with her thoughts. She was only half listening to their conversation. Thomas was recalling some incident that had happened at Barker's Pool. It was known for large crowds gathering to hear people voice their political concerns. Frances yawned. Her father would be leaving soon to collect her mother from the station, and she wanted to be fast asleep in bed before they returned; she didn't want to have to make small talk with her mother's mystery guest.

'You are quiet tonight, Frances; normally we can't get a word in,' teased Thomas.

'Am I?' she replied.

'Yes,' replied her father. 'You've barely touched your food. Are you feeling yourself?'

'I'm just tired. I might go to bed early if you don't mind, Father?'

'I thought you would come with me to collect your mother from the station.'

'Do I have to?'

'No, you don't have to, but it would be nice. You haven't seen each other all week and, besides, it would be nice to have your company,' he said.

'Fine, I'll come with you,' she sulked.

'Good that's settled then. We just have to drop Edna off at the tram stop along the way.' He picked up his cup and finished off his tea.

'Shall I go and see if Edna is ready to leave?' asked Frances.

'That's very good of you,' said her father.

Frances made her way to the kitchen, carrying a few plates with her. She startled Edna, who had been wiping down the sides.

'Ooh, you gave me a fright!' Edna said, clutching her heart. 'I didn't hear you come in.' Edna was permanently flustered and red in the face. It was mainly due to the heat in the kitchen, but her weight didn't help.

'Where would you like me to put these plates?'

'Just pop them in the sink,' she said, nodding. 'I'll wash them when I've finished here.'

'I can wash them. After all, I've nothing better to do,' replied Frances.

'Oh, would you, love? That would be a big help. I don't want to keep your father waiting. I know he has to collect your mother soon.'

'No need to panic; help is at hand,' replied Frances. She was in no hurry to collect her mother. Frances placed the dishes in the sink already filled with hot water and leisurely ran the dishcloth over them. She then sluggishly put the plates in the rack to dry.

'Hurry up, Frances love, your father will wonder where we are,' said Edna, hanging up her pinafore. She fastened her coat and pinned her hat to her hair.

'Finished!' declared Frances. 'Do you have any of those biscuits I love so much, Edna?'

Edna's eyes twinkled. 'In that tin over there,' she said, pointing to an old Rowntree's tin with a picture of King George V's coronation on it.

Frances took a biscuit from the tin. She followed Edna to the front door and out to the car where her father was waiting patiently.

'So, I've got an extra one to feed next week then Dr Eton?' said Edna from the back of the car.

'I'm afraid so, Edna. I hope it won't be too much trouble for you,' replied Edward.

'Do you know who it is?' Edna asked, turning to Frances.

'We have absolutely no idea!' Typical of mother, thought Frances.

'How's your son, Frank, and his wife?'

'He's well, Dr Eton, thanks for asking. Not long now before Joan gives birth. I just wish my Ernest were here to see his first grandchild.' Edna appeared to wipe away a tear. 'It won't be the same without him.'

'No, I'm sure it won't,' said Edward.

'I've been rattling around on my own in that house for far too long now; I can't wait to hear the pitter-patter of tiny feet again, to be wiping the sticky fingerprints off all the furniture and to be giving out cuddles. I'll be run off me feet!' Edna smiled to herself. 'Which brings me on to something, Dr Eton.'

'What's that, Edna?'

'Well, when Frank does have this baby, I might have to stop work—'

'No, Edna!' shouted Frances. 'You can't.'

'Now, now Frances. Let Edna finish.'

'At least reduce my hours,' Edna continued.

A lump gathered in Frances' throat at the thought of not seeing Edna again.

'Of course, I would miss you. After all, I've watched Frances grow into a beautiful young lady. But I need to think about my own family now.'

'Oh, Edna,' said Frances. 'It won't be the same.'

'You'll be fine on your own, Frances. You're tough as old boots.'

'But I would miss you,' said Frances.

Edna didn't respond; instead, she turned to look out of the car window. Frances thought she saw tears in her eyes.

'Do you mind if we keep this from Mrs Eton, just for now, Edna?' said Edward.

'As you wish, Dr Eton.'

It wasn't long before they had reached the tram stop. Edna climbed out of the car, and they waved her good night.

Frances watched as Edna seated herself at the front of the tram and closed her eyes. She looked more tired than usual. She knew Edna loved working for them. Edna had often told her that working for them had given her a focus, something to occupy her mind after her husband had passed. But Frances worried about her. She would hate anything to happen to Edna; she wasn't getting any younger and working in a hot kitchen all day seemed to be taking its toll. Maybe Edna thinking about starting to take things a little slower wasn't a bad thing after all.

'Edward, Darling!' enthused Frances' mother as she stepped down onto the platform in her crocodile-leather shoes, the sound of steam hissing in the background. 'And, Frances, you're here too.' She appeared amused. 'How sweet of you to come.' She was dressed to the nines in a new furred collar coat and hat. Frances noted something was off. Her mother seemed different. After a long journey, even travelling first class, her mother would normally be in a foul mood, but not this time – she was all smiles and kisses. 'I have missed you both. Have you missed me?'

'Of course, my love,' replied Edward. He kissed her cheek. Clarissa touched her father's arm with affection.

Stepping onto the platform behind her mother was a dashing young man dressed in a stylish dark grey suit with a grey fedora hat. He was about the same age as Thomas, give or take a couple of years, but his stylish pencil moustache and oiled, fashionable hair made him look more sophisticated and more grown up than Thomas. Her mother grabbed his hand, making him stand close to her.

'Edward, Frances, I'd like you to meet Robert. He's a distant cousin on my father's side. He'll be staying with us for a few days. Sorry I didn't tell you sooner, Edward; it was all last minute. You understand, don't you, darling?' Her voice grew cheerier. He wanted to breathe in some good clean northern air, and to meet... his family.' She glanced at Frances. 'Do make him feel welcome, won't you?'

'Of course, Clarissa. How do you do, Robert?' Edward held out his hand and shook it warmly.

'I can't complain.' Robert smiled and looked at Frances.

'This is Frances, Robert.' Her mother put her arm around Frances' shoulder and gave her a squeeze. Frances froze. 'Frances, say hello to Robert.' Frances looked at her mother and then Robert. 'She isn't normally shy.' Her mother laughed lightly.

'Shall we go to the car?' asked Edward. 'I'll grab your luggage.'

'Thank you, Edward. Robert, give Edward your suitcase.'

'It's fine, Clarissa, I can manage,' replied Robert. Clarissa, thought Frances. She'd only ever heard her father and one or two of her mother's close friends use her mother's actual name before. She was always Mrs Eton to everyone else. Sometimes, she'd heard her refer to herself using her maiden name Bennet, which Frances thought odd, being a married woman.

They walked to the car. Frances' father loaded all the cases into the trunk, leaving Frances alone with her mother and her mother's guest. Ordinarily, she would have been delighted to meet someone new, but something about this arrangement didn't sit well with her.

'Robert, tell Frances about your new job,' said her mother.

'Oh, I'm sure she doesn't want to hear about that.' He gave Frances a suggestive smile, causing Frances to hurriedly open the car door and sit down.

'Robert has got such a promising career,' said Frances' mother as she climbed into the front passenger's seat. Robert took the seat next to Frances. In the small confines of the car, Robert was bigger than he'd first appeared when he stepped off the train. Frances' mother turned in her seat to face Frances and Robert. 'We have had a wonderful time in London, haven't we, Robert?'

'A blast, Clarissa.'

'Such a shame you weren't there, Frances. Isn't it, Robert?'

As Edward started the engine, she turned back to face the front.

'Agreed,' replied Robert, turning his head to look at Frances.

As they drove home, Frances didn't quite know what to do. Usually, she was good at small talk but, right now, she couldn't think of a single thing to say. Her mother, with more enthusiasm than usual, chatted with her father about the events of the week, not paying the slightest attention to Frances' discomfort. Frances fidgeted in her seat and picked a loose thread from her coat. She pretended to be interested in the view of the passing buildings, ones she had seen a million times before. Frances caught a glimpse of Robert through the reflection in the glass and noted he had excellent posture. He saw her staring and she blushed. She wished her father would drive faster.

'Clarissa, I mean your mother, tells me that it's your birthday soon,' said Robert. His question disconcerted her and forced Frances to face him.

'Yes, it is,' replied Frances.

'Will you be having a party?'

'No, I think parties are fine for small children,' replied Frances, miffed that he would think she was still young enough to have a birthday party.

'Nonsense,' interrupted her mother. 'I think a party is an excellent idea. It would be a perfect opportunity for Robert to meet everyone.'

Frances inwardly cursed, annoyed that her mother had been listening to her brief conversation; the last thing Frances wanted was to have a party, especially one which her mother and mother's friends would hog.

'I'll start making plans tomorrow,' said her mother. 'It will be fun!'

'Fun,' echoed Robert.

Frances did not respond. She just slumped into her seat and sulked. Clearly, this was an attempt at marrying her off. Why else would she drag this stranger up to Sheffield? Well, her mother would just have to try harder because it was not going to work. Tomorrow she would convince her father that the whole fiasco was a terrible idea. Until then, she would just have to be patient and try not to get too annoyed with her mother and this Robert.

Chapter Eleven

It was decided that the party would take place the day after Frances's actual birthday. She had tried tirelessly to convince her father that the idea was a bad one, but he had argued that she should be grateful; her mother had gone to so much trouble to organise one in the first place. In the end, Frances had succumbed to the idea and admitted defeat. It was to be at the local church hall. Her mother, ever efficient, had sent out lots of invitations already, mostly to people Frances had never even heard of. Frances prayed that, as it was such short notice, none of her mother's friends would turn up. She had invited Agnes, Harriette and Alice, and her brother had invited a few of his friends. Frances' mother had organised a local dressmaker to come and measure her up for a new gown for the occasion. Ordinarily, this would have pleased Frances immensely but, for once, she thought it was all a lot of fuss for nothing.

To avoid running into Robert and her mother, who were

often having whispered conversations, Frances kept herself mostly to the confines of her room until the dressmaker arrived.

She arrived early Wednesday morning on a grey rainy day. Her dark hair, with just a few wisps of grey around the sides, was flat to her head underneath a wet hat. Frances took her coat and hat from her and showed her to the room where her mother was waiting. The woman held her head high, with a fearless dignity, and took in her surroundings. She didn't speak much, which suited Frances. Frances had to stand in the middle of the room. She watched as the dressmaker went about her business, taking her measurements. For a short, plump lady, she moved rather quickly, thought Frances. The whole process was over in seconds. Her mother then produced some magazines, and they all discussed styles and materials. Much to her annoyance, Robert looked on quietly from the corner of the room. He appeared to follow her mother everywhere.

'I really like this one, Mother,' said Frances.

'I know you want to be a Hollywood movie star, Frances, but that doesn't mean you should dress like a showgirl,' replied her mother. Frances clenched her jaw.

'Mother! If you insist on me having this party, then—'

'Yes?'

'Nothing.' She looked at the dressmaker. There was an uncomfortable silence for a few minutes. Robert coughed into his hand.

'How about this one?' asked her mother.

'It's so old fashioned,' replied Frances.

'I see,' said her mother. 'Old fashioned, am I?'

'I didn't mean anything by that, Mother.'

The dressmaker didn't comment, but when Frances looked at her, the corner of her lips curled, and her eyes appeared to light up.

'This one is nice,' said Frances.

'That's lovely,' said the dressmaker. 'Not difficult to copy.' Frances' mother said nothing.

'Let me see,' said Robert. He rushed over to them. 'Exceptionally glamorous.'

'Are we settled on this one then?' asked the dressmaker. Frances looked pleadingly at her mother.

Edna walked in with a tray of tea. She was halted in her tracks when she saw the dressmaker.

'Sorry, am I interrupting?' asked Edna. The two ladies nodded to one another like they were old friends.

'No,' replied the dressmaker. 'I've finished here for the day. It was nice to meet you all.' She looked again at Edna. 'I'll be back Friday for a fitting.' Frances thought that her mother must be paying her well to have a dress ready at such short notice. 'Goodbye,' said the dressmaker as Frances saw her out.

Frances walked to the dining room to join her mother and Robert. Her mother had started to pour the tea.

'Please don't argue with me in front of strangers, Frances. It's most disagreeable.'

'I'm sorry, Mother, I—'

'It pains me to say this, Frances, but as your mother, I feel I should. The style of dress you have chosen is all wrong. It reveals too much flesh. Don't you think so, Robert?'

'I can't say I noticed,' said Robert.

'Be that as it may, I feel it does. And the colour... well.'

Frances sipped her tea quietly. What's wrong with silver?

she thought. The style she had chosen was all the rage in Hollywood. It was a backless halter-neck dress, made of shimmering satin. She was, after all, turning eighteen. If she was going to have to endure this party, then she was determined to look her best. Although, maybe now was not the time to mention to her mother the idea of getting a permanent wave and some new shoes. Frances thought she would save that conversation for another day.

Edna arrived to collect the tray.

'Just the person,' said Frances' mother. Edna looked at her.

'Yes, Mrs Eton.'

'Now, Edna. I need you to make sure there is plenty of food for the party and, of course, the birthday cake for the birthday girl.'

'With all due respect, Mrs Eton, I need a lot longer than a couple of days to put a spread on. I'll need an extra pair of hands,' said Edna. 'You've not given me much time to get organised.' She straightened her pinafore. Frances could tell she was annoyed but her mother appeared not to care.

'Whatever you need, Edna,' replied Frances' mother. 'Hire whomever you see fit.'

'What food do you want me to put on? Salmon?'

'You know best, Edna. I trust you implicitly.'

'It's not on you know, leaving it all up to me, Mrs Eton,' grumbled Edna. 'I'm not happy about this.' She turned and walked down the hall, still muttering loudly, 'I've a good mind to hand my notice in today! It's not on!'

'Edna! Don't go!' shouted Frances after her but Edna had already slammed the kitchen door. Frances glared at her mother. Upsetting Edna was the last thing she wanted. Her mother went to her room, complaining about one of her headaches. Robert lit an awful, sweet-smelling cigarette and went out into the garden. Frances decided she would speak to her father about it all when he returned home from work. This party was not worth all the upset.

Anxious from all the commotion, Frances needed someone to talk to, so she telephoned Agnes and told her all about her day. She asked her to accompany her to the matinee show but Agnes was unavailable. Frances placed the receiver down and sighed.

'Not going out?' asked Robert. He leaned against the door frame.

'No, my friend is busy.'

'Too busy to spend time with you? That can't be right, surely?'

'Humph!' replied Frances. Robert laughed.

'I'll tell you what. How about if I go with you?' he said.

'Were you eavesdropping?'

'Moi?' He placed his hand on his chest.

'I see what you're doing, Robert, and no, I will be perfectly fine on my own,' Frances insisted.

'But I couldn't possibly let you do that,' he replied. 'It just isn't the done thing for a young girl to go wandering about the city on her own. What would your mother say?' He caught his reflection in the large ornate mirror that hung above the fireplace and smoothed down his already smooth hair. 'Besides, I would like to see what Sheffield has to offer.'

Frances dreaded the thought of being stuck in her room again all day, so she reluctantly agreed to let him accompany her.

'Alright, Robert, you can come with me. But I feel I

ought to put you straight on a few things. I don't know why you are here, or what plans you and my mother are deviously concocting, but I am not and will never be attracted to you! Is that clear?'

'Crystal,' he snorted. 'And for the record, Frances dear, the feeling is mutual.' Frances gasped.

With Frances a couple of steps in front, they walked the short distance to the tram. The tram stopped just outside the picture house, so they arrived in time for the afternoon show: a Three Stooges film. After standing silently for a short period in the queue, they passed the commissionaire with his familiar military-style uniform. Robert then walked forward to the ticket kiosk, while Frances admired the film posters. He bought two tickets from the smartly dressed woman who was seated behind a glass panel. Frances always thought the kiosk space was far too small for anyone to sit comfortably. A pretty usherette in a red uniform showed them to their seats in the upper circle, and they waited for the curtain to open.

The pianist was just finishing. Then came the newsreel: something about how well the Royal family's tour of Canada was going. After that were several short cartoons, which Robert appeared to enjoy thoroughly, and then finally the main feature. Looking around, she noted the auditorium wasn't as full as usual. She relaxed into her seat and stared at the big screen, longing to be a giant of the silver screen too.

. . .

It turned out to be a lovely afternoon, and she was enjoying herself immensely. It was almost perfect, and it would have been, she thought, if Robert didn't fidget constantly. During the interval, he kindly bought two tubs of vanilla ice cream, complete with small wooden spoons, from the usherette at the front of the auditorium, who looked weighed down by the heavy tray hanging around her neck.

When the film was over, they waited with the rest of the audience until God Save the King had finished playing and walked together side by side to the tram stop. Going to the pictures was just what Frances had needed to take her mind off her blasted birthday party. She was feeling so much better that she momentarily forgot she didn't like Robert.

'Oh, wasn't it funny. I couldn't stop myself from laughing,' said Frances as she climbed on board the tram and found a seat.

'I noticed,' replied Robert as he seated himself down next to her.

'Especially the scene...' She looked at Robert and her expression changed. 'Well, it was funny,' she said, more to herself.

'Indeed.'

'What I wouldn't give to star in my own movie one day,' she sighed.

'So, you fancy yourself as a movie star? Well, I daresay you've got the looks for it. What does your mother think about this dream of yours?'

Frances stopped talking. She realised she'd let slip too much about herself.

'I don't think that's any of your business,' she replied, folding her arms, and staring out of the window.

'Is that so?' he asked. Frances didn't reply.

'I once knew an actor,' said Robert. 'He was outstanding!'

'And?' asked Frances, eager for more information.

'And nothing,' replied Robert. 'Two can play your game.'

Frances huffed and turned back to look out of the window. Robert laughed. After a moment, Frances laughed too.

'Thank you, Robert.'

'For what?'

'For a nice afternoon.'

'My pleasure.'

Chapter Twelve

Frances was standing as still as humanly possible on a small footstool in the middle of the family room. Despite her aching legs, she didn't want to risk the chance of a pin pricking her again. The room was stifling. Fresh, sweet-scented flowers and bowls of potpourri with lavender oil made her feel queasy. Standing there, she was reminded of why she hardly ever came into that room. It suffocated her. It was more a shrine to the past than a family room – a museum full of old furniture and trinkets handed down through generations. She stared at the antique vase full of flowers and the delicate lace tablecloth it was placed upon in the bay window. The over-polished mahogany table gleamed in the morning sunlight. It was her mother's room, used only for 'special' visitors. So, it had come as a surprise when her mother instructed Jenny, the domestic help, to usher the dressmaker inside.

Frances tried her hardest not to move, but it was all too much.

'Ouch!' she cried as another pin stabbed her shoulder.

'I am sorry, but you must stand still,' replied the dressmaker. Frances looked at the woman's face. She could see her own frustrated expression being reflected in the dressmaker's spectacles.

'I'm trying,' Frances replied.

'Try harder,' said the dressmaker, forcing a smile, while holding pins between her teeth. Frances looked over at her mother, who was sitting by the fireplace, as poised as ever, in a tall velvet armchair, quietly observing. The grandmother clock ticked loudly in the background. Several times, Frances noticed her mother's lips part to say something, but then she would close them again. The dressmaker pinned away, oblivious to the tension in the room. Frances could tell her mother didn't like her new dress, but there was no going back now.

The telephone rang. Her mother excused herself and went to answer it.

'Not long now,' said the dressmaker. 'I know it's 'ard standing still all this time, but it'll be worth it in the end. You'll look lovely.'

'Thank you,' replied Frances. 'But I don't think my...' Frances stopped herself mid-sentence. Although Frances and her mother didn't always see eye to eye, it didn't seem proper discussing her with a stranger.

'You're done,' declared the dressmaker. 'You can take it off now, and I'll take it home to finish it. Be mindful of all those pins though. We don't want them falling out.'

'I'll be careful; it's the nicest dress I've ever owned. It

feels so soft. The colour is exquisite,' said Frances. 'See how it shines.'

'The colour compliments your eyes.'

'You're too kind. I don't think my eyes...' She blushed. 'I will treasure it forever, thank you.'

'You're welcome. Now, off with it!'

Frances stepped down from the stool as her mother re-entered the room.

'Who was on the telephone, Mother?'

'Charles. Such a nice young man. I've invited him to your birthday party; I hope you don't mind. I said you would call him back.'

'Ouch!' cried Frances as a pin scratched her arm. She was furious with her mother for inviting Charles.

'Are we all finished, Mrs Shepherd?' asked Clarissa. Frances had the dress mid-way over her head but stopped when she heard the name – Shepherd. Butterflies tickled her belly. She had managed to put Henry to the back of her mind for a few hours but, on hearing that name, she felt excited all over again. Her mouth went dry. Tomorrow she would go and meet him a second time.

'Hurry up, Frances, Mrs Shepherd hasn't got all day.' Frances sucked in her bottom lip as she handed the dress-maker the dress. Frances contemplated asking if she knew Henry Shepherd. She wanted to say, 'I know a boy with the same name – maybe you know him?' But surely it was just a coincidence. After all, Shepherd was a common enough name. Besides, if she did that, then her mother would discover her secret, and she would never be able to leave the house again.

'I'll be back next week with the finished dress,' said Mrs Shepherd.

'Thank you,' replied Clarissa. 'And thank you ever so much for managing to make the dress in such a short time; we do appreciate it, don't we, Frances?'

'Yes, thank you,' said Frances, changing back into her clothes.

'I'll show you out, Mrs Shepherd,' said Clarissa.

'I'll be on me way then. Goodbye.' The dressmaker nodded to Frances.

'Goodbye,' replied Frances.

As soon as her mother and the dressmaker had left the room, Frances went to her bedroom. She couldn't bear to remain in that room a moment longer. Frances ran down the hallway but slowed when she heard shouting coming from the dining room. The door was ajar so she peeked in. She couldn't see much, only Robert's back. He appeared to be having quite an animated conversation with someone on the telephone.

'I've told you,' shouted Robert. 'Things are complicated... no I don't mean you... I'll ask...'

Curious, she thought. I wonder who that could be?

Robert slammed down the receiver and turned towards the door. As quickly as she could, Frances continued on her way; she didn't want to be caught spying.

Finally alone, she sat at her dressing table and stared into the oval mirror. 'When did life get so complicated, Frances Elizabeth Eton?' she asked her reflection. She thought about her impending party and groaned. Soon she would be turning eighteen, and she hadn't the foggiest idea what she was going to do with her life. She ran her hand over the polished wood until it settled on one of her hand-painted postcards. Picking it up, she looked longingly at the faces of Clark Gable and Norma Shearer. They were standing close together looking stylish and beautiful. She sighed. Her dream of moving to America was slipping further from her grasp.

'Help me, God!' she prayed. 'Just send me a sign!'

'Can I come in?' asked Thomas, interrupting her thoughts.

'You're already in,' Frances replied, puffing out her cheeks and widening her eyes at him through the mirror.

'Indeed, I am,' said Thomas, grinning. 'Mother thinks you should come downstairs instead of sitting doing nothing in your room all day. Oh, and Edna wants to know if porky would like to give her a hand choosing your birthday cake.'

'Edna called me porky?' She pinched her cheeks and turned her head from side to side, checking her appearance.

'No, I added that bit,' said Thomas.

Frances turned in her seat, screwed up her nose and stuck her tongue out at him.

'Oh, Frances! You poor thing,' said Thomas. 'Show me your tongue again. Quick! It looks like you're coming down with lazy-itis and, being a medical student, I should know a case when I see one.' He laughed loudly at his joke.

'Go away, Thomas!' said Frances.

'Don't worry, I'm going,' replied Thomas. 'Some of us have things to do.'

'Where are you going? Can I come?'

'No, you cannot. I'd be the laughing stock if I were to bring my baby sister out with me. It was bad enough at the dance. Look how that ended up!'

'Oh, please!' begged Frances. 'I'll go mad if I have to stay in this house a minute longer.'

'No, sorry, not this time. I'll see you later.'

She was left sitting in her bedroom, wishing she had been born a boy. Life would have been so much easier, she thought. She envied the freedom Thomas was granted. 'Nobody ever speaks to him about marriage,' she grumbled. 'And Robert just comes and goes as he pleases. Maybe I should run away to Pinewood Studios – that would show them.'

Chapter Thirteen

Henry sat on the outdoor step and polished his work boots. The air was thick with soot and heavy with an acrid odour from the factories. His chest felt tight after an exhausting working day in the melting shop. He had a splitting headache too, caused by the noise of the machinery and the heat from the furnaces. He rubbed his tired red eyes. They still had marks around them from the protective goggles he had to wear. Henry watched as his mum swept the cobbled yard. He yawned and coughed. He wished he could find another job. The thought of working in the same place till he was too old to do the work filled him with dread. Today, one of the older men he worked alongside had almost lost his arm. He hadn't been looking what he was doing, and his sleeve had got caught up in the machinery. It was touch and go for a few seconds but, thanks to the quick thinking of the other men, they had managed to switch the machine off before it ripped the old fella's arm clean off.

'Evening, Edna.' Mary waved. Henry looked up and saw Edna, their friendly neighbour, always ready with a kind word.

'Evening, Mary.' Edna waved back. 'I was surprised to see you the other morning,' she added.

'Caught me by surprise too,' she said. 'I didn't know it was the same family you worked for when I took the job.'

'That reminds me, does your Margaret fancy giving me a hand? I know she's a good cook and I've got quite a lot of extra work on catering for the birthday party. What with her expecting, I thought she could do with some extra money.'

'I'll ask her,' replied Mary. 'So, the party weren't planned then? I thought not. When one of my other clients recommended me, I didn't expect to be having to make a frock at such short notice. Not that I mind; she's paying me well. Seem like a nice family.'

'They are,' said Edna.

'And she's a pretty little thing too. Mind, she's quite stubborn. The way she stood her ground with her mother over her frock,' Mary said.

'Yes, she is one in a million,' said Edna proudly. 'But I've decided that after the party I'm going to hand me notice in. I'm getting too old for it all.'

'Really? What will you do with thissen?'

'I'll find summat to keep me busy. I'll probably help our Frank and Joan when the baby comes. Are you back at the house next week?'

'Yes.'

'Might see you then; tell Margaret to pop over, if she wants work,' said Edna.

Henry left the two women to their gossip. All he wanted to do was go to bed and sleep.

Henry forced himself to eat the last of his breakfast; his stomach was in knots and his mouth was dry. He needed the toilet again. The last time he felt this anxious was when he attended his first football match with his dad and his brother Harold. They'd gone to Wembley to watch Sheffield United play Arsenal. It was the FA cup final. They'd travelled by train, laid on specially. The weather was good, but it was too windy, making play difficult. It was a nerve-wracking game. Sheffield United almost scored but, in the end, they had lost 1-0. Henry remembered that the train journey home had been a long and miserable one.

'You all reight, son?' asked his dad. 'You look a bit peaky.'

'I just need some fresh air,' Henry replied.

'Why are you wearing one of your best shirts again?' asked his mum. 'It's a bit early to be dressing in your Sunday best.'

'I'm meeting someone,' replied Henry, grinning from ear to ear.

'I thought as much. Who?' asked his mum.

'Remember that girl I told you about?' said Henry.

'Oh aye, that one you met out in Peak District?' asked his dad. His mum spilt a bit of her tea on the tablecloth.

'Yes,' said Henry. 'Well, I'm off to meet her today.'

'You alright, Mary love?' asked her husband.

'I've got a headache, that's all, George.' She went to fetch the dishcloth.

'Why don't you go and have a lie down,' George said. 'I'll wash the dishes.'

'I can't. I've got that dress to finish. It's not going to make its sen.'

'It's a lovely dress, Mum,' said Henry.

She patted Henry's hand and went through to the living room where her sewing machine was.

Henry followed her and looked at his reflection in the mirror. His mum watched from behind her sewing machine.

'What's up?' she asked.

'Nowt.'

'Come on, out with it!'

Henry turned around to face her. He shifted his weight from one foot to another. 'I've never felt like this before. I wish you could meet her; she's perfect, Mum. I don't want her to feel embarrassed about being with me.' He looked down at his worn shoes.

'Now look here, Henry!' she said, pointing her finger. 'I won't have you doubting thissen!' Henry met her gaze. 'You're just as good a man as anyone else. Do you hear?'

Henry nodded. 'Thanks, Mum.'

'You do me proud, son. You always have.' She turned away to wipe a tear that had appeared in the corner of her eye.

'Reight, I'm off,' he said. 'Wish me luck!'

With a steady hand, Mary added the final details to the dress.

'Good luck!' said his dad.

'Thanks, Dad.'

Henry's palms were damp with sweat as he stepped off the tram. He shielded his eyes from the sun and made his way to the gardens. The past few nights had been dreadful. He had hardly slept dreaming of this moment. Now it was finally here.

He reached the bottom gate but, before entering, he paused. He wiped his palms on the back of his trousers and took several deep breaths to steady his nerves and calm his erratic heartbeat. This is ridiculous, he thought. Mustering his courage, he pushed open the gates and strolled up the path to the pavilion. It was early. He had no idea how long he would have to wait for her to arrive, but he would wait all day if he had to.

Chapter Fourteen

It was a bright sunny morning. Light shone on the dust particles floating in the air giving them the appearance of dancing fairies. The birds were chirping outside. Edna and Jenny had the day off and the house was in disarray. While everyone fussed from place to place, Frances found sanctuary in the kitchen. She helped herself to bread and jam and waited for everyone to leave. Staring out of the kitchen window, she watched the neighbour's ginger cat climb down a wall and settle itself in a sunny spot in their garden and fall asleep. Her father was rushing around because he had a meeting to attend. Her mother and Robert were late for an auction somewhere close to the village of Dore, and Thomas was searching high and low for his tennis racket, blaming everyone because he had a match that morning. Frances was relieved the house would soon be empty. That meant she could get ready in peace and leave to meet Henry without anyone asking questions, but if anyone did care to ask, she was going to meet Agnes.

She started to think about the Botanical Gardens. Soon she would be there with Henry. Her stomach churned. Maybe she wouldn't go. After all, it had all happened so quickly. If she didn't turn up, he would soon get bored of waiting and go home. But he seemed nice, and Frances needed a distraction.

As it was a lovely morning, she thought she'd take a book, sit on one of the benches and wait for him to show. She chose a rose crepe dress with buttons on the short sleeves and just below the breastbone. She had always loved that dress because it fitted her so well and it was the one dress her mother complimented her on. Her mouth felt dry. She looked at her reflection in the hallway mirror for the last time and tried to smooth down the curls, before making her way out of the front door.

It was far too hot. Frances moved from the bench to the shade of a tree. Curling her legs round to her side, she tried to read her book. Her mind refused to stay focused, and she read the same line several times over. She kept on peering over the top of the pages to see if she could spot him, but all she saw were children playing and an elderly couple walking towards the pavilion. Maybe *he* has changed his mind, she thought.

Then she spotted him. He was walking across the grass, past the flowerbeds. Her heart began to flutter. The light of the sun reflected off his white shirt. He walked with his head high, his black hair sticking out from under his flat cap. Broad shoulders were held back, his arms down by his side, and his stride was long and purposeful. Frances felt her knees grow weak at the sight of him. He looked more handsome than the last time she saw him. As he neared, she pretended she hadn't been observing him.

'Hello,' she heard him say. Breathing in slowly, she lifted her gaze to meet his. She got a tickling sensation in her stomach when their eyes locked.

'Hello,' she said, her voice a little too high. She coughed to clear her throat.

'Mind if I join thee?' he asked. He seated himself down and rested his back against the trunk of the tree. His long legs spread out in front of him. Frances waited for him to speak first. She tucked her dress underneath her knees to cover her legs, closed her book and placed it down on the grass.

'Here, I picked this for you.' He handed her a delicate pink rose. She noticed bloodied scratch marks on his hand. 'It were worth it,' he said.

'Thank you,' she replied and sniffed the rose. 'You're lucky Bert, one of the gardeners, didn't catch you; otherwise, he'd have your guts for garters.'

Henry laughed lightly. 'It's a lovely morning,' he said.

'Yes, it is.'

'You look lovely.'

'Thank you,' said Frances. 'You look handsome too.'

'Have you been waiting long?'

'Not too long.'

Henry sat up and turned towards her. The hairs on Frances' arm tingled as he inched closer. 'What you reading?' he asked, nodding towards her book.

'Oh, it's nothing,' she said, quickly hiding it behind her back.'

'Don't be like that. Let me have a look.' He held out his hand for the book. 'Come on.' Hesitantly, she gave it to him.

'Let's take a look then.' He turned the book over and studied the title. Wuthering Heights,' he read. 'I've heard of this. What's it about?'

'It's sort of a love story, but it is also about revenge, I suppose, but I haven't finished it yet.'

'Appen I should read it then,' he said, smiling.

'You should... I can lend it to you, if you want.'

'Truth be told, Frances, I don't have the time to read books, even if I wanted to. I just enjoy the way your eyes light up when you talk about it. I read the papers because I like to know what's happening in the world, but I'm not a fan of books.' Frances' heart sank. 'I remember having to read Shakespeare at school; it sounded more Yorkshire with all that "thee'ing and thou'ing".'

'Books are magical. They're almost as good as going to the pictures,' she said.

'You like going t'pictures then?' he asked. Frances glanced at his mouth as he spoke. His smile was perfect.

'I love it!' she replied.

'You dirty, yellow-bellied rat!'

'I beg your pardon!' said Frances.

'No, not thee... I thought you might know it... I was doing an impression... never mind.' Henry blushed.

'Oh, I'm sorry,' she said. 'Do it again!'

'It doesn't matter now.'

'Please!' said Frances.

'I feel silly doing it now, moment's gone.'

'Go on, I won't laugh,' she said. 'I promise.' She crossed her fingers.

'You dirty, yellow-bellied rat!'

Frances screwed up her nose and tapped her chin. 'No sorry, I don't know who that is.'

'What? Come on! It's obvious!'

Frances shrugged. 'Sorry.'

'James Cagney?'

'Oh.'

'Everyone always said it were good,' he said.

'I've never seen any of his films,' said Frances.

'You've never seen a Cagney film? He's probably my favourite actor. It seems a lifetime ago now, but I remember when me and my brother, Arthur used to go on Saturday afternoons. Maybe we could go together some time?'

Frances dropped her gaze to the grass and was quiet for a moment. She wanted so desperately to say yes, but then she thought about how her parents would react if they found out. She knew they would not approve of Henry. But they don't have to know, she thought. She raised her eyes to meet his.

'I'd like to go with you.' She thought he looked relieved. He glanced around the gardens and at the people promenading.

'Do you fancy going for a walk?' he asked.

Henry rose to his feet and offered her his hand. She

placed her trembling fingers into his. The warmth of his hand sent a strange feeling coursing through her body. With ease, he helped her to her feet. They were standing close her hand still in his. The only sounds were her beating heart and the gentle breeze rustling the leaves on the branches of the tree overhead.

'Ready?' Henry said.

'My book,' she said. He handed back her book and their fingers touched. As they did, she felt him watching her, and shivers ran down her spine.

'Tell me about your family?' asked Frances as they walked together around the flower beds. If she was going to risk getting into trouble to be with him, then she wanted to know all there was to know about Henry Shepherd.

'There's not much to tell,' replied Henry. 'I'm the youngest of three. We had a sister, too, but she died at just three weeks when I was six. Her name was Helen, but I nick-named her Nellie. I used to think she looked like a porcelain doll. Although me mum puts a brave face on, I don't think she's ever got over it.'

'I suppose you wouldn't get over something like that,' said Frances.

Henry shrugged.

'So, what about your parents?'

'My parents are just my parents.'

But Frances noticed how his eyes lit up. 'You admire them,' she said.

'Of course, money might be tight, but there's always plenty of food on the table, and the house is always filled with laughter. They might never outwardly show their affection for one another, but I know they love and respect one another. To the rest of the world, me mum is a hard woman but, to me and me brothers, she's very loving. She's what keeps us together.' A mischievous grin appeared across his face.

'What?'

'Nowt, I was just remembering a time when Mr Shaw, the headmaster at our infant school, threatened to cane our Arthur. I ran as fast as a seven-year-old boy could all the way home to tell me mum, who said nothing but marched silently down to the school, with me running behind her. When she entered the headmaster's room, she grabbed the cane out of his hands and snapped it in two. Me and our Arthur looked on, our mouths open in horror. We still joke about it. Afterwards, she took us by the hand and marched us home. Unsurprisingly, not long after this, we were asked to move to a different school.' Henry laughed, causing Frances to laugh with him, but she felt a tinge of jealousy. She couldn't imagine her mother sticking up for her in that manner.

'Remind me not to get on the wrong side of her. And what about your father? What does he do?'

'He's worked as a grinder in the same small factory for most of his life.'

'How did your parents meet?'

'At a dance before the war. They married after me mum discovered she was pregnant with Harold. She had to leave her job as a seamstress at Cockaynes department store much to the disappointment of her mother.'

'Your mother used to be a seamstress?' Frances thought

back to the dressmaker, Mrs Shepherd. Was she Henry's mum? She had to be. It was too much of a coincidence.

'Still is, sort of, why?' said Henry. Frances swallowed hard. It was on the tip of her tongue to tell him that his mother might be the lady making her a dress, but she resisted the urge. She didn't want Henry to feel embarrassed.

'Tell me about your brothers,' she said, changing the subject.

'Harold is the eldest. He doesn't live at home anymore. He married his childhood sweetheart and moved in with her parents until they get a house of their own. They're expecting their first baby this year.'

'Are you looking forward to being an uncle?'

'Aye, I suppose I am. It's something good to look forward to in these dark times.'

'Dark times?'

'You know, with all that's happening in Europe,' said Henry.

'It's too dreadful to think about,' Frances replied.

'Yes, but we must.' Frances observed how quickly his expression and tone changed.

'But not today,' said Frances. She gave his hand a gentle squeeze. 'Today is our day. Tell me about your other brother?'

Henry laughed.

'What's so funny?'

'Arthur, is just Arthur.'

'What does that mean?'

'Nowt.'

'Please. I want to know all about you.' She gently touched the back of his hand.

'Well, let's just say he's spent most of his life in trouble with the police for fighting.'

Frances gasped.

'See! That's why I didn't want to tell you. I was scared you'd react like that.'

'I'm sorry,' Frances replied. 'Is he the one that caused the fight at the dance?' Henry nodded slowly.

'Don't look like that. He just has a temper but he's not a thug. His heart is in the right place. Once, when a man refused to apologise for swearing in front of me mum, he walloped him so hard that he fell back through a shop window. The man not only suffered cuts and bruises, he had been humiliated in front of the large crowd of people that had gathered. He was a well-known member of a notorious gang, and to take a beating from a young lad wasn't great for his reputation. When the man recovered, he went looking for our Arthur with some of his mates. They beat him until he was unconscious, but not before our Arthur had managed to get a few good punches in. He was in the hospital for weeks after, but he never told the police who did it, earning him the respect of Sheffield's criminal underworld.' Frances put her hand over her mouth.

'After that, he was known throughout the back alleys of Sheffield. He had built quite a reputation for himself. But the trouble with a reputation is that everyone always wants to chance their arm sooner or later. So, for Arthur, it's difficult to avoid trouble and hold down a steady job.' Henry reached for Frances' hand. 'That's my brother, Frances, not me. I'm not like him.'

Frances looked into his eyes.

'I know that, Henry,' she replied. Her stomach fluttered.

The more she discovered about Henry, the more she found she liked him. She would be lying if she said that his background didn't trouble her a bit, but not enough to put her off seeing him again. Being with Henry made her forget about the mundane things, at least for the time being. All Frances wanted to do was focus on the short time she had with Henry. She just hoped that she wouldn't live to regret it.

'Enough about me,' said Henry. 'Tell me about your family.'

Frances thought for a second. Her life was enormously different to Henry's; no one in her family had ever been in trouble with the police.

'Where do I start? My life is quite dull.'

'Pull the other one,' said Henry.

'It's true. We moved to Sheffield just after my eleventh birthday. It was a difficult time because I didn't know anyone, and I've never been good at making new friends. When Agnes approached me on my first day at my new school, I could have kissed her.'

'Is Agnes your friend?'

'My best friend.' Frances smiled. 'I have a brother, Thomas. He's older. He is in his final year studying medicine. The move to Sheffield didn't particularly bother him. He soon made lots of new friends. The person it hit the hardest was my mother.'

It was Frances' father's new job that was the reason they had moved. Her father was an excellent physician and had been earning good money previously. Still, when he was approached about a lecturing position at Sheffield University, he was delighted to be given the opportunity. Regrettably, she didn't see a lot of her father since their move to Sheffield because, as a general practitioner, and while lecturing students at the university, he had little free time. And as part of her father's new role, he had to travel sometimes, to London mostly, to attend conferences on the latest medical advancements. Frances missed him when he was away. When her father came home from work, her parents often argued.

'My father is a doctor. He also lectures at the university. Do you remember the girl I was with in the Peak District? The one who was driving the car?'

'You mean the snobby one who almost got you killed?'

'Yes, that's the one,' said Frances. 'Well, Harriette is her name. Her father is a professor at the university too. I've always thought that he resembles a walrus, with his whiskers and portly belly.'

'He sounds charming,' said Henry, laughing.

'Oh, he's not. He's far too stern. I don't know how Harriette puts up with him. He's nothing at all like my father; my father is kind.'

'You love him a lot?'

'I do,' replied Frances.

'And your mam?'

Her mother. What could she tell Henry about her mother? She wished she felt closer to her but that just wasn't the case – and now her mother had Robert.

'We used to be close, but things changed between us... I don't know why.' Henry held her hand. 'It's like she resents me.'

Frances thought about the woman her mother used to be; she was a different woman before they moved to Sheffield. It was the move that changed her. She always complained the air was too stifling and it gave her headaches. She also complained that Sheffield was not cultured enough – its people were far too unsophisticated. Everything was too dull and grey. Her mother would often go on about how she missed the excitement of London. Although she never openly said it, Frances knew her mother missed the grandeur of her past: her childhood home and the luxuries she was accustomed to. Frances believed all those things were superficial. Their Sheffield house was more than adequate. It wasn't a stately home, but it was one of the largest in the area. Frances often thought it was far too big for just the four of them.

Her mother had been a debutante, just like her mother before her. 'Quite a catch,' her father had once told Frances. She could have had her pick of suitable young men, but Clarissa's parents decided she would marry a man a few years older than her. He came from an aristocratic family, just like her own. Her parents knew his parents, and everyone adored Oliver Ralph Bower. Clarissa, who was sixteen when the engagement made the papers, appeared to like him too.

But then the war came, and her young fiancé became an officer and led a battalion of young men to the front line; he was shot and killed just months into the war. Her family was then dealt a second devastating blow when her mother's brother was killed too. The war stole the lives of many husbands, brothers and sons, changing England forever in the process.

As the war went on, women were encouraged to go out to work and keep the home front moving. Her mother and some of her socialite friends played their role too. They worked at a busy London station serving tea, buns and cigarettes to exhausted soldiers arriving back on boat trains from the trenches. It was Clarissa's job not only to smile and serve the tea but to chat with the men – even flirt a little. The pretty faces of the women were what lifted the men's spirits as they stepped off the trains and into the pandemonium of the walking wounded, bloodied and shell-shocked.

It was at that time Clarissa first laid eyes on Frances' father. He was home on a three-day leave. He emerged through the steam in his khaki uniform looking lost. He was travelling home to see his family, who lived in Cambridge. They chatted until Clarissa's shift finished; then he left to catch his connecting train home, but not before taking her home address. They wrote to each other for some time. Her letters gave him something to live for during those dark days. The second time they met was the Christmas of 1917. A mutual friend was throwing one of his lavish parties, despite the rationing. That night, swept up in the excitement, they kissed for the first time. It was her mother's first real kiss, Frances had discovered. She accidentally uncovered some of her mother's love letters to Frances' father in one of the boxes in the attic. The temptation to read them was too great. What she read in those letters were the thoughts and feelings of quite a different woman. They were full of romantic notions, her mother's longings and desires. She had been poetic and passionate.

'*My dearest darling*,' she wrote. '*I live to be held in your arms again...*' Reading those letters had made Frances blush for days after.

Her mother had been quite wild during the war years. She also read how Frances' grandparents were against the match and how Clarissa had suggested to Edward that they run away together, but Edward had been the sensible one.

Her mother was a different person back then—reckless. But the war made everyone reckless. It changed society – and people – forever.

Shortly after, Clarissa's father died and her mother, who was too grief-stricken to object, finally gave them her blessing – but not her money. They were married a couple of months after the war ended. Edward finished his medical training, and they bought a house close to his practice outside London. Thomas was born not long after that, the same year Frances' maternal grandmother died. Frances was born a couple of years later.

'I'm sure she doesn't,' said Henry. Frances spotted Mrs Blackwood walking towards them and quickly pulled her hand away from Henry's. Frances dropped her head and turned to the side hoping her mother's friend hadn't seen her, but it was too late.

'Hello, Frances,' said the woman.

'Hello, Mrs Blackwood,' replied Frances. The woman looked past Frances and settled her gaze on Henry. Mrs Blackwood was a tall, rather slight woman, with tight lips and cold eyes. She coughed into her hand and waited to be introduced. When the introduction didn't come, Mrs Blackwood appeared irritated.

'How is your mother?' she asked, her eyes still focused on Henry, who was standing quietly to the side.

'She is very well, Mrs Blackwood,' replied Frances.

'Do tell her I asked after her. Well, good day, Frances.' She nodded, her expression one of disdain, Frances shuddered.

'Good day, Mrs Blackwood.' Of all the people to bump into, she thought.

Frances waited until Mrs Blackwood had passed, then turned back to face Henry. 'I am so sorry, Henry, but I think I should leave now. If Mrs Blackwood tells my mother that I...' Frances began pacing.

'What's wrong?' asked Henry. 'Are you embarrassed to be seen with me?'

'No, not at all. But if my parents find out about you, well, it's not worth thinking about. One thing is for sure, we can't meet here again. It's far too risky.'

'You made it more awkward by not introducing me.'

'It's complicated... I think I should leave now.'

'Are you free to meet again next week?' asked Henry.

'Next week is awkward. It's my birthday, and my mother has organised a stupid party.' She groaned.

'Your birthday?'

'Yes.'

'When's your party?' he asked.

'Friday, at the church hall, not far from where I live.' Henry reached for her hand and pulled her behind a shaded tree. Frances breathed in deeply as his mouth neared hers. 'I really must be leaving,' she whispered. Henry's lips softly caressed hers.

'There's a dance in town next Saturday. Do you fancy being my date?'

Frances sucked in her bottom lip. 'Maybe.' He placed a delicate kiss on her lips again. 'Alright,' she said, looking longingly into his bright blue eyes. 'But I must be honest with you, Henry. I don't plan on staying my whole life in Sheffield. I wouldn't want you thinking—'

'It's just a dance, Frances, not a marriage proposal. I'll meet you here at seven,' he said.

'Well, just so long as you know. I think we should always be honest with one another.' She turned to leave.

'Happy birthday for next week, Frances,' he called after her.

'Thank you,' she replied and walked away, her heart singing.

Chapter Fifteen

Frances opened her cards and thanked her parents for the oval locket. It had scalloped edging and a delicate floral engraving on the front. It was beautiful. Her father helped her to fasten the gold chain around her neck. He kissed her cheek.

'Thank you, Father,' said Frances.

'Your mother chose it,' he replied before heading off to work, leaving Frances and her mother sitting at the dining room table, finishing their breakfast.

'Thank you, Mother; I adore it.' Her fingers touched the locket.

'I'm glad,' replied her mother. She took a sip of her tea. 'What do you have planned today?'

'I don't have any plans,' replied Frances.

'But it's your birthday. Are you not going out?'

Frances shook her head.

'Then how about we do something together?' She

reached forward and patted Frances' hand that was resting on the table.

'What about Robert?'

'What about him? I'm sure he can entertain himself for the day; besides, I think he mentioned meeting a friend.'

'A friend?'

Frances' mother nodded. 'Yes, someone he knows from London. So, do you fancy a trip into town?' asked her mother.

'Yes, if you aren't too busy, it would be lovely.' She didn't know what to make of it. Her mother rarely offered to spend time alone with her.

'It's your birthday! I can make time. Besides, it will be fun,' she said. 'We can have tea in town and do a bit of shopping. The dressmaker isn't coming till later, so we have plenty of time.'

'I'll fetch my coat,' replied Frances.

Frances and her mother spent the morning shopping at Cole Brothers before deciding to go for a cup of tea and a cream bun at a little teashop opposite the town hall. The conversation had been stilted to begin with but, as the morning progressed, Frances found she was enjoying herself. She hadn't seen her mother this relaxed in a long time. Her mother had been excited to buy herself a new handbag and a matching pair of gloves and, as a special treat, she had bought Frances a pair of shoes she liked. She would wear them Saturday night.

'Thank you, Mother. I have had a lovely day,' said Frances as she finished off her tea.

'It has been rather special, hasn't it? Just don't tell your father about our little trip to Coles.' She raised her eyebrows and the corner of her lips rose. 'It will be our secret.' Frances nodded. 'I remember my eighteenth birthday; my, how times have changed. It seems like only yesterday.' Frances thought she saw a tear appear in the corner of her mother's eye. 'Just look at you so grown up.' Her mother patted her hand. 'What I wouldn't give to have my time over again.'

Frances felt the urge to put her arms around her mother, but it was far too crowded, and she wasn't sure if her mother would welcome such public displays of affection.

The dressmaker arrived later that afternoon; Jenny showed her in. The finished dress was exquisite. Frances twirled this way and that and shrilled with delight. As her mother discreetly left the room, Frances could have sworn she saw her mother wipe away a tear.

'You look beautiful,' said the dressmaker. 'All eyes will be on you, no doubt about that, lass.'

'Thanks to you and all your hard work, Mrs Shepherd,' replied Frances.

'I'm pleased you like it,' said Mary. She helped Frances out of the dress and folded it back up into the box. As she dressed, Frances took a deep breath and decided to be brave and ask if she knew Henry.

'I hope you don't mind me asking, Mrs Shepherd, but do

you know a Henry Shepherd?' She had seated herself down in a chair to slip on her shoes. Mary took a second to reply.

'Why do you ask?' Mary narrowed her eyes. Frances' insides started to tremble.

'I... I, it doesn't matter. My goodness is that the time? Don't let me keep you.'

'I have a son called Henry.' Frances gripped the arm of the chair. 'But I wouldn't have thought you meant him. He doesn't venture to this part of town. Mind, it is a common enough name, I suppose,' Mary continued. Frances moved to stand next to the fireplace. Her palms grew sticky. She wished her mother would hurry up and return.

'I suppose it is,' agreed Frances. She pulled at a loose thread on the hem of her sleeve. She wasn't sure if it was the fire that was causing her to feel hot or the heat emanating from the glare of Mrs Shepherd's eyes on the back of her neck. Composing herself, she turned to face her. 'I don't know where my mother has got to. I'm sure you are a busy woman, Mrs Shepherd, so I'll show you out. And thank you once again; the dress is lovely.'

'You never know, you might meet a young fella tomorrow night,' replied Mary, her smile tight. Frances smiled nervously back and waved the woman goodbye. It was a relief to have her gone. The atmosphere had certainly changed between them after she mentioned Henry.

She was halfway upstairs, carrying her new dress, when the front door opened. It was Robert. Frances stopped when she saw another man standing behind him.

'Hello,' said Robert. 'Is your mother home?' he asked.

'I think she's in her room,' replied Frances, looking over his shoulder and trying to get a better look at the stranger.

'Sorry, let me introduce my old friend from back home. Frances, this is James.' He pointed to James, who took a step forward. 'James, this is Frances, the birthday girl,' said Robert. James nodded at Frances. He was shorter than Robert and wasn't as well-dressed. His complexion was quite youthful compared to Robert's too.

'Hello.' She held out her hand and James took it. His handshake was clammy and weak. 'Nice to meet you, James,' she said.

'Happy birthday,' he said. Frances noticed his accent. It reminded her of a London cab driver.

'Has the dressmaker gone?' came her mother's voice. She was standing at the top of the stairs.

'Yes,' said Frances.

'Sorry I abandoned you, Frances. I had one of my heads. Did I hear Robert come in?'

'Yes,' replied Frances.

'Tell him I'll be down in a minute.' Frances looked at Robert and James. Then her eyes fell on a small brown suitcase at James' feet.

'James will be staying for a couple of days,' he declared, noticing her stare.

'Does Father know?' she asked.

'Of course, James is a dear friend of mine,' replied Robert. Frances' eyes narrowed. Her father never willingly allowed strangers to stay in the house without meeting them first; Robert was the exception. Her mother had not left her father with any option but to allow him to stay.

'Where will he sleep? There's only one spare room, and you're in that,' Frances pointed out.

'He'll bunk up with me, won't you, James? You don't

mind, do you?' He put his arm around James' shoulder and ruffled his hair.

'No, I don't mind,' he replied blushing.

'So, if you'll excuse us, Frances, I think James would like to freshen up after his long train journey.'

'Of course,' she replied and stepped aside.

Edna was beating something in a bowl with vigour, the whisk gripped tightly in her hand. Her face was redder than usual. Another lady, a lot younger than Edna, with auburn hair in rollers and a scarf fastened round her head was standing next to her. They hadn't noticed Frances come in. The other woman was talking away and smiling, her hand on her belly.

'Hello, Edna,' said Frances. Both women looked up, surprised.

'Happy birthday, Frances!' said Edna. 'Come in, love. This is Margaret.' She indicated with her elbow, her hands full. 'She's helping me with all the catering for your party tomorrow.'

'Hello,' said Margaret. 'It's nice to meet you.'

'Hello,' replied Frances.

'So, you're the birthday girl,' said Margaret.

'Unfortunately, yes,' sighed Frances.

'What's the matter? Aren't you looking forward to your party?' asked Margaret.

'Not really.'

'That's a shame. The world's your oyster at this age.'

'You try telling that to my mother,' muttered Frances.

'I remember when I were your age,' she went on. 'I were

courting Harold, my husband, then – those were the days.' She blushed.

'Aye well, that's enough of all that, 'appen you should be getting home, Margaret love. You need some rest. You've been on your feet all day,' said Edna. She had finished and was wiping her brow on her pinafore.

'Congratulations,' said Frances.

'Thank you,' said Margaret. She looked down at her belly and patted it gently.

'You must be excited,' said Frances.

'We can't wait,' she replied. 'Hopefully, we'll have our own place by the time he or she arrives. Right, Edna, I'm off. I've got to pick up a quarter of bacon for Harold's tea on the way home.' She kissed Edna on the cheek, then turned her attention back to Frances. 'It was nice meeting you, Frances.'

'It was nice to meet you too,' said Frances.

'Bye, Edna,' said Margaret.

'Bye, Margaret love, take care,' said Edna.

Margaret left by the back door, and Frances walked to stand next to Edna.

'Right, young lady. I've got this new recipe from Woman's Weekly for a strawberry chiffon cake. I know how much you like strawberries.'

'Yummy,' replied Frances.

'I thought that's what you'd say,' said Edna. 'Are you happy with your dress? Mary Shepherd is a neighbour of mine. Margaret, who you've just met, is her daughter-in-law.'

Frances paused. 'Is Mrs Shepherd a nice lady?' she asked. She was thinking back to her earlier conversation with Mrs Shepherd and how unnerving she'd found the woman to be.

'What an odd question! What makes you ask that?' said Edna.

'No reason. I was just wondering,' replied Frances.

'Mary is a decent woman, but I wouldn't want to get on the wrong side of her, mind.' Edna took out a jar of flour from the pantry.

'What are you making?' asked Frances.'

'Some of those biscuits you like. Now come, tell me about your frock.'

'It's beautiful, Edna, really wonderful.' She spun around as though she was still wearing it. 'I feel like a Hollywood movie star in it.'

'You'll be the envy of all your friends,' said Edna, smiling. 'You might even meet a nice fella.'

'Not you too.'

'What's wrong with that? If I'd looked like you... well, never mind. Sometimes I think youth is wasted on the young.'

Frances held her tongue. She didn't feel that now was the right time to disclose her friendship with Henry Shepherd. But it felt odd to keep secrets from Edna. She wanted to tell her that she'd already met a nice 'fella'. She knew she could trust Edna. After all, Edna had kept her secrets in the past – like the time she had accidentally knocked over a vase in the dining room. Frances had been beside herself with worry, but Edna had helped her clear away the broken pieces. She never told on Frances. When her mother questioned her about it, Edna claimed she didn't know what had happened. There was also the time Frances had lied to her mother about being ill because she didn't want to go to school. And, on another occasion, Edna had caught her trying to steal biscuits but, instead of shouting at her, she just laughed.

'Just because I'm a woman, doesn't mean my first thought is marriage. Times are changing, Edna. I want to do things with my life. I don't just want to be someone's wife!'

'Nothing wrong with being someone's wife. There's not a day goes by when I don't think about my poor Ernest. We had some happy times together.'

'I'm sorry, Edna. I didn't mean anything by it.'

'No, I know you didn't love.'

'It's just Mother is desperate to marry me off.'

'I don't think that's true,' said Edna.

'It is so. All Mother ever goes on about these days is marriage. Originally, I thought that was why she invited Robert here, but now I'm not so sure. I don't know why he's here. And now he's brought a friend.' She placed one of her elbows on the kitchen side and rested her head on her hand. 'I can't help feeling that Mother wants rid of me.'

'Don't be daft. She doesn't want to get shot of you. Just because you don't see eye to eye doesn't mean she doesn't love you,' said Edna.

'Well, she has a funny way of showing it sometimes,' said Frances.

'What about her putting on this party for your birthday and buying you a lovely new frock? Of course she loves you. She's your mother.'

Frances thought about what Edna said and felt a little guilty, especially as they'd spent a nice morning together in town.

'I suppose you're right,' replied Frances. 'It's just, well, I hardly see her these days.'

Edna took hold of her and pulled her up into a tight embrace. Frances' head rested against her considerable bosom, and her arms didn't quite meet around Edna's waist. You're more of a mother to me, thought Frances, as she was comforted.

'Come now, cheer up! It's your birthday. Can't have you moping around here. I've got things to do. I want to leave early today. My lad and his wife are coming around for tea.' Edna released her.

'I don't know what I would do without you, Edna,' she said.

'You'll do fine.' Edna opened her mouth to say something but then closed it again.

'What is it?'

'It's nothing, only you know I won't be here forever.'

'But you're not leaving us just yet?'

'Well, I'm not getting any younger. Working in this kitchen all day... It's hard work.'

'I understand. I just never thought the day would come.' Tears filled her eyes.

'You are silly. Now go on before you set me off crying.'

Frances looked at her reflection in her mother's long mirror and admired her new dress. She hardly recognised herself, with her hair pinned up like one of her favourite screen goddesses. She wished she was going somewhere other than the church hall.

'You look so grown up,' said her mother, who was putting the final touches to her own outfit. 'Quite the young lady.

Although, I'm still not a fan off silver.' There was a tap on the door.

'Are we nearly ready ladies?' came her father's voice from behind. 'We don't want to be late.'

'Yes, we're ready,' replied her mother. 'You can come in now, Edward.' The door opened and in walked her father, looking dapper.

'My goodness, Frances, you look radiant, simply smashing. I can't believe our baby is so grown up, Clarissa darling, can you?'

'No,' she said wistfully.

'You look just like your mother – beautiful,' he continued, his eyes teary. He lovingly gazed at Frances, who returned his smile. 'As your proud father, I reserve the first dance young lady.'

'Of course,' replied Frances.

Chapter Sixteen

'Come on, Henry. We've been walking around here for bloody ages. My feet are killing me. Let's go and have a pint at that pub we passed on the corner,' said Fred, Henry's old school friend.

'It's round here. I know it. How many church halls can there be? We were standing outside the gardens when she said it were around t'corner.' Henry marched on in front.

'If it's not on the next road, I'm going home,' moaned Fred. 'I'm famished.'

Henry stopped walking and turned to face Fred. 'I just want to see her on her birthday.'

'You're a reight bampot!' teased Fred. 'You've only known her two minutes.'

'You'll never understand. Listen... do you hear that?'

'What? I don't hear owt.'

'Shush! It's coming from over there.' Henry pointed.

'Come on! I knew we were close.' He started to run towards the sound of the music.

'Hang on!' shouted Fred. 'I can't run as fast as you.'

They stopped in front of a large, single-storey, red-brick building. Hedges and small trees occupied the sides of it, and a large iron gate faced the road. Light shone from a long rectangular window onto the pavement where they were standing. They ducked into one of the bushes so as not to be seen.

'Things I do for thee,' groaned Fred. 'I'm gunna ruin me trousers.'

'Shush!' whispered Henry. He raised his head slowly so he could get a better look inside. It was full of elegantly dressed people. The party was in full swing. Most of the guests looked to be enjoying themselves. Henry scanned the room for Frances. He eventually found her dancing with a young man. Shivers ran up and down his spine. Enviously, he watched as the young man guided her effortlessly around the dance floor. She looked so beautiful in a shimmering silver dress. He let out a sigh; he wanted to be the one dancing with her. Blood surged around his body and his heart beat uncontrollably as jealousy burned within him. Her dress had no back; it revealed her creamy, flawless flesh. The young man had his palm placed on her skin. He fought the urge to run inside and cover her up with his jacket. He wanted to be the only one allowed to touch her. She was laughing with the young man as he placed his cheek next to hers like the lyrics were suggesting him to do. The band stopped playing, and Frances put her hand to her heart, breathless. Her dress looked familiar. He could have sworn his mum had been working on one just like it.

'Are you done yet?' whispered Fred. 'My knees are hurting, crouching down all this time.'

'Just two more minutes. I think they are about to light the candles,' replied Henry. 'I want to see her blow them out.'

Henry was right. A man carried the birthday cake to the centre of the room to where Frances was standing. Someone had turned the lights off. The candle flames danced and flickered as he walked. Despite only a dim light from the flickering candles, Henry could tell she was blushing. She had a particular look about her when she was embarrassed.

'Do you want a cig, Henry?' asked Fred. Henry nodded, and Fred passed him one and a box of matches. Henry lit it and inhaled. He blew the smoke out slowly and gritted his teeth as the young man she was dancing with earlier went to kiss her cheek. He saw the young man whisper something to Frances causing her to giggle.

Henry threw his cigarette to the ground and kicked the wall.

'What's got into thee?' asked Fred.

'Nowt. Come on, Fred. I've seen enough. You were reight; this were a bad idea. I don't know what I was thinking. Come on, let's get a pint.'

'Who's there?' shouted a male voice.

'Quick, Henry, let's get outta here!' said Fred.

'I know someone is there,' shouted the voice. The man had walked towards the bushes with another man following behind.

'Show yourselves!'

'Robert, come back!' whispered James. 'You don't know who is out here.' He placed a hand on his shoulder.

'Robert, there you are,' said Frances' mother. 'You missed Frances blowing the candles out. I was looking for you everywhere.'

'I needed some fresh air,' he said. 'Let's go back inside and have some cake.' He clasped his hands together and escorted her through the door. James followed.

As soon as they were inside, Henry and Fred made a run for it. Fred was laughing.

'They don't half sound posh,' said Fred. 'I didn't have you down as the kind to mix with their sort.'

'I don't care for their sort, Fred, only her. Now hurry up; I'm dying of thirst.'

❦

'Morning, son,' said his dad. Henry didn't respond. He just poured himself a cup of tea.

'What's up with thee?' asked his mum. 'You've got a face like a wet weekend.'

Henry just shrugged.

'I reckon it's girl trouble,' teased his dad.

'Who's got girl trouble?' asked Arthur as he entered the kitchen.

'The wanderer returns,' said his mum. 'Where've you been?'

'Out and about,' said Arthur. 'What's up with him?' He nodded towards Henry.

'Nobody knows,' said his dad. 'He woke up like that.'

'What's up?' asked Arthur, punching Henry lightly on the arm.

'Nowt.' Henry hunched his shoulders.

Arthur elbowed him in the ribs. 'Tell us?' he teased. 'Who do you need me to hit?'

'Leave him be!' said his mum and clipped Arthur round the back of his head.

'What were that for? I'm only kidding,' said Arthur.

'Well, he clearly doesn't want to talk about it,' she replied.

'Are you coming tonight?' winked Arthur. 'There'll be plenty of fillies to choose from.'

'I was planning to,' replied Henry. 'Are you going?'

'Of course, I wouldn't miss it.' He bit into a slice of bread.

'Reight, me and your dad are off down t'markets. We'll see you both later,' said their mum.

'Alreight, Mother,' mumbled Arthur, his mouth full of bread.

'Don't talk with your mouth full!' she said and clipped him round the head again.

'Ouch!' moaned Arthur. Henry laughed. 'Don't you laugh, or I'll give you a clout round thee lug'ole,' joked Arthur. 'Reight, I'm off out too. You can clear this lot away.'

'Get stuffed!' said Henry, but it was too late; Arthur had run out the door.

Henry was down to his last cigarette. His throat tightened when he saw Frances rushing towards him. He sucked in his breath and tried to ignore the butterflies in his stomach.

'I didn't think you were coming,' he said.

'I didn't think I would make it either. My father took

some convincing. He thinks I'm out with my friend.' Henry went to kiss her cheek, but she pulled away when she saw someone coming.

'Well, we need to hurry if we're to have any time dancing.' Henry reached for her hand. 'This way,' he said. 'I hope you've got your dancing shoes on?'

'I'm afraid my feet are a little sore after last night.'

'That's reight, it was your party. How did it go?' he asked.

'It was better than I expected,' she replied, cheerfully.

'Why's that then?' asked Henry. He suspected he knew why, but he tried to hide his feelings. As Frances told him about the party, Henry tensed. He ran his fingers through his hair, unable to remain quiet any longer. 'I saw you!' He stopped walking.

Frances stopped walking too. A crease formed between her brows as she looked at him. It was the tiniest frown. She looked more beautiful than ever.

'What do you mean, you saw me?' she repeated. 'How?'

'I was outside the church hall.' Henry shoved his hands in his pockets. 'I was only there a couple of minutes.'

'You were there?'

'I just wanted to catch a glimpse of you on your birthday.'

'But what if you'd been seen?'

'What if I had?' he grumbled.

Frances glared at him. 'We've only just met, Henry.'

Henry's shoulders sagged and he looked away. 'I didn't think it through. I should have listened to Fred.' He kicked the pavement.

'Fred?' asked Frances.

'A friend. He came with me.'

'Maybe you should have listened to him,' said Frances. 'If you had been seen... well, I'm not sure what would have happened.'

'I know, and I'm sorry. I'm not normally like this. You're confusing me, Frances. You're in my head all the time.'

Frances sucked in her bottom lip. 'I'm confusing you? Well, I'm sorry. I'll just go, shall I?'

'No! Don't be daft.' When Henry looked into her eyes, he resisted the urge to take her in his arms and kiss her. A faint grin touched his lips. 'It's crazy, I know we've only just met but...' He lifted his head, looked to the sky and sighed. He let out a long, low sound. 'Last night, you stole the air out of my lungs, but then I saw you with him. I know it's none of my business who you dance with, but you were laughing and smiling, and I couldn't sleep for thinking about the two of you together.'

'What are you going on about? Him?'

'Please, Frances put me out of my misery.'

'I should be angry with you. If you had been seen, I wouldn't be here right now.'

'I know and I'm sorry.'

'I danced with practically everyone last night, Henry. What time were you there?'

'I'm not sure. It was late, just before you blew out your birthday candles.'

'It was probably my brother,' she replied. 'You saw me dancing with my brother, Thomas.'

'Your brother?' Colour rushed to his cheeks. He hit the palm of his hand to his forehead. 'I'm such an idiot.'

'Yes, you are,' she teased. 'That is not to say I didn't

dance with other men last night, but you have nothing to feel jealous about.'

'Forgive me. I don't know what got into me. I'm not myself around you Frances. I wouldn't blame you if you didn't want to see me again.'

'Of course I want to see you again. I suppose I should be flattered.' She paused. 'I'm confused too. I don't normally sneak out of the house late in the evening or any other time for that matter to meet boys.' He closed the gap between them and, with a shaky hand, gently touched her face with the tips of his fingers, resisting the urge to kiss her in the middle of the street.

'You just can't do anything like that again, Henry. Do you hear?'

Henry nodded.

'Please try and understand, Henry. We have to keep this a secret for now.'

'I understand. You look so beautiful tonight,' he said. His eyes lingered on her mouth.

'We should get going,' Frances said.

'Of course. It's not far now.'

Chapter Seventeen

Frances handed her coat to the young lady in the cloakroom and turned to take in her surroundings. It was dark inside; the air was thick with smoke. She found Henry chatting to two young men; one looked vaguely familiar.

'Frances, come over here,' said Henry. 'This is my brother Arthur and his mate George.'

'Hello,' said Frances. Looking at the two of them side by side, she could see they were brothers. Although Arthur looked rough around the edges and slightly intimidating.

'I dint realise this were the lass you were meeting, Henry. You lucky beggar!' said Arthur. He turned to Frances. 'We've met before, love. It was at the City Hall dance.' Colour rushed to her cheeks. She instantly remembered the incident. She pursed her lips, unsure what to say.

'Nice to meet you again.' She held out her hand. Arthur tugged on his cigarette and took her hand in his. She couldn't help noticing how rough and big his hands were. They were not a gentleman's hands like her father's.

'Proper young lady, int she?' winked Arthur's friend George. Frances turned her head to the man standing next to Arthur. He was tall and lanky with blond hair. 'Pretty little thing an all.' George grinned at Arthur; then he winked at her. 'Done alright for thissen there, Henry.' He patted Henry on the back. He looked at Frances. 'You fancy a dance later, sweetheart?'

'You keep your greasy hands and eyes off!' warned Arthur. 'She's with our kid. She don't want to be dancing with the likes of you.' He turned to Frances. 'Don't worry about him, love; he's harmless.'

'I'm only asking her for a dance. What's wrong with that?' huffed George. 'You don't mind dancing with me, do you, love?' asked George. He wiggled his hips.

Frances looked at the faces of the men standing in front of her. She was unsure what to make of them. Fiddling with the tips of her fingers, she looked to Henry for support. 'I...I...'

Henry seemed to sense her unease and moved to stand next to her. He placed his arm about her waist. 'I'm afraid, George, she'll be too busy dancing with me all night, sorry, pal.' He turned to Frances. 'You ready?' Frances nodded.

'Sorry,' she said to George. George shrugged.

Arthur slapped him on the back. 'Come on, George; let's find some lasses of our own to dance with.'

Henry took hold of Frances' hand and led her to the dance floor. Every bit of available space was taken. And those who couldn't get on the dancefloor had to contend with tapping their feet around the edges. The music was intoxicating.

'There's not enough room, Henry!'

'Don't fret,' Henry shouted. 'Trust me, I know just the spot.' She was elbowed a few times, and a couple of people trampled on her feet, but Henry was true to his word and steered them to the side of the stage where they were able to dance more freely. 'Told you, hardly anyone comes to the front,' he said. Then, he placed his hands on her waist. Frances stiffened. Henry ran his thumb over her hip bone. She could feel the warmth of his hand through her dress.

Henry held on to her tight. Being so close to his body made her feel lightheaded. She closed her eyes briefly. What would her mother think? When she opened her eyes, Henry was staring at her longingly. She couldn't stop herself from smiling; never had she felt this alive and giddy. They danced until they were breathless. His movements were so precise, perfect and full of energy. She'd only learned to dance listening to the wireless with her friends, but Henry was a natural. He was so graceful and strong. Frances never wanted to be released from his arms. She loved the feel and smell of him. She didn't know if it was the music, the heat or being so close to Henry, but she felt wonderful; everything was perfect. She looked at his mouth and wondered what it would be like to kiss him. A strange tingling sensation rippled through her at the thought.

'Are you alright?' said Henry. Frances nodded.

'Never better,' she replied. 'Although I could do with a drink.' She fanned her face. Henry stopped dancing and took hold of her hand.

'Me too,' he said.

They walked together and found a small table. Henry pulled out a chair for her to sit down. 'I'll get us both a drink. I won't be too long. Will you be alright on your own?'

'I'll be fine,' she said, continuing to fan her face with her hand.

To Frances' relief, it wasn't long before he returned carrying two drinks. She watched as he gracefully manoeuvred around people, careful not to spill the contents of the glasses. He had almost reached her when a tall attractive redhaired girl leaped out in front of him.

'Well, Henry Shepherd, if I live and breathe. I haven't seen you since City Hall.'

Henry stopped walking, glancing over at Frances.

'Rose, nice to see you again,' he said. Rose beamed at him. She placed her hand on his chest and leaned in to kiss his cheek.

'Dance with me, Henry. I haven't been able to find anyone here half as good as you,' she pouted.

Frances was watching them both intently. The same small crease appeared above her nose.

'Sorry, Rose, but I can't; my date is waiting for me.' He signalled with his chin to where Frances was sitting. Rose turned her head and stared at Frances. Her smile faded. Henry shrugged apologetically at Rose and continued to move towards Frances; Rose followed behind.

He placed the drinks on the table. Frances eagerly picked up hers.

'Thank you,' she said. Frances moved her hair from her face and took a sip of her drink. All the while, she felt Rose's eyes on her.

'You don't mind, love, if Henry dances with me?' She had

placed her hands on the table and was leaning towards Henry but looking down at Frances. Henry had seated himself close to Frances.

Slowly, Frances lifted her head from her drink to gaze at Rose's face. She didn't like how forward she was behaving. Although the girl was smiling, Frances couldn't help but sense her aggressive manner. Rose by name, Rose by nature – thorny and dangerous, she thought. Frances looked at Henry and then back at Rose.

'We're old acquaintances, you see,' Rose added. 'Henry and I go way back, don't we, Henry love?' She grinned and appeared to gloat.

I bet you do, thought Frances.

'I work as a buffer not far from where Henry works. So, what d' you say? I'll only keep him a minute.' Rose reached out and squeezed Henry's cheek. Frances gritted her teeth.

'Fine,' replied Frances. 'My feet are hurting, anyway.' Rose beamed triumphantly in return and took hold of Henry's hand. Frances thought she had a wicked smile like a Siren luring a sailor to his death.

'Are you sure you don't mind?' asked Henry. Frances straightened herself.

'It's fine,' she said reassuringly. 'But don't be too long. I must leave soon.'

'I won't,' he replied.

'Come on, Henry!' yelled Rose. 'They're playing our song.'

Our song, thought Frances. How dare she? She watched as they danced together. They looked well matched. It was clear they had a history. Frances' throat burned, and her stomach churned with jealousy. She couldn't take her eyes off them. They moved together effortlessly like Fred Astaire and Ginger Rogers. She knew she could never compete with someone like Rose on the dancefloor. Henry looked so alive. A small group of people had gathered around them and were cheering them on. Rose glanced over at Frances with a smug look on her face, and Frances despised her even more.

Two dances later, they both returned panting and laughing. Rose had her hand placed on Henry's shoulder and was leaning into him. She whispered something in his ear and kissed his cheek.

'See you later, Henry,' she said, and then looked at Frances. 'Nice to meet you,' she said and then walked away.

'That guttersnipe!' Frances rose to her feet. 'I need to leave, Henry!' she snapped and marched towards the cloakroom. Henry followed her.

'Hold up!' he said.

'I'm going to be late!' She stomped up to the counter and handed over her ticket to the woman behind the desk.

'What's up?' asked Henry. Frances couldn't bring herself to look at him.

'Nothing!'

The woman gave Frances her coat, and Frances headed towards the exit.

'Hey, slow down, will tha!' said Henry. He pulled at her arm and took hold of her hand. Frances tried to shake him off.

'Let me go!' she said, gaining a few stares from people around them.

'Not until you tell me what's up,' replied Henry. He let go of her hand and tilted her chin upwards. Frances folded her arms and looked down at the floor. 'Look at me please,' he said.

Frances slowly raised her eyes to meet his.

'God, you are beautiful. Even when you're angry, your eyes sparkle. It's taking every ounce of my willpower not to take you in my arms and kiss you right now.'

'You do and I'll scream. I need to get home,' she repeated. 'Take me home, Henry!' Her eyes glistened as she struggled to hold back tears.

They walked the short distance back to Frances' home in silence. When they reached the Botanical Gardens, Henry took hold of her arm and dragged her into a dark corner.

'What do you think you're doing, Henry Shepherd! Let me go!' she demanded. She thumped at his chest and fought to free herself.

'No! Not until we've cleared the air,' replied Henry. He gently pushed her against the wall and pinned her body with his. 'Now, look at me!'

'No!' she whispered.

'Look at me, please!'

She squeezed her eyes tight. He ran his hand gently down the side of her face and stroked her mouth with his thumb. 'Why are you acting so mardy?' he asked. 'You said you didn't mind if I danced with Rose.'

She opened her eyes and breathed steadily. Henry's face was dangerously close to hers. He looked so handsome; his expression was one of hurt and confusion.

As she breathed out, her anger subsided. 'I didn't... I don't,' she whispered. 'I'm not mad at you. I'm mad at myself for behaving so childishly. But when you were dancing, I felt... you looked so...'

'She means nothing to me, Frances.' He placed a soft kiss on her cheek. 'Compared to you, she is nothing, nobody. She's just an old friend.' He kissed her other cheek.

Frances sighed. She could feel tears trickling down her face. Henry wiped them away with his thumb. 'Don't cry.'

'I'm not,' she replied. 'I'm just being silly.'

Henry brushed his lips delicately against hers. He pulled back and gazed into her eyes. Frances glanced at his lips. Henry bent his head forward once more and his lips pressed against hers, lightly caressing – the light touch made her body tremble. 'If you want me to stop, tell me now,' he whispered. 'Because I have wanted to kiss you forever and I don't know how much control I have left.'

She opened her mouth slightly but not to speak. Henry took this as acceptance. He kissed her, gently and carefully at first. His tongue touched the tip of hers. He groaned softly.

Frances, unsure how to respond, moved her hands slowly up his chest and rested them on the back of his neck like she had seen all the leading ladies do in movies. She'd never kissed a boy before but, with Henry, everything felt right, natural. His breath was warm against her wet lips.

Frances didn't want their kiss to end, but she was aware it was late, and she needed to get home. She placed her hands on his chest and moved her mouth away from his. She could feel his heart beating fast like her own. Both were breathless. He rested his forehead gently on hers, the tips of their noses just touching.

'I have to go,' she whispered. Henry moved his head a fraction so he could look into her eyes.

'When can I see you again?' he asked.

'Next weekend, maybe,' she said. Henry smiled, and

butterflies erupted in her belly. His lips melded to hers once more, but this time the kiss wasn't so gentle. This time it was more urgent. It pained her to have to push him away.

'Why not tomorrow?' said Henry.

'Tomorrow?'

'Yes, come to mine. Me mum will be doing a dinner.'

'Don't you think you should ask your mum first?'

'It'll be fine. She always cooks plenty. Say you'll come!'

'It's a bit strange me coming to your house; I mean we don't really know each other. What will your parents think?' Although Frances knew exactly what his mum would think. The thought of seeing Mrs Shepherd again scared her witless.

'It'll be fine. I'll meet you in town at Fitzalan square, at around half twelve and we can travel together to mine. What do you say?'

'I'm not sure. It's a bit soon.'

'Come on. It'll be fun.'

'I don't think fun is the correct term, but if you insist. Now, I really must go,' she said.

'You won't regret it,' said Henry. 'My mum makes the best Yorkshire puddings.'

They parted ways. Frances wrapped her coat around her body, feeling bereft of his warmth. She had just experienced her first kiss and it was just how she imagined it to be. She sighed and touched her lips. She couldn't wait to see him again; she just wished it wasn't with the rest of his family present.

Chapter Eighteen

Henry gripped Frances' hand to steady her as she stepped down from the tram. He followed the direction of her gaze. It had been raining. Left behind were stagnant, dirty puddles, like sheets of blackened steel. It wasn't the best day for her to visit. Attercliffe looked worse on rainy days. It was dreary. Thick and muggy air made it hard to breathe.

Henry watched her face as she took stock of her new surroundings. He knew she'd never braved this area of Sheffield before. She coughed into her coat.

'It's so grey – not a tree or bit of grass in sight,' she said.

'It's not much, I know,' said Henry, watching her. 'The grey doesn't bother me. It is what it is. I can't help it. We can't all afford to live in big houses.' For the first time since he had met her, Henry felt embarrassed.

'Sorry. I didn't mean anything. It's just...' Henry pulled her into his arms and kissed the tip of her nose.

'This...' He jutted his chin at his surroundings. 'This is not me, Frances.' He shook his head. 'It's where I was born, granted, but it won't be where I die. I plan to do summat with my life.'

She lifted her head and kissed his lips. Eyes wide, he looked down at her before kissing her back.

He took her hand and they started to walk towards his house. 'We'd better get a move on; we don't want to be late.' Frances stopped abruptly and pulled away from him. 'Come on!' She looked at him; the crease he loved so much appeared above her nose once more. 'What's up? Are you nervous? No need to be. It'll be reight. Come on.' He offered her his hand again but she didn't take it.

'I've got something to tell you.'

'Can't it wait? I'm starving.'

'I wanted to tell you before,' she said, looking at the ground. Darkness had swept across the sky, and black clouds loomed heavy overhead.

'It's gunna rain again soon; we'd better hurry,' he said. He grabbed her hand and tried to pull her along, but Frances wouldn't move. He rolled his eyes impatiently. 'What is it, Frances? Just spit it out!'

'I've met your mum before,' she whispered.

'What? When?'

'She made my dress for the party. She reacted oddly when I mentioned your name.'

Henry thought for a minute. He knew he'd seen the dress she was wearing before. But why hadn't his mum said something? It wasn't like his mum to keep secrets.

'Well, if that's all, can we get going now... please?'

'Is that it? Is that all you have to say?'

'Yes. Now let's hurry.' They started walking together again. Henry wasn't sure what to make of it. Did it matter that his mum hadn't mentioned it to him? She must have known it was the same girl he'd been seeing. When the time was right, he would ask her, but now all he wanted to do was get home. He had enough to worry about at present; introducing his family to Frances was a big deal, especially when they hadn't been forewarned.

'You're late,' whispered his dad. 'Gaffer's not happy. Where've you been?'

'I know, sorry. Dad, this is Frances – Frances, this is my dad,' said Henry. Frances stepped forward.

'Hello, love,' said his dad. 'It's nice to meet you. Let me take your coat.' Henry walked through to the kitchen to speak to his mum.

'Mum, there's someone I want you to meet.'

The food smelt delicious. Already seated around the table were Harold and Margaret, who were quietly chatting but stopped when Henry appeared. His mum gave him that look but didn't say a word.

'Do you remember that girl, Frances. I've invited her for dinner. I hope you don't mind.'

'It's a bit short notice, Henry love. I don't think meat's big enough.' She shook her head. 'I wish you'd have asked; the house is a mess.'

'House is spotless; it always is, and she doesn't eat a lot,' said Henry.

'It'll be noisy. Your brother's here.'

'Hang on a minute, what you trying to say?' said Harold.

'She's saying you're a noisy bugger,' laughed Margaret.

'She's here now,' said Henry. 'I can't ask her to leave.'

'No, I don't suppose you can. Show her in then, but she'll have to take us as she finds us.'

'Come on then, lad,' said Harold. 'Where is she? You haven't left her alone, have you?'

Henry darted back through to the other room. Frances looked like a startled deer. His dad was saying something to her, but Frances looked like she couldn't understand a word he was saying. Henry had to chuckle. Standing in his house, she looked out of place, like a beautiful delicate flower. For the first time, he began to have doubts about bringing her here. He walked over to her and gently took hold of both her hands.

'Are you ready?' he said. She nodded.

'Here she is!' shouted Harold. 'Bout chuffing time.' He held out his hand after receiving a scowl from Margaret. 'I'm Harold, Henry's older brother and, as you can see, the better-looking one.' Frances shook his hand. 'Your hand is like ice.' He placed his other hand on top of hers and rubbed it for her. Frances was unaccustomed to such familiarity. 'Don't worry, you'll soon get warmed up. This here is my wife, Margaret.' Margaret stood up to say hello. 'Sit down, she's not chuffing royalty,' he teased.

'Shut your pie hole, Harold, you're embarrassing the young lass,' replied Margaret. 'Besides, we've met before, haven't we, love?' Frances nodded. Henry watched on confused.

'Oh aye, when?' asked Harold.

'Never you mind,' she said and winked at Frances. 'You

don't go telling your husband everything, Frances. You have to keep 'em on their toes,' she teased.

'Reight, come on you lot, or this dinner will be ruined,' said Henry's mum. Frances looked at her and was greeted with a hard look; it made Frances' insides tremble.

'Frances, this is my mum,' said Henry.

Chapter Nineteen

'Hello, Mrs Shepherd,' said Frances, trying hard to stop her voice from shaking. It would have been the perfect opportunity for Henry's mum to say they had met before, several times in fact, but she never acknowledged it, so Frances didn't refer to it either.

'You can call me Mary.' She nodded. 'Now sit before it gets cold.'

Frances had never tasted Yorkshire puddings quite like them; they were delicious, even better than Edna's, although she would never admit that to Edna. Frances still couldn't believe that Edna had handed her notice in. It had been quite a shock for the family, especially Frances. She had given her notice the morning after Frances' birthday party but Frances' mother refused to except it. With Robert going back to London too, her mother had been in a foul mood the past few days.

It was so noisy around the table, not like it was in her

house. She loved watching how they interacted with each other, always joking and teasing. They appeared to enjoy each other's company. She tried to keep up with the conversation but understanding them was difficult at times, especially Henry's dad. She could just picture her mum's reaction if she'd been there. They asked her lots of questions and, after a while, she started to feel at ease and enjoy herself. It was only Henry's mum who made her feel uncomfortable. Now and then she would catch her looking her way.

'That were lovely, Mum,' said Henry. 'Thanks.'

'Yes, Mrs Shepherd, that was delightful, thank you,' added Frances.

'Mary, call me Mary.'

'Dunt she talk posh,' said Harold.

'Leave her be,' said Margaret, nudging him in the ribs. 'I think she sounds lovely.' She winked at Frances.

'Right, Henry, Harold, you can wash up,' ordered Mary.

'I can help,' said Frances.

'No, you're a guest, lads will do it.' She made her way to the front room. 'Can you make a pot of tea?' she asked, looking directly at Henry's dad, who nodded in reply. 'There's some cake in't tin. Come on, ladies; let's leave 'em to it.'

Frances couldn't eat another thing, but she wasn't about to tell Henry's mum. She seated herself in a high-back chair, opposite his mum, with her legs together and her hands placed in her lap. Frances glanced about her while she waited for his mum to start a conversation. It was a small room, about the size of her hallway, she mused, but it was cosy. Margaret had disappeared somewhere.

'Did everyone admire your dress?' she finally said. Frances

let out a breath she hadn't realised she was holding.

'Oh, yes, Mrs... I mean, Mary. Everybody commented on how beautiful it was.'

'Good, I'm pleased it went well for you.' She paused, looked away and then turned to face Frances, her gaze intensifying. 'Look, I'm a woman of few words. I'm not one for beating about the bush, so I'll say this once, and then I'll say no more on the matter. He's not right for you. You'll break his heart, and I'll not stand by and let you do it. He's falling for you; I can see that. I'm his mum. I'm not blind. Do us all a favour and end it now before it's too late.' She was interrupted by Henry's dad bringing in a tray with a teapot, cups and a delicious Victoria sponge on a plate decorated with blue flowers. He placed it down on a small table and went back into the kitchen. Frances' hands shook. Such a personal rebuke from Henry's mum had taken her by surprise, and she was not sure how to respond.

'I was one of thirteen children; I had a difficult childhood,' she continued. 'I know what it's like to try and be heard. If you're doing this to get a reaction... attention from your mother, well I won't stand by and let you use Henry this way.' Frances bit her bottom lip to stop it from quivering. 'Look, you're a nice girl, and I don't want to upset you, but nowt good will come of this.' She leaned forward and started to pour the tea. 'Tea?' she asked as if nothing had just occurred.

Margaret re-entered the room, touching her small baby bump, oblivious to the tension.

'Ooh, cake,' she said.

'Do you want a slice, Margaret love? Where are the plates, George?' she shouted.

'Reight gaffer!' called Henry's dad who came rushing in with plates and a jug filled with milk. Henry's mum cut Margaret a slice, and Henry's dad passed it to her. Frances was a tiny bit envious over how they fussed over Margaret and how warmly Henry's mum spoke to her. She tried to put Mary's words to the back of her mind, at least until she was alone. Henry and Harold walked in, and she was relieved to see a friendly face. She stood and asked to go to the bathroom.

'Is it upstairs?' she asked. Everyone looked at her. 'What is it?' She blushed, looking at Henry.

'Nowt,' he said. 'Come on; I'll show thee.' She noticed his accent had become thicker in the short time he'd been with his family.

Henry led her outside. 'Where are we going?' she asked. It was raining, and Frances was annoyed he hadn't mentioned bringing her coat. They walked across the yard, and Henry pointed to a wooden door attached to a small building.

'Bathroom,' he said, smiling.

'Sorry? You mean...' Henry nodded.

'I'll wait for you outside,' he said. Frances opened the door and looked in. It was basic, with just a toilet and news-paper cut into squares for toilet paper. She made her way inside and closed the door. She took the paper and wiped around the seat, then lifted her dress, took down her under-garments and lowered herself down. Nothing.

'I can't go with you standing outside, Henry!' she said.

'Don't be daft. I'm not listening.'

'I still can't,' she moaned.

'Well, I'm not leaving you. I don't know who'll turn up.'

'You mean other people use this toilet too?' She couldn't

disguise the disgust in her voice.

'Yup.'

Frances shot up and righted herself. She opened the door and walked outside. 'I'll wait.' She folded her arms and marched past him.

'Suit thee sen.' He chuckled.

When they re-entered the house, Margaret and Harold were leaving.

'It was nice to meet you,' said Harold, shaking her hand.

'Yes, we hope to see you again soon,' said Margaret. Frances looked at Henry's mum, who looked away. 'We'll be off then, Mary, catch you later. I'll pop round next week for those bits you've been knitting for the baby.'

'Yes, you take care of yourself,' replied Henry's dad. 'Make sure Harold does all the lifting, Margaret love.'

'I will,' she said, and they left.

'We should be going too,' said Henry. 'Frances has to get home.'

'Well, it were lovely to meet you at last, Frances love. Our Henry hasn't shut up about thee,' said Henry's dad.

Henry blushed.

'Look at him; he's gone red,' teased his dad. 'Don't be a stranger, Frances. You know where we live now.'

Henry fetched her coat. His mum was silent.

'Thank you for having me over. The food was delicious.' She looked at Henry's mum. Henry helped her on with her coat. 'Well, goodbye then.'

'Yes, goodbye, Frances,' said Henry's dad. His mum just nodded her head and watched as they both walked outside.

Chapter Twenty

It was a glorious morning. Frances and Henry were huddled together on a busy train heading towards Hathersage. They were happy to leave behind the endless skyline of monstrous factory chimneys breathing out black smoke. What lay in wait for them was the fresh air of the rolling countryside.

'It's Edna's day off. I still can't believe she's handed in her notice. I blame my mother. Anyway, I was able to sneak the picnic basket from the pantry and fill it with some goodies. I've got sandwiches, chicken drumsticks, biscuits and cake.'

'Crikey! Who are you feeding, the five thousand?'

'Is it too much? I just want this day to be perfect.'

'And it will be.'

'It's so romantic,' she said, relaxing into her seat as the train blew its whistle and chugged along.

They held hands discreetly under the table and admired the picturesque green landscape. Frances began to hum.

'That sounds so pretty,' said Henry. 'I've heard it before. What's it called?'

'"Where or When", I think.'

'Aye, I remember now. Why don't you sing it?'

'I couldn't. There are far too many people around.'

'If you want to be an actress, you'll need to get used to an audience.'

Henry watched her as she began to quietly sing the words. He was captivated by her hair, which fell in waves to her shoulders; her delicate features; and the green dress which matched her eyes and fitted her in all the right places. He loved the sound of her voice and her sweet intoxicating scent.

'My eyes never tire of looking at you, Frances. I wish I had a camera to capture you at this precise moment; I would treasure it forever. Everything about this moment is perfect.'

'For someone who doesn't like to read books, Henry Shepherd, sometimes you sound like a poet.'

Henry loved the countryside but, sitting next to Frances, everything around seemed to lose its lustre. He couldn't stop fantasising about kissing her in the coach compartment where they were seated. He watched her mouth part and her chest gently lift and fall, every time she noticed something new. He wondered what it would feel like to kiss her neck and along her collarbone to her breasts. With that image, he had to cross his legs, feeling his trousers tighten.

Frances turned in her seat. 'We're almost there.' She beamed. Lucky for Henry, she was oblivious to the discomfort he was in. He could only manage a nod as he adjusted his position and tried to compose himself before they disembarked the train.

They left the train station and headed towards a picnic spot Henry favoured. Henry carried the basket and held her hand as they climbed over stiles into the open fields. They trundled over the uneven terrain until they came to a stream with trees on both sides and large stepping stones giving access across the water.

'Here we are,' said Henry.

'This is glorious!' Frances announced with her arms stretched out wide, smiling. 'Shall we sit over there?' She pointed to a lush patch of green grass.

'Looks good to me,' replied Henry. He followed Frances, who had taken the basket from him and had proceeded to spread out the blanket. 'Here, let me help you,' said Henry rushing to her side. He grabbed one of the corners to help lay it flat.

'Thank you,' said Frances.

'No bother,' said Henry.

Frances took out the food she had prepared and placed it down.

'It's probably the poshest picnic I've been on. We normally only have beef dripping sandwiches.'

'I don't think I've ever eaten that,' said Frances. 'Is it nice? It doesn't sound particularly appetising.'

'It's lovely,' he replied.

Henry stretched out his legs and leaned back on his elbows. He watched as the summer breeze blew her hair from her face and gently kissed her cheeks. A hint of warm yellows and golds surrounded her. He couldn't remember the last time he'd felt so relaxed and happy.

᛭

The sun beat down as they rested. The food was delicious, but Henry couldn't eat another bite. He flicked a bug away that was crawling on his arm and relaxed back. He let out a satisfied sigh and placed his hands on his stomach. Frances lay on her side with her head resting on her hand. He could sense her staring at him. Her hand hovered tentatively close to his face.

'Enjoying the view?' he asked, the corners of his mouth turning upwards into a subtle smile. He could see she was blushing. She quickly withdrew her hand and sat upright. She plucked some daisies from the ground and started to make a chain.

'Thank you,' she murmured. Henry turned slightly.

'For what?' he asked.

'For being here with me today.'

'It's me that should be thanking you,' he replied. He took the daisy chain from her grasp and placed it on her head. 'You are my fair lady, and I am your humble servant.' He kissed her hand. 'What do you want, Frances? Whatever you want, just tell me, and I will give it to you.' Henry knew what he wanted. He wanted to take her in his arms and kiss her all over, but he knew she wasn't ready for that. Frances inched her body closer to Henry's and rested her head on his chest, her body parallel with his

'Do you think you will always live in Sheffield, Henry?' Henry shrugged.

'Some days when I've had a hard day at work, I wish I could leave. It can be dangerous in the factory. What about you?' He lightly stroked her hair.

'I like living in Sheffield, don't misunderstand me, but I want to see the world and experience new and exciting things,' replied Frances.

'Like what?'

'I don't know – to start with maybe visit the Eiffel Tower or the Taj Mahal.' Frances rested on her elbows and looked down into his eyes.

'And then what?'

'It has always been my dream, from being a little girl when my father first took me to the pictures, to go to America! One day I want to see my name in lights! It's no secret.'

Henry couldn't help smiling at her. He loved her passion for life; in fact, he was beginning to realise he loved everything about her.

'Haven't you ever wanted to travel?' she asked.

'Yes, of course, but you need money to be able to travel,' said Henry. 'I haven't got enough for a trip to the coast, ne'r mind travelling round the world.'

'I realise travelling costs money.' Frances sat up and hugged her knees. 'But I don't want to live my life through someone else's. I don't want to just experience life through books and films.'

'And when you've conquered the world, what then?' Henry asked.

'Does there have to be a 'what then'? Can't I just live in the moment?'

'There's nothing wrong with dreams, but they won't satisfy all of your needs.'

'Well, I haven't thought that far ahead yet.' She turned her head away, looked to the sky and sighed.

'I have,' said Henry. Frances turned back to face him.

'You have?'

'Yes.'

'Aren't you going to tell me?'

'You'll think me daft.'

'No, I won't. I shared my dream with you,' she said.

'Well, in my future, I see a home, and two people who are madly in love and I see children.' He rubbed a palm over his mouth and waited for her reaction.

'That doesn't sound terribly exciting,' pouted Frances.

'Maybe not to you,' said Henry, disappointed by her response. 'And maybe not right now, but one day you might change your mind.' He pulled Frances down, on top of his body, then switched positions so he could see into her beautiful, beguiling eyes, a dreamy expression on his face. 'That's not all I want. One day I would like to own some land and be self-sufficient. Somewhere far away from all the smog. I'd like a few animals and I want to wake every morning and see nothing but green for miles around, none of the mucky blackness.'

'You should do it!' said Frances.

'I've never told anyone that before.'

'You're quite a romantic,' said Frances.

'Gi o'er! Are you saying I'm soppy?'

'No, not at all. It's just nice to know you have ambitions. I like that about a person,' said Frances.

'You don't want someone with money then?' he asked.

'Money isn't everything.'

'That's easy for you to say – you don't have to worry

about it.'

'It's important, yes, but it shouldn't define a person. I think you can do anything if you put your mind to it.'

'Well, that's all well and good but I'd need more money than I'm earning now to be able to afford to buy some land,' said Henry.

'You could take out a loan,' she suggested.

Henry shook his head and laughed. 'Who in their right mind is going to give me money?'

'You never know,' replied Frances.

'Could you marry someone without money?'

'I want to marry for love, not wealth or social status.'

'Can you see yourself living on a small farm?' asked Henry.

'I'm not sure. It would be awfully smelly.' Frances wrinkled her nose.

'No more than living in Sheffield,' said Henry.

'My father wants me to be a nurse and my mother wants me to marry a wealthy man. Nobody has asked me what I want. All I know is that, right now, I'm happy being here with you.'

'Me too. But all the books you read, what do they have in common?' The small crease appeared above her nose, and she shrugged. Henry kissed her nose. She took his breath away.

'Love, Frances. They all have love in common. I don't need to travel around the world to find what I'm looking for. I'm not rich but, one day, who knows? I might own that bit of land. And if I need to wait for you while you travel the world, I will, because when you find the one, you'll do anything to keep them.'

Henry placed his mouth over Frances' and delicately kissed her. She tasted sweet; her lips were soft and inviting. Henry knew he didn't need to see any man-made wonders because his eyes already beheld a wondrous treasure.

'You say the sweetest things, Henry.'

'I only say what's true.'

'I'm hot,' she said, smiling. 'Do you fancy dipping your toes in the stream with me?' Henry lifted his weight from her body. Frances sleepily stretched out her arms and leaned forward to slip off her shoes. Henry gulped at the sight of her bare flesh as she peeled down her stockings.

'I'm good. You go. I'll stay and look after the things.'

Henry watched her saunter towards the stream and onto the stepping stones. Gingerly, she hopped onto a giant rock. With her dress hitched above her knees, she sat down and dangled her legs over the side. Henry watched lustfully.

'The water is cold,' she squealed. Henry laughed. The sunlight reflected off the surface, making it sparkle. He watched as she dipped her fingertips in to create ripples. It was such a beautiful day; he didn't want it to end, but he knew it had to, and soon. She'd be worrying about her parents.

Just then, he heard male voices coming from the opposite end of the stream. He turned his head sharply and saw two young men heading in Frances' direction. Frances jumped up and pulled down her dress. She almost stumbled into the water as the two men reached the stepping stones. They had seen her but not Henry.

'Hey, what's the hurry, lass?' one of them yelled. Frances turned to walk away.

'Don't go! Me and my mate need a hand getting across

the stepping stones,' he sneered as Frances hurried to the grass.

'Slow down, we won't hurt you,' added the other one smirking.

Henry shot upright. Frances ran towards him, seated herself on the blanket and started to put her stockings and shoes back on.

The two men, both smaller and older than Henry, approached, laughing and staring directly at Frances as they neared. Henry moved towards them his eyes full of fury.

'You alright there, pal?' one of the men asked Henry. Henry remained silent. 'We mean no harm. We were just admiring the view. 'Nice little filly like that needs to be admired, don't you think, Stan?' He turned to his friend and winked. 'We've been walking for ages. You don't have a drink we can have, do you?' he asked.

'There's nothing for you here!' warned Henry. He was standing with his shoulders back, his fists clenched. He narrowed his eyes, ready to fight.

'That's a shame,' the one called Stan said. Frances watched on, clutching the edges of the blanket. 'We'll be on our way then,' he said and winked at Frances. 'If you fancy a real man, miss, then why don't you come along with us.' Henry took a step closer. Frances reached out and held him back by the hem of his trousers. The man sniggered. 'No? Oh well.'

The two men then proceeded to walk on, smiling and laughing to themselves. Anger surged through Henry. His skin was tingling. He wanted to rip their heads off for embarrassing his girl like that.

'Are you alright?' he asked, turning to Frances, who was

trying to fold the picnic blanket.

'Yes,' she replied. 'Are you?'

'Come on! We need to leave.' He reached down and collected their picnic things.

Very few words were uttered on the way back to the station.

'Are you going to talk to me?' Frances asked as they walked back through the fields.

'What do you want me to say?'

'Anything. Why don't you start with why you're so mad at me?'

'Mad at you? I'm not mad at you. I'm mad at missen because I should have hit them for leering at you. If our Arthur were here, he wouldn't have hesitated.'

'Lucky for the both of us you're not Arthur,' she said.

'What's that supposed to mean?' he snapped.

'Nothing. Henry, please don't be angry. Nothing happened.'

'Don't you get it?'

'Get what?'

He reached forward and took her hand. 'I love you.'

'You love me?' Frances' eyes widened.

'Yes, why is that such a surprise?' He gazed at her. 'I don't expect you to love me back, not yet anyway. If anything were to 'appen to you – well, I don't know what I would do.'

'You love me?'

'Yes,' he said with a playful smile. He pulled her into his arms, and they kissed.

Chapter Twenty-One

'Oh, I wish this blasted rain would go away!' Frances pressed her forehead to the glass and looked out at the sodden flower beds in her garden. Her breathing caused condensation to form on the windows. 'I hate having to stay indoors.'

'You mean you hate not seeing Henry,' teased Agnes.

Frances quickly turned to face her.

Agnes was reclining on Frances' bed, flicking through magazines.' She paused to look up at Frances. 'I know that look. You're in love.'

'What if I am?' She wrinkled her nose and playfully stuck out her tongue.

'I bet you haven't told your parents about him yet.' Frances shrugged. 'I thought not, and I bet you aren't going to, are you?'

'Oh, I don't know, Agnes.' She made her way to the bed and plopped herself down. 'I want to, really I do, but it's not that easy. You know what Mother is like.' She picked up a magazine and then placed it back down again.

'Well, you can't go sneaking around forever, Frances Eton. They'll find out sooner or later. You're lucky to have kept the secret this long. You can't keep pretending you're meeting me. What if you get caught? Wouldn't that be even worse?'

'You're right. I know you're right. But now just isn't the time.'

'What are you waiting for? You know there's a war coming.'

'Oh, don't say that, Agnes! I don't want a war.'

'Nobody wants another war, silly, but my father says the Nazis aren't playing fair.'

'Let's not talk about it. It gives me the chills.'

'When are you meeting him again?' asked Agnes.

'Sunday. We're going to the pictures. Do you want to come?'

'And play gooseberry? No thanks.' Agnes licked her finger and turned another page. 'Look at that!' She pointed to a picture of a glamourous model wearing a straw hat with a wide brim covered in flowers. 'I like that!'

'What is it?' Frances leaned over her to get a closer look.

'Do you think it would suit me?'

'I don't see why not; all hats suit you, Agnes. Look.' She pointed to a picture of Cary Grant and Jean Arthur. 'Don't they both look dashing?' She folded her arms. 'I'm fed up with reading about other people's lives. I want people to be reading about mine. I'm never going to be a Hollywood star at this rate.'

'You've spoken about it long enough, Frances. If it means

that much to you, why don't you just go! What's stopping you?' Frances bit her bottom lip. 'Well?'

'What do you think?' replied Frances.

'You've got it bad,' teased Agnes.

'I know. What am I going to do?'

'Let's read our horoscopes. Maybe the answer will be in there.'

'What for? It's all just made-up nonsense.'

'Come on, it'll be fun!' Agnes flicked through the pages till she found the right place. 'Cancer, that's you...ha. You won't believe what it says.'

'What?'

'You will meet a tall, dark stranger.'

Frances rolled her eyes.

'See, I said it was nonsense,' said Frances.

They carried on looking through the magazines and didn't speak for a few minutes.

'Did I tell you that Henry's mother practically warned me off? She claims I am going to break his heart.'

'She's probably right.'

'What do you mean?' Frances stared down at her. Agnes closed the magazine and gazed at her.

'What I mean is you still haven't told your parents about him, which probably means your ashamed of him.'

'I'm not!'

'Look, it's none of my business, but if it was me and I was serious about a boy, then I would tell the world. Life's too short not to!'

'I know you're right, but I just don't feel now is the right time. I like Henry. I like him a lot, but we haven't known each other long.'

'Well, you know best,' said Agnes. 'Look, the rain has stopped! I must be going soon.'

'Father said he would drive you home so no need to rush. He's taking Mother to the station. Robert telephoned to say he needs her help with something; it sounded ominous. Father doesn't mind driving you home.'

'What time is he leaving?'

'I think he said about two o'clock.'

'What do you have against Robert? I thought he was a gentleman when we met at your party.'

'I don't know. I don't not like him. Only...'

'Only?'

'It's just Mother acts so differently with him.' Frances walked over to her dressing table and looked at herself in the mirror. 'It's like she cares only about him.'

'I'm sure you're just imagining it, Frances.'

'Maybe you're right. Did I mention Father wants me to become a nurse?'

Agnes nodded. 'Are you considering it?'

'Absolutely not! I mean, can you see me studying anatomy?'

'I think it would be a good thing to do. We could train together.'

'What about America?' asked Frances.

'We're on the brink of war. The country will need more nurses soon.'

'You sound just like my father.' They were interrupted by a knock on her bedroom door. 'Who is it?' said Frances. The door opened.

'I've come to tell you I have to leave now; something has come up so if you still want a lift, Agnes, you'd better come right away,' said Frances' father. He smiled at the two girls, but his eyes had lost some of their warmth.

'What's the matter, Father?'

'Nothing for you to worry about, dear. Right, I'm going downstairs. I'll wait for you there, Agnes.'

'Thank you, Dr Eton,' replied Agnes. He walked out of the room, closing the door behind him. Agnes jumped off the bed. 'Right, I'm off. If the weather is nice, do you fancy meeting Friday? We could go into town.'

'Alright,' said Frances.

'I'll telephone you, and we can finalise the details,' said Agnes.

They left Frances' bedroom and walked down the stairs to her father who was standing in the hallway, waiting.

The friends hugged goodbye.

She waited until she heard the car drive off and then headed to the kitchen. She wanted to catch a glimpse of Edna's replacement. Edna was showing her around the kitchen that afternoon.

'It's all very posh!' Frances heard a woman exclaim. She waited in the doorway and listened, observing the woman from behind the door. The woman was smaller than Edna and, although she was younger, the passing of time hadn't been so kind to her. She was sallow and skeleton-like.

'You did say you've cooked for a family before, Mrs Vickers.'

'I did, but it weren't a big kitchen like this one.'

'Aye, well. You'll get used to it, and don't worry, Jenny can help you if you get in any bother,' replied Edna. 'Right, do you have any questions?'

'I don't think so. You've been quite thorough,' said the woman. Frances tapped lightly on the door.

'Hello, Edna, only me,' she said as she entered.

'Hello, Frances dear. Good timing. This is Mrs Vickers. She's the replacement cook. Ivy, this is Frances, the youngest of the Eton children.'

'How do you do, Mrs Vickers?' Frances held out her hand. Mrs Vickers took it.

'Nice to meet you, miss,' she replied.

'When will you be joining us, Mrs Vickers?' asked Frances.

'Next Tuesday.'

'And don't be late!' warned Edna. 'Dr Eton is a busy man, and he likes breakfast early.'

'Yes, of course. Well, I must be getting off home. Thank you for your time, Edna, and it was nice to meet you, miss.'

Edna opened the back door and handed Mrs Vickers a key. She waited for Edna to close the door before she spoke again.

'Oh, Edna! Do you have to go? It just won't be the same without you here.'

'Now, now. We've talked about this, Frances. You're a grown woman now. You'll be just fine when I'm gone.'

'Can we at least see each other occasionally?' moaned Frances.

'Of course we can. Besides, a little birdy tells me you've been seeing quite a bit of Henry Shepherd.' Edna gave her a knowing look. Frances blushed. 'Don't be embarrassed. He's a lovely lad. You could do a lot worse.'

'Who told you?'

'Never you mind.'

'Do you know him well?' asked Frances.

'You could say that,' replied Edna.

'What does that mean?'

Edna pretended not to hear and instead started to collect various pots and pans in preparation for dinner.

'Edna!' cried Frances. 'Tell me! What do you know?' She came to stand in front of the older woman, placing two hands on her arms. 'Please, I beg you.'

'Fetch some potatoes from the pantry and get peeling and I'll tell you everything I know,' she chuckled.

Frances hugged her before running to the pantry. 'I'm going to miss our chats, Edna!' she said.

'Aye, me too, love, me too,' she said sadly.

Chapter Twenty-Two

⚜

It was a busy Saturday afternoon. Shoppers of all ages hurried on their way, caught up in their own demanding lives. Trams rang their bells as they stopped to let people on and off. Families and friends queued outside the cinema, hoping to catch the latest movie.

Henry and Frances walked out of the dark into the bright sunshine. Henry reached for Frances' hand; she hesitated for a moment before she let him hold it.

'Did you enjoy the film?' He grinned.

'Yes, thank you. I've had a lovely time.' Secretly, though, she would have much preferred to see anything other than a Tarzan film.

'Where to now?' asked Henry. Frances shrugged. 'Shall we grab a cup of tea somewhere?'

'That sounds lovely.' She didn't understand why she suddenly felt nervous. When their were watching the film, she didn't mind him holding her hand because no one could see them but, here, standing for all to see, she felt uneasy. She'd never held a boy's hand in public before. She looked at their connecting fingers, her gloved hand so small in his.

'Are you alright, Frances?' asked Henry.

'I'm fine.'

'You make me feel like the luckiest man alive. I want to beat my chest and scream, just like Johnny Weissmuller. 'I love Frances Eton!" He lifted her hand to his mouth and placed a soft kiss on the back of it.

'You are silly, Henry.'

'We'll head down Dixon Lane if you don't mind?'

'No, I don't mind,' she said.

Henry pulled out a wooden chair for Frances and waited for her to take a seat. A young waitress with an ample bosom and wide hips approached their table, smiling at Henry.

'What will it be, love?' she asked, pushing a strand of hair back under her hairnet with her pencil.

'Tea for two please?' He turned to Frances. 'Do you want summat to eat?'

'No, just tea, please.'

Frances looked with interest at the young waitress, who appeared to be openly flirting with Henry.

'Sure?' he asked. Frances nodded. Henry turned his attention back to the waitress. 'I'll have a cream bun, please.'

'Right you are, love,' replied the waitress. 'Coming straight up.' Frances was pleased that Henry seemed oblivious to the young woman's best efforts.

It was a small café that had seen better days. They had

decided to take a table at the back of the room for more privacy. It was alive with noisy customers talking and the clatter of crockery – far too distracting. She took off her gloves and looked around. Henry appeared unfazed. He leaned forward in his seat and took hold of her hand once more.

'Have I told you just how lovely you look today?' He gently rubbed his thumb over the back of her hand.

'Yes, at least a dozen times already,' she teased.

'Well, it's true,' he replied. 'You are lovely.' He gazed longingly into her eyes.

'Don't look at me like that,' she whispered.

'Like what?'

'Like you know what I'm wearing under my dress.' She sucked in her bottom lip and gave him a half-smile.

'I can't help it. Especially when you smile at me like that.'

The tea and cake arrived. Frances quickly pulled her hand away for fear the waitress would see, but she paid her no attention. All her focus was on Henry.

'You pay at the till over there when you've finished, love.' The waitress lightly touched Henry's shoulder and pointed to a counter close to the entrance.

'Thanks,' replied Henry. She giggled and walked away.

Frances placed the tea strainer over the cup and began to pour. She could feel Henry's eyes on her.

'You're watching me.'

'It's not a crime, is it?' teased Henry. 'Besides, I could watch you all day.'

'Stop, or you'll make me blush. Or worse, I'll spill the tea.'

'Do you know that it's been almost a month since I first met you?'

Frances paused with the milk jug mid-air and looked at him. 'It doesn't feel it,' she said.

Henry picked up a couple of sugar lumps and dropped them into his cup.

'It doesn't to me neither, but it is.' Henry tilted his head. 'I would have never imagined I would be sitting down Dixon Lane with thee, drinking tea.'

She watched as he devoured his cake. She felt the urge to reach out and wipe away the tiny bit of cream that was sitting on his chin – any excuse to touch him – but she quickly remembered herself. Instead, she just pointed to her chin and waited for him to catch on.

'What? Do I have something on me face?'

Frances nodded. He was so handsome, so uninhibited and free. Henry wiped away the cream and Frances wondered what her mother would have thought of Henry at that moment.

As though reading her mind, Henry asked, 'What did you think of me when you saw me on that first day?'

'I... I can't remember,' replied Frances. But she could. She remembered every detail of his handsome face that day and exactly how she felt.

'Come on! I won't be offended.' Frances picked up her cup and blew on her tea. Henry stared at her and waited. Frances could feel her cheeks burn.

'I thought... I thought that you.' Why she felt embarrassed, she didn't know. Henry had been nothing but honest with her. She knew how she felt about him, so why was she finding it so difficult to put it into words?

Frances placed her cup back onto its saucer.

'Go on,' he said encouragingly.

'I thought that you were extraordinarily handsome.'

'Phew! That's a relief,' he joked. 'I wondered what you were going to say for a moment.' He looked amused.

Frances pushed her hair back from her face. His eyes twinkled. She gazed at him, at his mouth, and suddenly the air in the café became stifling.

'Frances,' said Henry. Frances looked at him. The way he said her name, so slowly and intimately made her weak at the knees. He reached for her hand. His eyes fixed on her face. 'I feel like the luckiest man alive.' Frances looked back into his eyes and could barely breathe.

'We should get going,' said Frances.

'So soon?' Frances nodded. 'Finish your tea and I'll pay the bill.'

They walked in silence. Henry reached into his pocket, pulled out a packet of cigarettes and offered her one. Frances declined. She watched as he lit his cigarette and drew heavily on it.

They reached the tram stop. In one swift movement, Henry crushed her to his chest, his mouth close to her ear.

'Do you want to know what I thought of you on that first day?' he whispered. She nodded. 'That you were the day to my night, the stars to my moon.' Frances held her breath and closed her eyes; her throat tightened as his lips moved from her ear to her cheek. 'I thought I would die if I never saw thee again.' His lips finally found hers. His kiss was slow and tender and Frances kissed him back. 'Meet me tomorrow,' he mumbled through kisses. 'We can go to Millhouses Park.'

She opened her eyes and wrapped her arms around him. 'But we're not allowed to swim together there, remember?'

'I know a secret place,' he said with a sparkle in his eye.

'Oh, Henry,' she said softly. 'You'll get us into trouble.'

'I'll look after you.' She kissed him, no longer caring who saw or what her parents might think if they found out. All she cared about was him.

Chapter Twenty-Three

The sun shone brilliantly, making the water on the boating lake sparkle. Henry waited for Frances in the shade of a tree. Tiny beads of sweat glistened on his forehead. He stared at the water longingly, ready to jump into to the cool water. He saw Frances approaching from across the grass, wearing a cornflower-blue summer dress. Her hair was shimmering in the sunlight. Her head held high, she looked like she was walking on air. His heart filled with pride.

'Frances!' he called out as she neared him. 'Have you not brought your bathers?' he looked lovingly at her

'No, but you go ahead. I'll be happy just dipping my toes in.' He raised his hand to her face, ran his fingers down the side of her cheek and along her jaw, and placed a soft, delicate kiss upon her lips. They walked towards the swimming pool, which was segregated with iron bars, men on one side women on the other.

Henry took her hand and led her through some trees. When they neared a small embankment, close to the edge, Henry quickly slipped off his trousers.

'What are you doing?' gasped Frances.

'Getting changed,' said Henry.

'What here?'

'Where else?'

'But? There are people just over there.'

'Don't worry. I have my bathers underneath my trousers.' He unbuttoned his shirt. The corners of Henry's mouth twitched upwards, amused at her discomfort. She'd probably never seen a man half naked before. Making the most of it, he took off his shirt and began to stretch. Frances' lips parted and she gasped. Henry had to try hard to suppress a grin.

'Edna was right about you,' she said.

'What do you mean?' asked Henry, his hands on his hips.

'A proper exhibitionist.'

'A what?'

'Nothing... Edna was telling me stories of you running around the yard naked when you were little, that's all.'

'She did, did she?' Henry took a step closer to her and pulled her to him. Colour rushed to her cheeks. All that was between them was the thin layer of his bathers. Henry could tell she was unsure where to place her hands. 'What else did she say about me then?' he asked.

'That's for me to know,' she teased.

'Is it now? I'm sure I could get it out of you. I have my ways.' His eyes darkened and a mischievous grin spread across his face.

'What are you going to do?' Frances tensed in his arms. She tried to push him away, but it was too late. He gently knocked her to the ground and started tickling her. Frances squealed.

'Stop, Henry!' she screamed through giggles. 'Please! If we get caught, we'll get thrown out.'

'Relax.'

'It's easy for you to say.'

Henry leaned back and gazed lovingly down at Frances lying on the grass. The sunlight made her skin glow. She was so pure and innocent.

Henry allowed her to get her breathing under control and she looked up at him from under her long eyelashes.

'What?' she asked, still giggling.

'Nothing,' said Henry, but the smile didn't quite reach his eyes. He brushed her hair away from her face and sighed. 'It's just that sometimes I don't feel I'm enough.'

'What do you mean?' Frances sat up. She cupped his head in her hands.

'I mean, what do I have to offer the likes of you?'

'Henry Shepherd, you are not to say that again, do you hear?'

'But it's true.'

'You are more than enough. You are kind and you say the sweetest things.'

'If that's true, then why not tell your parents about me?'

Frances lowered her eyes.

'That's what I thought.' He pushed himself up from the ground and turned away, exhaling slowly.

'Henry!' Frances tried to grab his hand, but he pulled away from her. 'It's just not that simple.'

'Why not? You've met my family.'

'Yes, and look how that turned out.'

'What's that supposed to mean?' He tilted his head.

'It doesn't matter.'

'Clearly it does. Don't you like my family?' His body tensed.

'Yes, of course I do. It was just something your mum said. Forget I said anything. Look, I promise, I will tell my parents, just not yet. My mother has this unrealistic plan for my life. We argue all the time because she wants me to be more like her. You must understand, Henry. Telling her is not going to be easy.' She moved to stand next to him and tried to place a soft kiss on his lips, but he pulled away to hide the hurt in his eyes.

'I have to know that we're in this together, Frances.'

'We are... I am, Henry. Look at me please. I'm yours. You must trust me and give me more time,' she pleaded.

Henry looked at her. He wanted to believe her. But even if she had no intention of telling them, it wouldn't make a difference because, deep down, Henry knew that even if she never told her parents, he would accept it. He was in too deep. He pulled her into a tight embrace and kissed her. She wrapped her arms around his neck and kissed him back.

'Ignore me. I shouldn't have brought it up. Right, I'm off for a swim. Will you be alright on your own?' Henry looked at her glowing cheeks. 'It looks like you need to cool off too.' He placed a kiss on the top of her head while breathing in her intoxicating scent.

'I will,' she replied. 'In a minute.'

He ran to the edge of the pool and jumped in, only to reappear a second later, pushing his wet, dark hair back from his face. He watched as Frances sat on the grass and stretched out her legs. His feelings for her were growing deeper by the day. He didn't want to remain her dirty secret. He wanted the world to know he loved her.

'Why don't you dip your toes in?' he called.

'Maybe.' She reached forward to take off her shoes and stockings, causing Henry to lose his balance in the water.

'Over there looks good!' He pointed to a spot close to the shallow end and in the shade, away from the crowds. The park was a cacophony of laughter, screaming, and splashing water.

Frances walked to where he'd pointed, sat on the edge and dipped in her big toe. Henry chuckled as she shivered, her body tensing with the cold. He watched as she waited a second before repeating the action. While she was focused on the water, Henry swam over to where she was sitting.

'What thee dithering about at?' asked Henry.

'Just give me a minute,' she said. Henry watched on as she tentatively placed her whole foot into the water. 'Gosh, it's cold!' she cried.

'It's not that bad,' he said. Frances frowned at him. But, to prove his point, he disappeared underneath the water only to reappear directly at her feet.

'Show off!' she said.

Henry was standing before her, the top half of his body on full display under his tank top. He placed his cold hand on her foot and gently stroked her ankle with his fingers. Then he played with it, turning it this way and that before lifting her foot out of the water and placing a wet, warm kiss on the underneath.

'I wish you were in the water with me,' he said. A roguish grin spread across his face. Frances swallowed hard. Henry pulled her other leg down into the water, then draped her legs around his waist.

'Henry,' whispered Frances. 'People can see.'

'So what? We're not doing anything wrong,' he replied.

'But it looks indecent, me with my bare legs wrapped around you.'

'So what?' he repeated. He looked down at her dress; it was pushed past her knees. His breathing quickened. He slowly moved his wet fingers to her thigh but she didn't stop him. The water had warmed around him; blood soared through his veins and settled in his groin.

'Henry, stop,' she whispered. But he continued to move his hand higher. She firmly put her hand on top of his. Then she lifted her legs out of the water, straightened her dress, and quickly walked back to the spot she'd left her shoes and stockings.

'Frances!' shouted Henry. 'I'm sorry!'

Getting no response, Henry jumped out of the swimming pool and followed her. When he reached her, she had already pulled on her stockings and shoes and looked ready to leave.

'Frances, don't go! I'm sorry. I got caught up in the moment. I didn't mean—'

'What if someone I knew saw us? Or worse a friend of my parents?' She put her hat on and glared at him. 'I'm not like other girls.'

'I know you're not. I'm sorry,' he repeated. 'It won't 'appen again. Stay... please.' His brow furrowed.

'You need to dry off,' she snapped. 'I'm going to go for a walk while you get changed.'

'Does that mean you're staying?' he asked.

'I'll see you over at the boating lake,' she added and stormed off.

The sun had dipped behind a cloud, offering momentary relief from the heat. Henry found Frances sitting on a bench; she had her eyes closed.

Henry, his feet still bare, his wet hair swept back from his face and his swimsuit dripping in his hand, seated himself next to her and started to pull on his socks and shoes.

'Do you forgive me?' he asked, without turning to face her. Frances turned to him and reached out to touch his arm.

'Of course,' she said. 'I shouldn't have let it get that far.'

'Now I feel even worse. You did nothing wrong. It was all me,' he said earnestly. 'I'm struggling to control myself around you, Frances. I can't seem to think clearly.'

'It's fine,' she said. 'Come on, let's get ice cream. My treat this time.' She jumped up and held out her hand. He hesitated before accepting it.

'You're going to be the death of me, Frances Eton,' he said.

They ate their ice cream in the shade of a tree. Henry's gaze was drawn to Frances' mouth as she struggled to stop her ice cream from dripping down her fingers and onto her arm.

'This is ridiculous!' she sighed.

'Nonsense, you're not doing it right,' teased Henry. 'You can't afford to act like a lady when there's ice cream at stake. Watch me!' Henry stuck out his tongue and, in one swift circular movement, licked his ice cream to prevent any from dripping.

'Show off!' Frances tried to copy him. She stuck out her tongue and slowly licked around the bottom, and then placed her tiny mouth over the top and softly sucked and smoothed it down with her lips. Henry gulped.

They relaxed in contented silence, observing the other visitors to the park as the sun beat relentlessly down.

When they had finished their ice creams, Henry rested his back against the trunk of the tree and stretched out his legs. Frances put her head on his chest, so Henry placed his arm about her. Blissfully, they stayed nestled in each other's arms for the rest of the afternoon.

Chapter Twenty-Four

'Morning, Frances,' greeted her father from behind his newspaper. 'Sleep well?'

'Good morning, Father,' she replied. 'I did, thank you.' She pulled out a chair and seated herself at the dining room table. 'Good morning, Jenny.'

'Good morning, miss,' replied Jenny as she wrapped the used bits of coal in newspaper and left the room, taking the dustpan and brush too.

Her father folded his paper and placed it in front of him, a pained expression reflected in his eyes.

'What's wrong?' asked Frances.

'Oh, nothing dear. Just more news about the dreadful things that are happening in Europe. Germany's expansion and Hitler continuously pushing his luck.'

'It's so worrying,' declared Frances.

'I wish I could tell you that you have nothing to fear my dear, but...' Frances watched her father rise and make his way towards the door. Dark circles under his eyes gave him a tired and worried look. He stopped, turned his head and forced a smile. 'Sorry, Frances. Listen to me, all doom and gloom. There's always hope. There has to be, otherwise what is the point? Oh, I nearly forgot – there's an article in the paper about that film you mentioned the other day; I thought you might be interested. Oh, and not a word to your mother, but I've circled an advertisement; a local theatre group are holding auditions.'

Frances stretched her arm across the table and grabbed the paper eagerly. 'Thank you, Father.'

'Right you are. Tell your mother I will see her tonight. Goodbye, Frances.'

'Father, wait!' She ran over to him.

'What is it, Frances? I need to get going.' She put her arms around his waist and squeezed him tight. 'What's brought all this on?'

'Nothing. I just wanted you to know how much I love you.'

He smoothed his hand over her hair and kissed the top of her head.

'Silly girl.' He blinked away tears. 'I love you too. Now I really must be going. I'll see you later.'

It was Edna's last day. Frances was about to go down to the kitchen with the present she'd bought for her when the door opened and in walked Robert.

'Robert!' she said, rather too loudly.

'In the flesh,' he gave a wolfish grin. 'Miss me?'

'Hardly. Where's mother and what in heaven's name happened to your face?'

'What this?' He pointed to his black eye. 'You should have seen the other fella,' he joked. 'Clarissa, your darling mother, is paying for the taxi.'

'Why are you here?'

'Got myself in a spot of bother. Your darling mother had to bail me out. Police don't care much for my sort. Do you fancy a trip out?'

'With you?'

'Don't be like that. Life is so dull and northern here.'

'So why did you come back?'

Robert placed his hand over his heart. 'Ouch. Now be a dear and fetch a fresh pot of tea will you.'

Frances was almost glad he had a black eye. She just wished whoever had hit him could have wiped that smug look off his face.

'I will do no such thing. What did your last slave die of?' She flounced out and left him sitting at the dining room table.

Robert chuckled loudly. 'Answering back!' he said and picked up the newspaper.

Edna was looking out onto the garden, her back to the door.

'He is so infuriating!' cried Frances. 'Urgh! I don't know why Mother entertains him. He's so conceited.'

'Who?' asked Edna.

'Robert! I thought we'd got rid of him, but he's back again.'

'Breathe!' said Edna. 'You'll burst a blood vessel. Just ignore him, love. He's not that bad.'

'I wish I could. I know he isn't all bad, but he just has the knack of getting under my skin.' Frances let out a deep sigh. She looked at Edna. 'Have you been crying?'

'No, no. I was cutting some onions.' Edna quickly wiped a tear from the corner of her eye with her pinafore.

'Oh, Edna!' Frances walked over to her and wrapped her arms around her waist. 'I am going to miss you!'

'I'm going to miss you too.' Edna sniffled, putting her arms around Frances.

'But I will see you again, especially now I'm with Henry.' She pulled away and looked at the woman's blotchy face. 'Don't cry, Edna, or you'll set me off.'

'Are you going to tell your parents about Henry then?' She blew her nose into her handkerchief.

'I want to, but what if they try to stop me from seeing him?'

'You'll never find out if you don't tell them. Henry's a good lad; what's not to like?' said Edna.

'Yes, but you know what Mother's like.'

'It's your life, Frances. If Henry makes you happy, then what's to worry about?'

'I know you're right, but... oh never mind.'

'Right, I'm off. My son is coming over with the baby, and I don't want to be late. He's so tiny, Frances. I didn't think I could love anyone as much as I do our little Peter.'

'Oh, I nearly forgot. I've got you a present.' Frances reached into her pocket and pulled out a small box.

'You shouldn't have,' said Edna, beaming

'It's not much. I wanted you to have something to remember me by,' said Frances.

'I don't need a gift for that. I'll never forget you, Frances Eton.' Another tear trickled down Edna's cheek as Frances passed her the box.

'Now I'm crying,' said Frances. She used the back of her hand to wipe away the tears from the corner of her eyes.

'Oh, it's beautiful. Thank you so much. Here help me to pin it onto my coat.'

Frances unclasped the pin on the back of the round fili-gree brooch, with its pastel rhinestones and small white shells, and carefully pinned it to Edna's coat.

'Come here,' cried Edna. She opened her arms and Frances went to her. 'I will miss you and don't worry about your mum. Just give her a chance. She might surprise you.' She kissed the top of Frances' head. 'Now, I really must go.' She held Frances at arm's length. 'You are a smart, beautiful young lady, Frances Eton. You'll do what's right for you and don't let anyone tell you otherwise.' She walked out the back door. Frances waved and wiped away more tears.

It was early morning. Frances' father had left already for an important meeting at the university and had taken Thomas with him. It was just Frances and her mother downstairs. Robert was still in bed. Frances watched as her mother busied herself at her writing desk. She finished sticking the last of her stamps on an envelope and looked up.

'Why the long face, Frances? Sit up and tell me what has you looking worried.' Frances gazed at her mother. She wished her father was present – he was always the voice of reason and remained calm in these situations. 'What is it, Frances? Do spit it out!'

'It's rather hot in here, isn't it?' Her palms grew sweaty, and she twisted her hair around her finger.

'Why don't you open a window?'

'I'd like to invite a friend over for tea,' Frances said, her voice wobbling slightly.

'Is that all? Really, Frances. Why do you have to be so melodramatic? Of course you can have a friend over. It wouldn't be the first time. Now if you have finished...'

'It is not one of my usual friends.' Frances wrung her hands. Her mother narrowed her eyes. 'I have a new friend and his—'

'His?' asked her mother. Frances nodded. 'I see. What's his name?'

'Henry. He's nice. I know you'll like him – once you get to know him,' said Frances.

'And where does Henry live? Do we know his parents?' Frances' mother folded her arms and glared.

'Does it matter?' replied Frances.

'Of course it matters, Frances. Now, where did you meet him? Does he have a good job?'

'I only want to invite him over for tea, Mother; I'm not marrying him. He's just a friend.'

'Be that as it may, I don't want my daughter associating with just anybody. What will people think?' She placed her hand over her mouth. 'Of course, it all makes sense now.'

'What does?'

'You've been sneaking around and acting differently for days now. I thought Mrs Blackwood had lost her senses when she told me I ought to keep a more watchful eye on you. Now I understand. Frances. I demand that you tell me just how long this 'friendship' has been going on!'

'Mother!' cried Frances.

'Don't Mother me!' She folded her arms and stared at Francis. 'Well?'

Francis took a deep breath and told her mother almost everything, just skipping the kissing parts. Her mother listened poker-faced and waited patiently for Frances to finish.

'I will have to tell your father when he returns. In the meantime, you are to have nothing more to do with him. Do you hear?'

'What? No! Weren't you listening to a word I've just said?'

'Don't you raise your voice! I heard everything, and it is abundantly clear that you have feelings for this young man. Oh, I am sure he's delightful, but he is not for you. You, who can have her pick of any fine young man, are not going to associate with a common steelworker. Now, I must go.' She moved to stand up.

'Mother, please!' Frances reached for her hand.

'I have said all I am going to say on the matter, Frances. I do not want you to see him again. Now goodbye.'

Frances picked up her handkerchief and wiped away the tears that had begun to roll down her cheeks. She didn't notice Robert walk in.

'Are you alright, Frances?'

'Robert! Have you been listening?'

'Not exactly,' he replied. 'You've been crying.'

'What if I have?'

'I know all too well what it's like to have people oppose the ones you love,' said Robert.

'You were listening! That was a private conversation; you had no right!' yelled Frances.

'You're right, I'm sorry. But I didn't get this black eye for nothing,' he said, rubbing his face.

'What happened to you?' asked Frances, her anger quickly waning.

'I was attacked.'

'Attacked? Who would want to attack you?' Frances burrowed her brows.

'Lots of people,' he said. He pulled out a chair and sat down. 'I won't go into detail but, if it wasn't for your mother, I'd probably be dead in a ditch somewhere. She's not a bad person; on the contrary, she's my guardian angel. She'll come around. I'm positive. She just wants to protect you. If you'd like, I can speak to your mother on your behalf.'

'Do you think she'd listen to you?'

'I don't see why not.' He shrugged. 'We're friends, after all.'

'I don't understand. What's in it for you?'

'Frances, what do you take me for? All you need to know is that I am offering my help.'

'I don't trust you.'

'I know that. But know this, I'm not the man you think I am.'

'Fine, talk to her if you must. But she won't listen.'

'At least let me try.'

Chapter Twenty-Five

✿❀✿

It was late Saturday afternoon when Robert knocked on Frances' bedroom door, startling her. She'd been listening to Anne Lenner and lamenting her lost love. She'd only ventured out of her room once since the argument and that was only to help poor Mrs Vickers in the kitchen. Frances had given up all hope of Robert changing her mother's mind. But when she opened her bedroom door to him, she discovered he'd somehow miraculously managed the impossible.

'That's wonderful, Robert! Thank you. I could kiss you,' said Frances.

'Now, now let's not go overboard,' he said.

'How ever did you manage it?'

'I have my ways.'

'But what did you say?'

'Nothing, I just reminded her of a few things. So now you owe me.'

Frances frowned.

'Don't look so worried. You owe me to do all the things you've dreamed of doing. Live your life and love whomever you see fit. Promise me that.' Frances nodded. 'Life's far too short.' He winked and turned to walk away.

'Wait!' she said, stopping him in his tracks. 'If you get bored, I mean if you find yourself at a loose end. I would be happy for you to come with me to the pictures again...'

'Are you sure you want to be seen with me?' Robert teased.

'Of course, I would like it if we could be friends.' Robert nodded his head before leaving.

'Now all I need is to figure out how I can get a message to Henry and fast. If only he had a telephone,' she groaned.

Frances believed it to be divine intervention when Edna called round on Monday to collect some things she'd left behind. Frances quickly wrote a letter to Henry and dashed to the kitchen to give it to her. Frances was thrilled to see her old friend again. Mrs Vickers was pleased to see her too as she was still struggling with the oven. She was used to an old-style range but was getting better at gauging how hot to have it and how long to leave cakes in the oven before they burned.

'Edna, you must give Henry this as soon as you return home,' instructed Frances. 'You mustn't forget because it's imperative Henry receives it today!'

'Calm down! Where's the fire?' asked Edna.

'Mother has agreed for Henry to come over for tea,' said Frances.

'My goodness! That's a turn up for the books. How on earth did you manage that?' Edna took the letter and placed it in her coat pocket.

'It was Robert. Maybe I misjudged him after all. Don't ask me how he managed it; all I care about is that he did. I'm so nervous, Edna!' She rushed to put her arms around Edna's waist. Edna pulled her into a tight embrace.

Mrs Vickers screamed; Edna and Frances ran over to her.

'What is it?' shouted Frances.

'A mouse! A mouse ran into the larder!' She was standing on a stool with her skirt hitched up above her knees.

'I warned you! You must remember to put traps down,' replied Edna. 'And make sure there are no crumbs left about. You'd better keep things sealed too; otherwise, you'll get more.' Edna tutted and shook her head. 'Get down from that chair, you silly chuff before you fall off!' She turned back to face Frances. 'It was lovely to see you again, and don't worry; Henry will get your letter. You can depend on me.'

'Calm down!' ordered her father.

'Henry, he's here!' Frances declared excitedly.

'Well, go and wait in the dining room with your mother. I will answer the door,' he replied.

'But, Father!'

'No buts, now go!' He fastened his suit jacket and shooed her down the hall.

Frances waited with her mother, her palms sticky. Her

mother didn't say a word. She heard low muffled sounds coming from the hall and her whole body tensed. Then the door to the dining room opened. Henry looked nervous. Frances tried to reassure him with a smile. Her mother stood up and held out her hand.

'Hello,' she said. 'I'm Mrs Eton, Frances' mother. It is nice to meet you, Henry.' Henry's hands were shaking as he went to reciprocate the handshake.

'Hello,' he replied. 'It is nice to meet you too, Mrs Eton.'

'Take a seat, Henry,' she said. 'Shall I pour the tea,' asked Frances' mother. Henry pulled out a chair, his eyes never leaving Frances' face.

'You have such a beautiful home, Mrs Eton,' said Henry. 'Such beautiful things.'

'Thank you. It's nice of you to notice. How do you take your tea?'

'Milk and sugar please.'

'So, Henry, Clarissa tells me you work in the factories. What do you do there?' asked Edward.

Henry accepted his cup of tea from Frances' mother and then proceeded to answer the question. It went on like that for some time, Frances' parents asking him questions and Henry politely answering each one. She patiently waited and listened in the background as her parents practically interrogated him. Frances was proud of how calm and composed Henry was under her parents' watchful eyes. He stole glances at Frances when her parents paused or took a bite of their sandwiches. Frances had to stop herself from giggling as Henry tried to disguise his usual broad Yorkshire dialect.

When it was time to leave, Frances walked with Henry to the front door, her parents close behind.

'It was nice of you to invite me for tea, Dr Eton,' said Henry, shaking Edward's hand.

'Yes, well, take care of yourself, young man,' said her father.

As Henry left, Frances turned to her parents. 'Well?'

'He seems nice enough,' said her father. 'What more do you want me to say?'

'I don't know. Do you think he could call again?'

'Ask me another time,' replied her father.

'Thank you again, Mother, for allowing Henry to come for tea.' Her mother didn't respond. 'I'm going upstairs to my room now.'

'Righto,' said her father.

Frances waited for her parents to go back to the dining room before she quietly opened the front door and ran down the street after Henry.

'Henry!' she shouted. 'Wait!'

Henry stopped walking and ran towards her. He wrapped his arms around her waist and held her tight.

'How did I do?' he asked.

'You were wonderful,' she said. She reached up and kissed his cheek.

'Do you think they like me?' he asked.

'What does it matter what they think? I think you're wonderful.' She grinned.

'I'm serious, Frances.' His smile faded from his eyes. 'I need them to like me. All I have to offer is this.' He spread his arms out wide and looked down at his body. 'This is all I have.'

She tried to touch him, but he took a step back.

'You don't understand! You live in a fine big house with

more rooms than you have use for. You even have a cook and a cleaner! What can I give you that you don't have already?'

'You,' she said, staring into his eyes.

'Am I enough, Frances? You're all I need, but am I enough for you? For your parents?'

'You make me happy, and I want to be with you; what more proof do you need? Now kiss me,' she demanded, laughing.

'It's not funny. I'm serious,' said Henry.

'As am I,' she said. They kissed and held each other tight.

'I've wanted to do that all evening,' he whispered against her ear. 'Come to mine again tomorrow,' said Henry.

'What about work?'

'I'll finish early. Come after lunch.'

'Alright. I must dash.' She kissed his cheek. 'See you tomorrow.'

She ran back up the street. Before she entered her house, she turned back and blew him a kiss. Henry pretended to catch it.

Frances crept up the stairs and collapsed on her bed. She was bursting with happiness. Henry was simply wonderful. Now, she just needed to convince her parents of that too.

Chapter Twenty-Six

'I 've just got some things to take to a neighbour, said Henry.

'What things?'

'She's just had another baby and me mum has given me some old clothes and blankets to take round. Apparently, it's her fifth. They're not as well off as most. Her husband's always in and out of work. Youngest are always running about with no shoes on no matter the weather.'

'How dreadful!' said Frances. 'Can I help?'

'You can come with me, if you want?'

They arrived at a small house, with two tiny windows, one upstairs and one down.

'Surely, they all can't fit in there?' Her eyes narrowed. She clutched the front of her coat.

'You can wait outside if it's too much,' said Henry. 'Reckon it'll be a bit of a shock for you.'

'I can handle it.' She glared at him and straightened her back.

'Please thee sen.' Henry knocked on the door.

'Only me, Mrs Smith, Henry, Mary's son.' He opened the door and let himself in. Frances followed behind. She almost gagged at the stale smell that greeted them. The place was dark apart from a little broken sunlight coming through the net curtains. Frances had to stop herself from pinching her nose. Her skin itched; she shuddered when she saw something crawling in the children's hair and bites on their skinny arms from bed bugs.

'Oh, Henry, nice to see you,' called Mrs Smith. The poor woman looked awful. She was stretched out on a worn chair; her hair was flat to her scalp and her skin was clammy. In a wooden drawer on the floor beside her lay the baby. Frances forced a smile. Mrs Smith followed Frances' gaze as she took in her surroundings. 'I would have tidied up, if I knew you were calling, Henry.'

'Don't be silly, Mrs Smith, you need your rest. Where do you want the blankets and other stuff putting?'

'Put them on the table there.' Mrs Smith pointed to a table next to the fireplace. 'I'll see to them when you've gone.'

'Me mam said she'd call on you later. Check how you're getting on.'

'God bless her. She's such a good woman your mam, Henry.'

Frances had no idea that people still lived like that. Living on the other side of the city, she had never encountered such poverty before. She had grown up not wanting for anything. She knew, at times, she had taken her lovely home for granted. Now Frances felt ashamed. It wasn't right for people to have to go without. It made her sick to the stomach when she saw the cramped conditions this family lived in. The two small children, a boy and a girl, pulled at Frances' dress to get her attention.

'Go and play outside! She doesn't want to be bothered by the likes of you,' shouted Mrs Smith.

'It's fine.' Frances coughed. The little girl's eyes lit up when Frances pulled out two coins from her purse.

'Two thruppenny bits, John!' the little girl exclaimed excitedly. It was all Frances had in her purse. Part of her felt guilty that she didn't have more money to give, but she knew that handing out money was only a short-term solution. She knew she should do more to help, but part of her just wanted to go back home and forget that today had ever happened.

'That's kind of you,' said Mrs Smith.

'It's no bother,' said Frances.

'What's up with you?' asked Henry as they walked back to his house.

'I still feel itchy.' Frances shuddered. 'It was like a scene from a Dicken's novel. How can people live like that? So... dirty.'

'Some people don't have a choice,' said Henry.

'I realise that, but—'

'But what? Not everyone is like you, Frances.'

'What do you mean, like me? I was simply saying that—'

'I thought you were different, but you're just like the rest of them. I know exactly what you meant. I'm lucky, Frances, my parents have always worked but my life could have been different. That could have been me in that house. Would you have looked at me with such... disgust?'

'Henry, don't!'

'Don't what? Come on, I think I should walk you to the tram stop.'

Frances reached for his arm, but he pulled away.

'Henry. You've got me all wrong.'

'Maybe I have.' He shook his head.

'What did I do? Tell me! I don't understand what's happening here?' She looked at him. She placed her hand over her heart as it beat like a trapped bird fluttering its wings frantically.

'I...' He closed his eyes and sighed. 'I don't know.'

'Will I see you again?'

Henry gave her a long look she couldn't interpret before he turned and walked away, leaving her standing at the tram stop. She wrapped her arms around her body, determined not to cry. She closed her eyes and tapped her foot again and again on the ground.

'Where is this blasted tram?' she shouted.

'I don't know what I did wrong, Agnes.' She twisted the telephone wire around her finger and watched as her tears fell and smudged the ink on a newspaper left on the table.

'Don't worry, Frances. It's probably just a storm in a teacup as my mother is fond of saying. Henry will come around, you'll see.'

'What if he doesn't want to see me again?' She looked at her red face and puffy eyes in the mirror.

'He loves you, Frances. He probably just felt embarrassed. Who wouldn't after seeing your house?'

'That's just silly. Well, if he doesn't come round, his loss.' She sniffed.

'You don't mean that,' replied Agnes. 'You love him too.'

The worst part was Agnes was right, she did love him but now she wouldn't get the chance to tell him just how much.

Frances had almost worn holes in her bedroom carpet. No matter how many times she'd checked, Henry was nowhere to be found. He wasn't waiting at the Botanical Gardens, nor was he walking up her street ready to apologise. It had been two days. Every time she swallowed, it was like she was having to keep down fragments of her broken heart.

When she had almost given up hope of ever seeing him again, her mother shouted her from the hallway.

'Frances dear! You have a visitor.' Frances ran as fast as her legs could carry her. She thought her face would break from the huge smile she could no longer contain. She wanted to appear cool, but her heart would have none of it.

'Henry!' Her voice cracked and her eyes widened. She placed her hand on the banister to steady herself. 'Charles, what are you doing here?'

'Your mother asked me to call. Said you needed cheering up. I daresay, you're looking a bit peaky.'

She fixed her smile. 'My mother shouldn't have troubled you. I'm fine.'

'It's no trouble. I haven't seen much of you lately. I've been meaning to call on you. Are you sure you're alright?'

'Absolutely.' Her voice was a little too high pitched.

'Are you going to keep your friend standing his entire visit, Frances?' called her mother.

'Where are my manners? My mother is quite right. Would you care for tea?' she asked.

'That would be lovely.'

'After you.' She gestured to the dining room, her hand trembling. She quickly dropped it to her side and followed Charles to where her mother had already arranged for Mrs Vickers to serve up tea and cake. Frances clenched her fists. She wanted to scream and smash the plates but, instead, she handed Charles a napkin.

'So nice of Charles to visit, don't you think, Frances?'

'Yes, Mother.' She gritted her teeth. Now more than ever she was determined to leave this house and never look back.

'You should call more often, Charles,' said Frances' mother. 'Do help yourself to cake.'

'Thank you, Mrs Eton.' He looked at Frances. 'I would like nothing better than to call again.'

'What does it matter what I think?' she mumbled under her breath.

'I didn't quite catch that,' said her mother. 'Do speak up Frances!'

'I said I should ask Mrs Vickers for more hot water.'

Chapter Twenty-Seven

'A ren't you seeing that young lass of yours tonight?' asked Arthur as he pulled on his trousers.

'No, not tonight,' replied Henry.

'Why not? If she were mine, I wouldn't be able to get enough of her, if you know what I mean?' He made a moaning sound, grabbed his crotch and started to move his hips.

'She's not like that!' Henry threw his pillow at him.

'I'm only teasing. Prim and proper type, is she? Buy her some flowers or summat, that ought to seal the deal.'

'Besides, I'm not sure she is my lass, not anymore.'

Arthur was combing his hair in the small mirror as Henry stretched out on his bed, looked up at the ceiling and sighed.

'Lover's tiff? You've got it bad,' said Arthur. 'Come on, shake thissen.'

'I've done something stupid.'

'Whatever it is, I'm sure she'll get over it. Girls like to sulk a bit, but she'll come round.'

'I hope so, Arthur, because I love her.'

'Crikey, you'll be asking her to marry you next,' teased Arthur.

'Would that be such a bad thing?' asked Henry. Arthur spun round to face him.

'Now hang on a minute!' Arthur threw his comb at Henry. 'Don't talk outta your arse. You can't get married. What do you have to offer a young girl like that? She's from a different class. You still live at home with your mum. You're only just out of short trousers!'

'Surely, if you love someone that should be enough? Why should it matter that I'm not rich?' said Henry.

'Because it does and if anyone tries telling you otherwise, they're lying. You've got some living to do first, kid. Why would you want to tie yourself down? She's a good-looking girl, granted, but there are others out there. Take that Rose for example. Besides, there's a war coming; you mark my words, and what if you get called up? What good would you be to her then?' Henry shrugged. 'Exactly,' continued Arthur. 'I don't suppose her parents want her to marry someone like you either,' he said, pointing his finger at Henry. 'You listen to your big brother. Come on, get dressed! I think you could do with a night out.'

'You're right, I know you are, but I've tried staying away from her and it's killing me.'

'Try harder.'

'Where are you going tonight?' asked Henry.

'London Road again, fancy it? I've got some booze I picked up from this bloke who owed me money. I'm meeting

George, and he's bringing along some birds. It'll be a laugh. You could do with taking your mind of this Frances for one night.' He straightened his tie and pulled on his jacket.

'Go on then. I'll quickly get changed and meet you downstairs.' He jumped off the bed and went to the washbasin.

'You won't regret it.' Arthur winked.

Arthur was seated at the kitchen table, chatting with their mum, when Henry walked in, ready to go.

'Bout bleeding time,' said Arthur. He shot up and headed to the front door.

'Watch your mouth!' warned his mum.

'Where's Dad?' asked Henry.

'Pub,' replied his mum.

'Come on, Henry!' said Arthur. 'Dance will be over by the time we get there.'

'Frances!' Henry rummaged around for tiny stones and threw them, hitting her bedroom window. A light went on and Frances pulled back her curtain. Henry looked up from the pavement below. He lightly threw another stone. She pulled up the shutter and looked outside.

'Psst, down here, Frances,' he shouted.

'Henry?'

'Aye, it's me! You look beau...ti... ful.'

'Shush! Henry, you'll wake the whole street! What are you doing here at this hour?' she whispered.

'I'm... rescu... rescu... I'm saving you,' he spluttered.

'You're drunk.'

'Just a teeny-weeny bit.' He hiccupped and pinched his forefinger and thumb together to show her how much.

'I haven't heard from you in days. Go home! Do you want my father to see you? Are those people with you?' Henry looked at the other figures behind him in the street, who were laughing and now appeared to be waltzing together. 'This is a respectable neighbourhood, Henry; someone will call the police. Tell your friends to be quiet.'

'I'm... sorry... truly... truly... cross my heart,' he shouted.

'Shush! What are you going on about?'

'I want you to know... I'm a...' He stumbled forward and landed in the privet. 'I'm alright... I'm alright,' he slurred.

'Henry, please be quiet, I beg you,' said Frances.

'Will you?' he shouted. He was sprawled in the hedge grinning up at her.

'Will I what?' said Frances as the next-door neighbour's dog started barking, and their lights came on.

'Forgive me?'

'I can't talk about that now. Go home!'

'I didn't mean any of it... I know... I know you're not like that. Forgive me... please.'

'If it will shut you up. Now please go away!'

'I'm going... good night... parting is such... good night... I can't remember the rest.'

Frances giggled and closed the window as Henry staggered back towards Arthur and George.

Chapter Twenty-Eight

Henry and Frances were lying on their backs, close together on the lush green grass, watching the clouds float by. It was a peaceful, picturesque morning; there was no one else around for miles.

'I really am sorry, Frances. I don't know what I was thinking.'

'I know you are. You've told me a thousand times. I forgive you. There! That one looks like a dragon!' declared Frances, pointing to the sky. 'Look! Do you see it? Just there!'

'I see it,' he said. He rolled onto his side and stared lovingly down at the heavenly creature by his side. Daisies and dandelions framed her face like a halo. He wanted to make love to her there and then, to wrap her up in his arms, touch her delicate skin and hold her naked body against his own. Just the thought of having her caused his blood to simmer through his veins.

'Ooh, that one looks like a...' Henry cupped her face and pressed his tender lips to hers, silencing her. He pushed his tongue gently into her mouth, then stopped and gazed at her shocked expression before kissing her again; this time, his kiss was hard, demanding. He playfully nipped her bottom lip between his teeth.

Frances gasped as he rolled his body onto hers and pushed his weight into her. She opened her mouth to accept his fervent kiss, gripping his shoulders. But as quickly as he had started, he pulled away.

'What's wrong?' asked Frances.

'Nothing.' He pushed himself up and sat with his legs bent, his arms folded around his knees.

'It doesn't look like nothing.' She rolled onto her side, her head resting in her hand.

Henry took a deep breath. Slowly he reached into his trouser pocket and pulled out a blue velvet box. Earlier that day, he had made a purchase at a pawn shop. He had spotted a ring in the window. It wasn't anything fancy, but it was all he could afford. It was a delicate silver and rose-gold marcasite ring. He just hoped he had done the right thing and that she liked it. 'Marry me, Frances!' Henry got down on one knee, opened the lid, and held out the ring for her. Frances gasped. She looked at the ring and then back at his face.

'I had planned it all differently, but I couldn't wait. Those days apart from you were the hardest I've ever had to deal with. I just want to get on with living our lives together.' Henry felt like he was treading water in a storm as he waited for her to speak. 'Say something, anything.'

'But I'm not ready to be someone's wife,' she said. 'I've already told you that.'

'Not someone's – mine,' he said.

'But there are things I want to do with my life... places I want to visit, like America. I thought you understood.'

'We can do all those things together...'

'Where will we live? How will we—'

'We'll work something out, even if we have to live in a cardboard box; what does it matter as long as we're together. You said yourself money wasn't important.' Momentarily, his heart stopped as he held his breath. Frances bit her bottom lip. The tiny crease appeared above her nose.

Henry feared he'd messed everything up. He felt like he was losing her; he had to think fast. 'Just try it on for size.' He carefully placed it on her finger. 'We don't have to get married straight away; we can have a long engagement.' He stood up and brushed the grass from his trousers.

Frances looked at the ring on her finger, turning her hand from side to side, and then she made the smallest movement with her head.

'Is that a yes?' said Henry, grinning.

'It's a maybe. I think you should speak to my father first. If we are going to do it, I think we should do it properly.'

Henry picked her up and spun her around, making her squeal.

'You won't regret this, Frances Eton. I am going to devote my life to loving thee. Today you have made me the happiest man alive, and I promise I will spend the rest of mine making you equally as happy.'

He cupped her face tenderly and brushed his lips softly against hers. His breath was hot against her mouth; she tasted so sweet. Then he parted her lips with the tip of his tongue. She placed her hands at the back of his neck and gently gripped his hair, forcing his mouth closer to hers. Henry thought he would combust with desire.

Reluctantly they ended their kiss. Henry looked longingly into her eyes.

'I love you, Henry,' whispered Frances.

'Do you mean it? I don't want you to say it because you feel you ought to.'

'With all my heart.'

'That's all I needed to hear, Frances.' He kissed the tip of her nose. 'Right, now let's make a move. That cloud over there looks like a right big scary monster that's going to gobble us up.'

A large, thunderous cloud had gathered overhead. Henry grabbed Frances' hand, and they ran back through the fields towards the station. A cold splash of water landed on his arm and then another. Soon it was coming down heavy.

'Get a move on, Frances!' shouted Henry as he pulled her along. Frances stopped abruptly, almost causing Henry to fall backwards. 'What's the matter?'

'Hang on a minute. I can run much faster if I take off my shoes.' She bent down and slipped them off her feet, then started to run again. A clap of thunder echoed around them. 'We're not going to make it!' said Frances.

In one rapid movement, Henry reached down and swooped Frances up in his arms. He flung her over his shoulder and started to run.

'Henry! What are you doing?' she squealed. 'Put me down!' She bounced about in an unladylike fashion. 'Henry!' she yelled.

'Almost there,' he said.

Henry didn't see the stone; he slipped and fell backwards.

Frances screamed. Henry quickly positioned her so that his body hit the ground first to cushion her fall.

'Are you alright?' he asked. The ground was wet and muddy beneath him. Henry pressed his lips together to suppress his laughter when he saw Frances' face covered with mud.

'I hate you, Henry Shepherd! Look at me!' she replied, sitting up.

'A minute ago, you loved me,' he said grinning.

'What? What is it? Do I have something on my face?'

'Only a little bit of mud. Here let me help you wipe it off.' He used his shirt to try to rid her of the dirt, but it only made it worse.

Taking a mirror from her bag, she looked at her reflection. 'Look at the state of me! How am I going to explain this to my parents?'

'It's not that bad,' said Henry.

'Not that bad? Well, if it's not that bad, why are you laughing?'

'I'm not,' he said, trying to suppress another grin.

'Look at my clothes!' Frances stood up. 'My dress is ruined.'

The rain was coming down fast, soaking them both.

'It could be worse,' replied Henry.

'How? How could it possibly be worse?' snapped Frances.

She looked at Henry, lying on the ground and covered in mud. He had the biggest smile on his face. Frances burst into laughter. 'Yes, I suppose I could look like you.'

'Give us a hand up then?' said Henry. Frances held out her hand, and Henry took it. He pulled her down on top of him and Frances screamed with laughter. His wet lips sought out hers, and they kissed. Henry dragged her closer and buried his face into the curve of her shoulder. 'I will remember this day for the rest of my life,' he said and kissed her neck.

The platform was empty of people, so nobody saw the state they were in, not that it mattered to Henry. The platform offered little protection from the rain so they huddled together under Henry's coat to keep warm as they waited for the next train back to Sheffield. Frances shivered in his arms. He tried his best to keep her warm.

'We do look a state,' she said. She wiped the water from her face and pinned her wet hair behind her ear.

'Not you, you look like a mermaid princess,' replied Henry. He squeezed her tight against his body.

'You are crazy, Henry Shepherd,' teased Frances.

'Aye, crazy about thee.'

Chapter Twenty-Nine

Frances held her shoes in her hands and crept up the stairs to her bedroom. She didn't want her parents to catch her looking the way she did. She twisted the door handle and was about to walk inside when movement in her room caused her to stumble backwards.

'Good lord, Mother! What are you doing here? You gave me a fright.' Frances put her hand to her heart and quickly hid her ring.

'You should change,' she said flatly. 'Your dress is filthy.' Her mother was sitting on her bed, waiting for her.

'I was about to,' said Frances. 'Why are you in my room?' Her mother stood up and walked towards the window.

'I didn't realise what a wonderful view you have from here,' she said, peeling back the net curtain.

Frances didn't say anything.

Her mother turned to face her. 'I'm going away. I'm going

to stay with my cousin Rachel. Remember her? She lives in a lovely house in Paignton overlooking the sea.'

'That's nice,' replied Frances. 'How long will you be gone?'

'I haven't decided yet. I miss the ocean.' She looked at Frances. 'I think it will be good for my health; your father agrees with me.'

'When will you go?'

'That depends.'

'On what?'

'You.' She looked Frances squarely in the eye.

'I don't understand,' replied Frances, a tiny crease appearing between her brows.

'You're coming with me!'

'But I don't want to go with you... I need to be here,' cried Frances.

'Why? So, you can chase after *that* boy?' said her mother with a harsh, derisive laugh.

'What's so funny?'

'You are! Just look at you. You're a mess! I know you've been with him. I saw you together at the bottom of the road. Like I said, your window has an excellent view.' She took a step closer to Frances. 'What about poor Charles?'

'Charles?'

'Yes. He's a nice decent man. He has a good future ahead of him, unlike... you know who.'

'Henry, his name is Henry, Mother.'

'Your father and I agreed to meet him, but that was all. He's not good enough for you, Frances. In years to come, he will only disappoint you.'

'You know nothing about it. Henry loves me!' said Frances.

'I don't doubt he does, in his own way. I saw the way he looked at you when he was here; the boy's besotted, but he's not right for you.' She reached out to touch Frances' face but she pushed her hand away.

'You can't stand to see me happy,' she cried.

'Don't be ridiculous; you're my daughter. I want nothing more than for you to be happy, but with the right person. That's why your father and I think you should come with me to Devon, until you're over your little girl crush.'

'No, I won't, and it's not a crush. I love him!'

'No! You cannot love him. You don't even know him.'

'Well, I do, and don't act like you don't know what it means to be in love. I've seen your letters to father.'

Her mother went rigid, and the colour appeared to drain from her face.

'You had no right! Those letters were private.'

'I'm sorry,' said Frances.

'I was... times were... it was a long time ago. It doesn't change anything now.'

Frances pushed past her mother. 'I beg to differ. Now I would like you to leave, please! I need to get changed.'

'This nonsense has gone on long enough. Don't you realise there is a war coming? What will you do if Henry has to fight? You have no idea how it feels to lose the people you love... It is best that you end it now and save yourself the heartache.' Her mother's ice-blue eyes implored her.

'Don't try to pretend you care about my feelings. You have no idea what is best for me. It is best for *you*, you mean.

You don't want me to embarrass you in front of your friends!' replied Frances. Her mother sighed heavily.

'Why must you insist on making me the villain?' She turned back to the window. 'The weather will be lovely this time of year. Robert has offered to accompany us.' And, with that, she left Frances standing in the middle of her bedroom and made her way down the stairs.

'I won't go!' said Frances. 'You can't make me!' She slammed her door and pulled her wet dress over her head and ripped off her stockings. She looked at the ring on her finger before taking it off and hiding it in the bottom of her drawer. 'I won't go,' she whimpered.

After Sunday service, Frances waited until her father was alone before she broached the subject of Devon. She found him in his study, reading. He looked at her briefly when she entered, but then returned his eyes to the pages of a worn medical journal. With her arms clasped behind her back, Frances casually perused the shelves, feigning interest. She kept one eye on the many books and the other on her father.

'Are you here to admire my dusty shelves, or do you want something?' he asked, his pipe between his lips, smoke hovering in the air.

'Now that you mention it, Father...' She turned swiftly to face him.

The corners of his mouth twitched. 'Yes?'

'About Devon...' She leaned forward, her hands resting on his desk.

'What about it?' he asked, licking his finger and turning a page.

'Do I have to go?'

Her father placed down his journal and puffed on his pipe. 'Your mother and I think you ought to go. A change of scenery would do you the world of good.'

She walked around to his side of the desk and rested on its edge. 'It is awfully far away. I would miss you and, besides, who would help poor Mrs Vickers in the kitchen?'

'You mean you would miss that boy.'

'Yes, but I would miss you more.'

'I'm afraid, Frances, that on this occasion, I agree with your mother. You need to put some distance between you and Henry.'

'But, Father, I thought you understood. I thought you liked him.'

'I said he seems like a nice boy and that he does, but that doesn't mean I want you spending any more time with him.'

Frances listened to her father with horror. She had been sure he'd understand. Her hands began to tremble and tears pricked at her eyes as his words started to sink in.

'In time, you'll forget all about him. Soon, when the time is right, you'll meet someone more suitable.'

'I don't care what you and Mother say. I won't go to Devon, and you can't make me! Henry is who I care about.' She ran out of the room crying.

'Frances! Come back this instance!' shouted her father, but it was too late.

Frances was up with the lark and out of the house before her parents could notice she was missing. Suffice to say her mother had not changed her mind, and she was expecting Frances to be ready to leave after breakfast. Luckily for her it wasn't raining because she hadn't the foggiest where she was going to hide out until her mother had left for Devon. Never had Frances acted so rebelliously. Now the guilt was overwhelming but she reassured herself that her mother would have to forgive her eventually.

She glanced at her watch. Breakfast would be on the table now; soon her absence would be noted. She walked quickly to the tram stop and jumped onto the first tram heading into town.

It was a bright, sunny morning. Frances tried to relax in her seat, but her conscience wouldn't allow it. Scattered light shone through the branches of the leafy trees, glittering onto the pavement: birch, chestnut and ash all lined up like old soldiers on parade. Frances stared absentmindedly at the houses she'd passed a million times before. She wished her mother would understand. Frances didn't care for money – not in the way her mother did. The tram filled with people as it got closer to the town centre, each of them going about their business, unaware of her turmoil. When the tram approached Frances' usual stop, she didn't get off. Instead, she stayed on as it drove past the impressive town hall and continued down the High Street and on past the bustling markets. Mother will be livid right about now, she thought. As the tram approached the Wicker Arches, Frances recalled the stories Edna had told her about Sedgwick's elephant, Lizzie, who was loaned to Thomas Ward during the war years to move scrap metal around Sheffield because there was a shortage of horses: all the horses had been sent to the frontline.

As the tram turned on to Saville Street, Frances noticed that the sky had changed from blue to light grey to black as giant plumes of smoke and steam came into view. She hadn't intended on travelling this far, but it was too late now. This was Henry's part of town. On the left side she could see an endless sea of factories, some small enough to fit inside railway arches; others, like Sheffield's founding companies, spread all the way down to Tinsley. Names such as Firth, Vickers, Cammell and Taylor, merged to become English Steel. On the right were hundreds of grim back-to-back houses. Frances signalled to be let off at the next stop, gaining a look of bewilderment from the driver. She smiled in response and climbed down.

Sullied buildings, gritty streets and the screams of whistles greeted her. The shouts of men were heard over the clanking of iron. The air was thick with the smell of sulphur. The whole scene was bleak. As she stared at men's grey faces, with only the whites of their eyes visible, she too wondered just what she was doing there. The men tipped their caps at her. Some of the younger ones wolf-whistled, but she ignored them and set off walking, to where, she didn't know.

'Ay up!' she heard someone shout. She ignored it and carried on walking. 'Hang on a bit, love!' came the voice once more. She turned her head slightly to ascertain where it was coming from but, with so many people milling about, she wasn't sure. Then she heard her name. 'Frances!' Her heart stopped. A man was walking towards her and waving.

'It's me, Frances, Henry's dad.' His face was black. 'This is no place for you, lass,' he said as he drew nearer. 'What you doing here?'

'Hello, Mr Shepherd,' she said, relieved to see a familiar face. 'I'm not sure. I stayed on the tram too long and I ended up here. How did you know it was me?'

'Cause you stand out like a sore thumb, that's why. You don't want to be hanging about here, love. It's too dirty and dangerous for the likes of you. Let me walk you back to the tram stop.'

'Is Henry here?' she asked, as they walked side by side. He chuckled.

'Young love, eh?' he teased.

Frances blushed.

'Don't mind me,' he said. 'I were young once. In answer to your question, no. He works in a factory over back.' He pointed in the opposite direction. 'I can tell him you were looking for him if you'd like. I'll see him in t'pub at lunchtime.'

'It doesn't matter,' she said. 'I'm not quite sure why I came really.'

'Reight, tram going into town is on other side of road. I'll leave you here cause I've got to get back before anyone notices me gone. It were nice to see you again. Maybe you could visit our house again soon,' he said.

'What are those men doing, Mr Shepherd?' she asked, pointing over his shoulder.

George turned his head. Dozens of men were running towards the entrance of one of the factories. A large crowd had gathered. 'I don't know. I'd better go and take a look,' he said.

'What do they make there?' asked Frances.

'That one makes cannons for t'big ships. I've got to go, Frances. You take care, love, bye.' As George turned to leave, a bell ringing in the distance caught their attention.

'Must have been an accident. That's an ambulance coming,' said George.

'I hope nobody is seriously hurt,' said Frances.

George ran as fast as he could back along the path towards the factory as the ambulance came speeding past.

'Goodbye, Mr Shepherd,' she shouted. Frances stood for a moment longer and watched as the ambulance came to a standstill and two ambulance workers rushed inside the building. Her heart went out to whoever they had come to help.

She didn't go to the tram stop. Instead, she walked further along past houses and pubs until eventually she came to a lively, bustling street. She weaved her way through the crowds of women with scarves around their curlers, factory workers and families. Frances stopped to look in a corner shop window of an old department store building. She didn't go inside, although she was tempted to. Deciding it was time to head back, she considered her options. Going home was not at all appealing. She didn't have the strength to deal with the aftermath of her little rebellion, but she knew that if she wanted to be taken seriously then it was about time she stood up to her mother and started acting like a grown woman.

Chapter Thirty

'War, war, war! If I hear another bloody word about it, I'm going to chuffing scream!' Mary slammed the newspaper down on the table. 'Int it bad enough that decent folk are being killed here, without having to go to war? It were only the other day that Mrs Smith's brother-in-law was crushed to death by an eight-ton piece of metal, after a chain came loose. Poor bugger didn't stand a chance, your dad said. As if that family haven't had it hard enough.'

'I heard, but war's going to 'appen, Mum. I'm single, and I don't have a job. I don't know how I managed to avoid military training back in April. Just look at what the paper is sayin'.' Arthur pointed to a page in the Star. 'A second batch of men, it says there. We've all known it's been coming, ever since Hitler marched into Czechoslovakia.' Arthur leaned forward with both hands on the table. Henry sipped his tea and listened quietly.

'I'm sure Harold could get you a job working in the factory. You'd be helping the war by making stuff for aeroplanes and tanks. You wouldn't have to fight then.' Mary reached forward and rested her hand on Arthur's. 'Owt's better than this.'

'Yes, but I want to go, Mum. I need to, don't you see? I want to do something good for once. I'm not like Harold or Henry. I don't have a reason to stay.'

'Aren't I reason enough? Me? Your mother? Do you want to break my heart?'

'Come here! Don't get upset.' He reached forward and held his mum in his arms. Her head rested on his chest. 'Of course you are, but we can't let them Jerries win. You taught me how to stand up for missen. What sort of a man would I be if I didn't fight for King and country?'

'You'd be safe, here, with your dad and me. I've seen what war does to men, Arthur. You're still so young. You've got your whole life ahead of you.' She squeezed him tight.

'I couldn't live with missen if I didn't go, Mum. You understand, don't you?'

Mary sighed and nodded. Arthur kissed her cheek. 'Talk some sense into him, Henry,' said his mum.

'What? He's not a baby any more. He's old enough to make his own mind up.'

'And what about you, Henry, fancy joining me?'

'Stop that right now!' shouted his mum. 'I've enough on with you wanting to be a chuffing hero!'

'Look, we're going to need as many men as we can,' replied Arthur. Mary glanced first at Arthur and then at Henry. Her eyes filled with tears.

'Don't worry, Mum. It might not even happen. I thought

Chamberlain was still negotiating,' said Henry. He glowered at Arthur.

'Appen, thee might be reight, Henry. It probably won't come to owt.' He glanced at his mum, who was wiping away a tear that had worked its way down her cheek.

'What you both up to today?' she said, sniffing.

'I'm off out,' replied Arthur. 'Got a bit of business to take care of.'

'Don't you go getting yourself in any trouble,' warned his mum.

'Me? Trouble?' He grinned and walked away.

'What about you, Henry love?' She emptied cold tea down the sink and rinsed out the teapot.

He shrugged.

'If you've got nowt better to do, you can give me hand hanging this washing out!'

'I've got summat to tell you.'

Henry was standing in the yard holding a basket of wet clothes. Mary looked at him. 'I've asked Frances to marry me.' Mary's lips tightened into a thin line and she resumed pegging the washing on the line with more vigor.

'But why the rush?' she asked. 'She's not pregnant is she, son?'

'No! What do you take me for?'

'Then why?' repeated his mum.

'Because I love her, and she loves me.'

'What do her folks say?'

'We haven't said anything to them yet. I'm going to ask her dad for her hand. Well? Aren't you happy for me?'

'You've only known each other two minutes,' continued his mum. 'Marriage is a commitment.'

'We know that,' said Henry. 'I want to spend the rest of my life with her. Isn't that commitment enough?'

'Where will you live?' His mum hung the last bit of laundry.

'I'll sort something. 'Do I have your blessing or not?'

'If it's what you want.'

'It is,' replied Henry. 'More than anything else.'

Chapter Thirty-One

'I wouldn't want to be in your shoes when your mother returns,' said Agnes.

'What have I done?' Frances flopped onto Agnes' bed.

'Well, it's no good crying over spilt milk. Show me the ring then!' said Agnes.

'I can't. I've hidden it in my drawer at home, so my parents don't see it.'

'So, are you going to marry him then?'

'I don't know,' said Frances. 'I have to tell my parents first.' She stood up and began pacing the room. 'They're bound to object. Mother already despises the idea of me even dating Henry, and no doubt I'll be in hot water for not going to Devon with her.'

'You could always elope. I'd come with you; you could go to Gretna Green.' Agnes came to stand next to her and put her arms around her. 'If you love him, you'll find a way, I'm sure of it.' She started to laugh.

'What's so funny?' asked Frances.

'You are,' Agnes said.

'I don't see how. This is serious,' said Frances.

'I know, but only a short time ago, you were so adamant that you were never getting married and now look at you.'

'I suppose it is sort of funny,' said Frances. 'But I do still think marriage is nonsense. Only, Henry is different. I'm different when I'm with him.'

'Well, I think it's romantic. I hope I find someone to love soon and who loves me the way Henry loves you.' Agnes gave Frances a hug.

'I'm sure you will, and when you do, we can be two old married maids together,' said Frances and she hugged her friend back. 'Right, I must dash. Henry is calling tonight; I need to change my dress. He plans on asking my father for my hand. We stand a better a chance of persuading him with my mother out of the way.'

'Good luck,' said Agnes.

'Thank you. We're going to need it.'

'No, no, no, no, no!' Frances' father pounded his fists on his desk. 'You barely know each other. You are too young, and you...' He pointed his finger at Henry. 'I'm sorry, Henry, you seem like a decent person, but this is no time for talk of marriage. Maybe, when you can provide properly for my daughter, but my answer now is no!'

'But, Father!' cried Frances.

'Frances, my answer is no! What do you know about love? It seems like only yesterday you were daydreaming of going to America. You were so against marriage. What's changed?'

'Henry. Henry is what's changed. Have you forgotten what it's like to fall in love? You weren't much older than Henry is now when you married Mother.'

'Things were different then. I knew I could provide for your mother. You are acting far to rashly.'

'I will get a better job at the factory, Dr Eton,' said Henry. He had screwed his cap into a tight roll. 'I'll work every day and night if I need to. I love your daughter, and I want her to have a good life.'

'I'm sure you do, Henry, as do I, but I'm afraid marrying you would not give her the life she deserves. She is my only daughter, and I want what is best for her.'

'I love him, Father!' Frances touched her father's arm; tears had begun to pool in her eyes.

'I'm sorry, Frances, but I cannot and will not give you my blessing. Goodbye, Henry.' Frances' father held out his hand. 'Please try to understand; it is nothing personal, but for you two to get married would be a grave mistake.'

'Bye, Dr Eton.' Henry didn't shake his hand. He turned to walk away but then turned back, his fists clenched. 'Forgive me, Dr Eton, but I am going to prove you wrong. I will show you that I am deserving of your daughter's hand.' And with that, he stormed out of the study; Frances ran after him.

'Henry, wait!' shouted Frances. Henry turned sharply, his lips pressed together in a thin line.

Frances ran over to him and touched his face. 'Don't be angry. We can still be together.'

'How? I will never be good enough for the likes of him.'

'For my parents, maybe, not me. I love you.'

'And I love you, but it's not enough in this world. I want your dad to see me as an equal, not to look down his nose at me like the rest.' He ran his fingers through his hair.

'He'll come round; just give him a day or two. He's under a lot of pressure at work, but he'll change his mind. I'm sure he will.' She reached forward and kissed his lips. Henry turned away.

'Do you think I don't know that you deserve better than me? Do you not think I want to see you in a nice house surrounded by beautiful things?'

'Don't be angry, Henry. It's you I want. Money doesn't matter to me. All that stuff means nothing.'

'You say that so easily because you have no idea of the real world... of what it's like to have nothing.'

'I thought we'd got past all this?'

'We have, but...'

'We could run away,' Frances suggested.

'And prove your father right? No, thank you. This is not a game.'

'Then what do you want? You said you wanted us to start our life together; what's changed? I'm willing to put your feelings before my parents. Doesn't that count for something?' Her voiced trembled. 'I can't win!'

'This is not a game, Frances.'

'I know.'

'I was an idiot to think I could get your father to welcome me with open arms.'

'I'm sorry,' said Frances. 'Let's not quarrel, Henry. I love you, and you love me, and nothing and no one is going to change that.' She moved forward to kiss him again. She kept on kissing him this time until the tension disappeared from his face. Henry kissed her back. 'Better?' Henry nodded. 'Good "you yellow-bellied rat!"'

Henry shook his head. 'That were terrible.'

Chapter Thirty-Two

By the time her mother had returned, her little rebellion was yesterday's news. The Prime Minister had made his dreaded announcement. He had given his final notice to Hitler to withdraw his troops from Poland, but Hitler had shown no sign of complying. The Prime Minister's 'long struggle to win peace' had failed. Britain was now at war with Germany. Months of speculation was over.

Her father had had far more pressing matters than to give her quarrel with her mother and her plans to marry Henry a second thought. He was helping with the relocation of hospital patients and the transferring of babies, all to free up space in the casualty hospitals in the city. Frances had tried and failed on several occasions to talk to her father, but his study door was firmly closed.

Her father had given Thomas the task of buying as much blackout paper as he could find, after he had heard reports of crowds of shoppers rushing to get their hands on it. It was also Thomas' job to put brown sticky tape on the windows too. Everyone in the house had to ensure they always carried their gas masks with them. Frances couldn't get her head around the idea that German bombers could drop poisonous gas bombs on England at any time. Everything was normal last week; now people were running around frantically, preparing their homes for the worst. Barrage balloons made the place look like a scene from science fiction. Fear was the official word on everyone's lips. Frances must have read the government leaflet on how to maintain your gas mask over and over. The words, 'It is possible that in war your life might depend on your gas mask' constantly played on her mind.

Frances needed something to occupy her time. She'd offered her help to Thomas and Robert, who had the arduous task of putting together an Anderson bomb shelter in the garden, but they sent her away.

On the day war was declared, the sirens went off, sending everyone rushing to their nearest public shelter, but it had been a false alarm, leading to a chaotic few hours, with half the street crammed inside a small space. Afterwards, her father decided that they would have their own. The neighbours thought he was mad, but he didn't care. The papers had shown photos of men building more communal shelters in the city and stacking sandbags outside. Frances was shocked to read the Home Office's announcement that family pets would not be allowed in public ones. Luckily, they didn't own a pet, but a lot of her neighbours did. She remembered the night a few months back when they had been testing the air-raid sirens and her neighbour's dog kept on howling.

Her mother hadn't said two words to her since her return. The news that Henry had asked for her hand only made things worse. She'd left early the next day to attend a Women's Voluntary Service meeting to discuss the evacuation of children and women with babies to hostels and country mansions in remote parts of the county. A worthwhile task, but Frances thought she cared more about strangers than her own daughter.

She hadn't heard or seen anything of Henry in days; she so desperately wanted to be with him, but fear prevented her from leaving her home. She knew she was behaving ridiculously; it was perfectly safe to venture out during the day. It was only at night when all the lights were out that it became more hazardous. She thought back to the RAF air-raid precaution exercises in July; she had been terrified, but her father had reassured her that all would be fine.

Frances knew she would eventually have to go out because it was Henry's birthday soon and she hadn't bought him anything yet. One idea was to buy him a new compass because his old one didn't work. She decided she would brave it the next morning and venture into town; she didn't want Hitler to think he had won the war already by scaring the British people to death.

Luckily for Frances, and thanks to Henry's bravery, or rather his stupidity, she didn't have to wait long to see him again. After saying goodnight to her parents, Frances climbed the stairs to bed. She'd only just closed her eyes when she heard tiny stones hitting her window. She rushed over and peeled back the corner of her curtain. Standing below was Henry. Grabbing her dressing gown, she tiptoed to the front door and outside and led Henry down the side of her house to reduce the risk of anyone seeing them. He was still wearing his work clothes and he smelled of sulphur.

'What are you doing here?' she whispered. 'It's dangerous to be out after dark.'

'I had to see you, Frances. I've been going out of my mind ever since they announced we were at war. I fear the world is changing too fast.' He pulled her into his arms and pressed his lips to her cheek. 'I've missed you,' he murmured, his voice mellow.

She didn't have a chance to respond because his lips moved from her cheek to her mouth, covering it with his own, his kiss an all-consuming fire that heated her body. He pushed his hand under her dressing gown and cupped her breast. Her nipple hardened as he rubbed it gently between his finger and thumb. She gasped.

'Should I stop?' he asked. Frances shook her head. He pushed her up against the side of the house; cold stone made her shiver. His other hand tightened at her back and pulled her against his thighs. Frances' stomach knotted. Her cotton nightgown was no protection against his searing touch; her skin tingled. When his hand moved leisurely from her breast and teasingly travelled over the flat of her stomach, his fingers splayed, the tips touching the tip of her pubic bone. She panicked – she wasn't wearing any underwear, but she didn't want him to stop; it felt so good. Henry cupped her sex with his palm, sending a new, strange heat deep inside her. She felt his fingers probing, softly rubbing over the thin fabric of her dress. She lifted her hands behind his neck and hooked her fingers in his white neck scarf, allowing his mouth to claim hers. Nothing else mattered. She whimpered as Henry moved his fingers closer to the entrance of her sex. She couldn't breathe. She heard him moan.

'Stop!' she whispered. 'We can't, not here.' He pushed his hardness into her soft flesh, sending her dizzy with desire. Her body reacted naturally to the sweet sensation, and she opened her legs slightly and pushed herself closer to him, enjoying the feeling.

'I love you, Frances,' he moaned into her mouth, his breath hot against her lips.

'I love you too, but we have to stop now before we do something we both regret.' It took all her willpower, but she pushed at his chest and slid her body away from his. She pulled her dressing gown tight across her chest. 'I think you should leave now.'

Henry looked at her lips like he was about to devour her again. Frances took a step back.

'I love thee. I have from the moment I saw you and, while I live, I will love no other. I can't wait till we are married.'

He took a step closer to her and cupped her face tenderly in his hand. 'You make me want to be a better man.' He kissed the little frown line above her nose. 'I'll see thee tomorrow morning. I'll wait for you at Cole's Corner. We can go to the cinema.'

She nodded. 'I'll be there.'

'Good night, Frances.' He kissed her cheek and grinned. 'I'm never going to wash this hand again.' He placed a kiss on the back of his fingers.

'Good night, Henry,' she said, blushing.

Chapter Thirty-Three

Henry opened the scrunched piece of paper he had shoved in his pocket and recalled the words over again. He had received his conscription papers that morning. He left his house without telling anyone, afraid that if he told someone, it would make it more real.

He waited patiently in front of the large display windows on Cole's Corner. He leaned against the glass, gaining himself some disapproving glances from the swathes of people toing and froing through the building's busy entrance. Shoppers hurried about their business. It was like any other noisy Saturday morning. Cars whizzed past, honking their horns, but there was no sign of Frances.

While he waited, he read the headlines on the placards; the Germans had seemingly reached Warsaw. It wasn't looking hopeful for Poland. Henry thought about his brother Arthur and his plans to volunteer. The thought of fighting used to excite Henry but not now he had Frances in his life.

Arthur, on the other hand, couldn't wait to kill the enemy. The image of killing another man, let alone risking his own life, made Henry shudder. But regardless of his fears, he knew he couldn't ignore his letter. But going to war would mean leaving Frances, the idea of which tore at his heart. To not see her would be torture, more so than having to endure military training and being shipped off to some godforsaken place in Europe.

He glanced up at the distinctive clock face above the Telegraph Building. They had five minutes before the movie started. He wondered what was keeping her; then, across the street, he spied her golden hair and her beautiful face emerging from behind a tram and his heart stilled. She waved and he waved back; he felt like the luckiest man alive.

Henry watched her as she fought her way across the busy road, swerving cars; his palms grew sweaty.

'I'm so sorry I'm late; I forgot my gas mask. I don't think I'll ever get used to having to carry it around. It doesn't go with any of my outfits,' Frances joked. 'It's pandemonium in my house. I thought my parents would object to me coming to meet you, but they are so distracted with the war effort. Father's new role is now examining new recruits.'

He placed his hands on her waist and pulled her close. 'Never mind,' he said, smiling. He kissed her cheek. 'You're here now; that's all that matters. But we'd better get a move on if we're to catch the start of the film.'

After the film, Henry took hold of Frances' hand and walked with her up the High Street to her tram stop; they were still laughing at Will Hay's performance. Henry had temporarily forgotten about the war. The streets were now almost empty of shoppers. Most people were making their way home, not wanting to be in town after lights out.

'There's a dance on tonight if you fancy it,' said Henry. 'Me and some of the lads are planning to go. I think it's our last one together for a while.'

'Why's that?' asked Frances. Henry was silent for a moment.

'I don't know how to tell you.'

'You're scaring me, Henry. What has you looking so worried?'

'I... I received my conscription papers this morning.'

Frances stopped walking and turned to face him. 'Please tell me that doesn't mean what I think it means?'

'I don't have a choice. I'm young, not married. I've no ties.'

Frances gave a heavy sigh and shook her head in despair. 'Why did this have to happen?' She put her hands to her cheeks and closed her eyes; when she opened them, they were teary. 'I've had to listen to Thomas go on about it all week. He can't wait to offer his services to the Navy as a medic, and Harriette tells me her cousin Charles has already left. It's madness!' She swallowed hard to fight back the tears.

Henry moved her into a shop doorway and out of the way of oncoming people. 'If we get called up to defend our country, then we must go. It's our duty. It doesn't mean we have to like it.' Frances glared at him, her eyes sparkling with the fresh build-up of tears. 'I already know some fellow who's in the BEF. He's already in northern France.' He pulled her into his arms and tilted her head back so he could see into her eyes. With his thumb, Henry gently wiped away a tear that had started to fall. He kissed her forehead. 'Besides, I might not pass the medical,' he joked, his lips close to her skin. 'And if I did, it wouldn't be forever, just until we stop Adolf.'

Frances rested her head against his chest and closed her eyes.

'What if something happens to you?' She placed her hand over his heart. 'I couldn't bear it.'

'Nothing and no one could keep us apart, Frances. My lucky compass found you, and it will always bring me back to you because our souls have been bound together.' He squeezed her tight against his chest.

'Compass?' She sniffled. Henry nodded. 'But isn't it broken?'

'Yes, but on the day I met you it was working; don't you see? Not the way it was supposed to, I know. Call me crazy, but I think I got lost that day for a reason and that reason was you. My broken compass led me to you, and that's why I will never throw it away.'

Frances lifted her head to look at him. 'Do you truly believe that?' she asked.

'With all my heart,' he said.

'It's a good thing I didn't buy you a new one for your birthday then,' she said.

'I don't need a new one. If... when I go to war, I know it will guide me safely home.'

'What would you like for your birthday?' asked Frances.

'I have all that I need standing in front of me.' He reached for her and placed a chaste kiss on her lips. 'I love you, and you loving me back is more than enough. You do love me, don't you?'

'Of course,' replied Frances. 'Never mind my parents... let's get married, Henry, the sooner the better.'

'Why the rush?'

'Because as you've just said, we're meant to be together. Let's not waste any more time. I want to be your wife.'

'If you marry me, your mum and dad might never speak to you again. I couldn't be the reason for you falling out with your family, Frances. We can wait until the war is over; by then your parents might have come around.'

'I don't want to wait, Henry. I love you. Times are changing. Who knows what the future will bring. Besides, it will be romantic, just like in the movies.'

'I'm not sure. It takes months to plan a wedding.'

'It doesn't need to be grand. I have some money put away. Come on, what do you say?'

'I think you're crazy, Frances Eton.'

'I'm not crazy, Henry, I'm in love.'

Henry kissed her soft lips and held her tight. 'I could hold you in my arms forever, Frances. I pray this war ends soon.'

Chapter Thirty-Four

Mrs Vickers was leaving the house in a bit of a hurry when Frances returned home. Her coat was unfastened, and her face was all flushed.

'Hello, Mrs Vickers.' Frances said.

'Ow do, Frances,' she replied. 'Look after thissen.'

'Whatever do you mean? Are you not coming back?' asked Frances, startled.

'Can't say I will be. All this travelling to and fro in the dark is playing 'avoc with me nerves. I've told your mother. It's 'ard enough without a bleeding war on!'

Frances watched as Mrs Vickers walked down the street, muttering to herself.

She found her mother sitting at the dining room table, her eyes transfixed on a painting that hung on the wall. She looked horrified.

'I've just seen Mrs Vickers,' said Frances.

'Wicked woman!' replied her mother. 'Queuing around the block at the corner shop for bacon and butter was horrifying enough, but the thought of having to cook brings me out in hives. I cannot expect Jenny to do everything. I feel one of my heads coming on.'

'I can help.'

'You might have to. I can't ask Thomas, and your father is never home these days.' She looked at Frances. 'Where have you been? I suppose you were with *that* boy. I'm too upset to think about that now. Robert was looking for you.'

'I wanted to talk to you about something, Mother, but I see now is not the time. What did Robert want?'

'How would I know?'

'I thought you and Robert shared everything.'

'What do you mean by that?'

'Nothing. I like Robert, but I'd just like to know how long he intends on living with us.'

'That's none of your concern,' replied her mother.

'Clearly.'

'I beg your pardon!'

'I think it's about time you told me just what is going on with you and Robert!' said Frances.

'Going on? What do you mean? Nothing is going on.' Her mother smirked.

'What?' asked Frances, her arms wrapped around her waist.

'You! You act so grown up, but you know nothing of the real world. Of just how cruel the world can be.'

'What's that supposed to mean?' Frances' cheeks smarted as though she had just been slapped in the face.

'It doesn't matter; you wouldn't understand.'

'Try me!'

'Very well, things aren't always what they appear. Life is not a fairy tale. It's not like in the *movies*.'

'I know that.'

'Robert has had a hard life... an awfully bad start to put it mildly. He is... the illegitimate child of one of my dearest friends, Emily. There, are you happy now?'

Frances gasped.

'Emily met Robert's dad during the summer of 1916 – things happened, and she never saw him again. It was quite a scandal. Robert has had a tough time. When Emily married another man, Robert went to live with Emily's mother, but she died, and so I took it upon myself to look out for him.'

'What about Robert's mother?' asked Frances.

'When she married, she never told her husband about him. Robert was her guilty secret.' She sighed.

'How dreadful!' said Frances. She took a seat closer to her mother.

'Yes, it was. But people are rarely able to keep secrets forever.'

'So, you weren't trying to match make?' asked Frances, relieved.

'Absolutely not! Whatever gave you that ludicrous idea?'

'You're always together whispering.'

'How hilarious.'

'Why so?'

'You wouldn't understand. Robert is different; he's special. He always has been. I do not fully understand myself, nor do I care to. I certainly don't approve of his choices, but he's a grown man so I guess they are his mistakes to make.' Frances burrowed her brows.

'Why was he arrested?'

'I don't know, but he's no longer friends with James, not since James ran off and left Robert to face the police by himself.' Her mother pushed back her chair to leave. Frances' heart was beating fast. She had to stop her mother from leaving. She knew she would never have this moment again.

Frances breathed in deeply and slowly let out the air through her nose. She couldn't believe her mother had gone to so much trouble to protect Robert, when she seemed to have practically disowned Frances.

'Am I invisible?' she asked, feeling the muscles in her body tense.

'What are you going on about?' Her mother sounded irritated by the question. 'Of course not.'

'Then why?' replied Frances. Her throat burned.

'Why what?'

'Just because I was born a woman! It's not fair that Robert and Thomas are allowed the freedom to decide their own fate.'

'Life is not fair, Frances, and the sooner you accept that, the better it will be for all of us.'

'I wish you would change your mind about Henry, Mother.'

'I can't, Frances. I'm sorry; I just can't.' She swept out of the room, leaving Frances sitting alone at the table.

She had been so excited when she left Henry. All Frances really wanted, was to share her wedding plans with her mother. She imagined her wedding day, her mother putting her arms around her and telling Frances how beautiful she looked. A tear fell onto the table as realisation hit. Her father would never walk her down the aisle. The thought of being alone on her wedding day and lying to her parents had her rushing to the bathroom to be sick.

Chapter Thirty-Five

'A re you sure this is what you want?' asked Henry. 'It's not too late to change your mind.'

'I'm sure!'

'I've told you I'm happy to wait.'

'Henry, you need to report to Leeds for training in two weeks and then only God knows what will happen. Life is too short. It was only the other day I read about a man who was knocked down and killed by a bus during the blackout. We don't know what waits for us around the corner – we need to do this now!' He raised his hands in surrender.

'Are *you* sure?' she asked, suddenly concerned he'd changed his mind.

'Me?' Henry chuckled. 'Since the first time I saw you, it's always been you. But I don't want you to marry me out of fear or any silly obligations, Frances. I know you love your family. Wouldn't it be nice to have them here?'

'Yes, but if I wait for them to come around to the idea, I

could be waiting forever.' Frances dropped her eyes to the ground and sighed. She looked up at Henry through a veil of tears. 'My mind is made up; I want to marry you today. Agnes and Arthur have agreed to be witnesses, so let's just do it!'

'Your parents might change their minds.'

'Maybe. But I think we stand a better chance of them accepting you if we're married.' She dabbed her eyes with her handkerchief.

'As long as you're sure.'

'I'm sure.' She kissed his cheek.

'Frances Elizabeth Eton and Henry Enoch Shepherd!' called the registrar.

'Enoch! There's no backing out now,' she said, giggling. 'Here!' she shouted.

Agnes walked over to Frances and started to straighten her headdress. It was her mother's. Frances had sneaked it out of the house, along with her mother's lace veil; she'd always admired the headdress as a child. It was exquisite. It had ivory pearls, marquise stones and glistening opals and crystals.

She had dressed at Agnes' house. Together they had concocted a plan whereby Frances would pretend she was staying with Agnes for the night. It wasn't unusual for them to stay over at each other's houses. Besides, Frances' father had been so distracted, it wasn't difficult to get him to agree to the idea. Agnes had pinned her hair up and helped her into her dress. She wore the creamy, champagne-coloured dress she'd worn for the City Hall dance. Together they had made their way into town and to the registry office for noon.

Agnes had gathered some flowers from her mother's garden that morning and used a bit of gardening wire to create a small bouquet, while they were away visiting her sick grandmother in Cleethorpes.

'Don't go getting upset,' warned Agnes. 'You go all flushed in the face when you're upset. Henry, you'd better get inside and wait with Arthur. It's bad luck to see the bride.'

Henry nodded and walked through the main doors to where the registrar and Arthur were waiting. 'Right, Frances Elizabeth Eton, are you sure this is what you want? It's not too late to change your mind,' said Agnes.

'I'm certain,' said Frances.

'Do you have something blue?' Frances nodded. 'Borrowed? Old?' Again, Frances nodded.

'Right, what are we waiting for?' said Agnes.

Back at Henry's house, his mum and Edna had made some sandwiches, a trifle and other bits for the wedding guests. Edna had baked a wedding cake with ingredients she already had in her pantry. Margaret had decorated the house with bunting and flowers with help from Harold. Henry's dad put on the wireless, and everyone cheered when Henry carried Frances through the door. The house looked beautiful. It couldn't be more perfect, Frances thought. Arthur opened a couple of bottles of champagne he claimed fell off the back of a lorry. It was a wonderful afternoon.

'Here's to the bride and groom!' Arthur toasted. Everyone clapped. Henry took Frances in his arms and kissed her.

'You take my breath away, Mrs Shepherd.' He kissed her again. He then moved around the room holding her, dancing the foxtrot. Frances thought back to the first time they had danced together in that smoky dancehall; so much had changed since. She was now Mrs Shepherd. It was going to take some getting used to. Henry slowed the dance down, so they were barely moving to the Al Bowlly song that was playing. He placed his lips against her ear causing her to shiver and began to sing, 'The Very Thought of You'.

'I didn't know you could sing.' She smiled.

'I wouldn't call it singing.'

'You have a lovely voice.'

'Not as lovely as you.'

'You look handsome too.'

'Thank you.' He kissed her cheek.

'Everyone is staring,' said Frances, smiling at Edna and Henry's mum. Edna had tears in her eyes.

'Because you are so beautiful,' said Henry.

'They do make a handsome couple,' said Edna, sipping her sherry. 'Just think of the lovely grandkids you'll have, Mary.' Mary took a bite of a sausage roll. 'It's a shame her parents couldn't be here. It breaks my heart, the poor love.'

'Aye well, it is what it is,' Mary tutted.

'Come on, Mary love!' said George. 'Let's show these two lovebirds how we do it.' He grabbed her by the hand and tried to pull her into the centre of the room.

'What is your dad doing?' giggled Frances. Henry turned to look.

'He's probably had too much champagne,' said Henry, laughing.

'Your mum doesn't look happy,' said Frances.

'Get off me ya daft sod!' said Mary. She swatted his hand away like a fly but George reached forward and pulled her into an embrace. He looked into her eyes. 'We were young once.' He grinned.

'Yes, and look where that got us!' She tried to push him away.

'I wouldn't change a single thing, Mary Shepherd. We've had some happy times. Now give us a kiss!' He bent his head and tried to kiss her, but she turned her face away.

'Get away, ya daft bugger!' She tried to squirm free.

'You know you want to.' He laughed, making Mary laugh too. George pecked her on the cheek and pinched her bottom before releasing her. Mary squealed.

'You silly sod! I don't know what's got into you.'

'I'll dance with thee, George,' said Edna. 'I haven't had a good knees-up since my husband passed, God rest his soul.' She put down her glass and hitched her skirt up.

'Come on then, Edna!' he said. He grabbed her by the waist, and they started to dance to a livelier song.

Henry and Frances stopped dancing. Henry fetched Frances a glass of champagne and Frances watched as Arthur put down his beer and walked over to Agnes, who was standing by the fireplace. She heard him clear his throat. He looked nervous. Agnes glanced at him, then went back to watching George and Edna dancing.

Arthur coughed into his fist. 'Do you fancy a dance, Agnes?'

Agnes turned her head to look at him.

'I would love to.' She giggled coyly.

Before long, those who could were dancing, knocking into one another. The party was in full swing. Edna's son, Frank and his wife had arrived carrying their baby, along with several of Mary's neighbours. It was far too cramped, but no one seemed to care. Mary started to clear some plates away and put the dirty dishes into the sink.

'Are you alright?' asked Frances, going into the kitchen to fetch another plate of sandwiches.

'I'm fine.' Mary wiped away a tear that had broken free.

'I can give you a hand tidying up if you like,' she said.

'No need. You go back in and enjoy yourself. It's your wedding day,' said Mary, her smile tight. 'Don't mind me.'

Frances lifted her chin and pushed her shoulders back, feeling brave after the champagne. 'I know you don't like me, but I love your son, and I'm his wife now, and we are going to be very happy together, whether you like it or not.' She slurred a little.

Mary raised her eyebrows. 'Well, well, so you have a little fire in your belly. That's good; you're going to need that,' said Mary. 'I might have underestimated you, Frances. 'Appen, you might be happy.' She nodded. 'Cause life's not going to be easy for the pair of you.' She sat down and indicated for Frances to join her. 'It's not that I dislike you, Frances; I s'pose I'm a bit jealous.' Frances pulled out a chair and sat down. 'I'm losing my boy. I know he's not a boy to you; he's a man now and your husband but, to me, he'll always be my little Henry. You won't understand because you're not a mother, but I worry about him. I'll be losing him to you, and probably to this blasted war. I don't think my heart can take any more.' She tried to hold back her tears. Frances reached across the small table and touched Mary's hand.

'I know it's not the same but try not to think of it as losing a son, more like gaining a daughter,' said Frances. 'I'm not asking you to replace my mother, but she doesn't approve of Henry and me, so it would be nice to have someone to talk to when Henry goes away. I know I'll miss him dreadfully. I love him so much.' Frances blinked away tears.

'Now, don't you start,' said Mary. 'You'll set me off again. It's your wedding day. It's supposed to be the happiest day of your life.'

'It is,' said Frances, snivelling. 'But it would be even better if my father was here.' She wiped away a tear that had trickled down her cheek. Mary stood up and went over to hug her.

'I know,' she said, patting her back. 'Your father will come around; he loves you. She hesitated. 'And I'm sorry I haven't been welcoming. I promise to try harder. We're family now.'

'Thank you,' said Frances.

'Right, enough moping, let's go and join the others,' said Mary.

'Turn off the wireless a minute, Dad!' shouted Harold. 'I'd like to make a toast.' He cleared his throat and looked at Henry. Henry beckoned to Frances to stand next to him. She hurriedly left Mary standing in the doorway and went to hold Henry's hand. 'To our kid brother, Henry. I didn't think you had it in thee. Frances is a reight beauty; you've done alreight for thissen. To Frances, look after him; he's a reight soppy pillock who's always worn his heart on his sleeve, but we wouldn't want him any other way. He'll always do reight by thee because he's dependable and loyal. Ours might not be the richest family, but where we lack wealth, we make up for in love. I wish you both all the happiness in the world. If you're half as happy as Margaret and me then you'll be blessed. Raise your glasses to Henry and Frances everyone!' The room erupted with whistles and cheers.

'Oh, Harold, that were lovely. Give us a kiss,' said Margaret.

Henry's dad stood up and wobbled slightly. 'You make a lovely couple,' he said, wiping a tear from the corner of his eye.

'Sit down! You're drunk,' said Mary.

'I am not.' He hiccupped. 'I'm reight as ninepence.' He turned to Henry. 'Henry, me lad, we've all chipped in and got you summat.' A big smile spread across his dad's face. Henry looked at Frances and shrugged. 'We've booked you a room above the 'Rose and Crown'; we don't want you to miss out on your wedding night.' He winked at Henry. Frances turned scarlet. She didn't know where to look. Arthur patted Henry on the back, then winked at Agnes, who also blushed. 'They're expecting you there now, so what you waiting for?' his dad shouted.

'I don't know what to say,' said Henry. 'Thanks, everyone.' He whispered 'sorry' in Frances' ear.

'Turn the wireless back on!' shouted one of Henry's friends.

'Shut thee gob!' shouted Arthur and glared at him. 'Before I shut it for thee.' Henry's friend apologised profusely, upped and disappeared to the kitchen for another drink.

Edna started to sing a Gracie Fields song. When it got to the chorus, everyone joined in.

'Edna,' said Frances. 'I didn't know you had it in you.'

'There's a lot you don't know about me, Frances love,' said Edna, winking.

After Edna sat down, George stood up and told a rude rhyme.

'George Shepherd, there are young ladies present!' said Mary and clipped him around the back of his head.

'Sorry about that, Agnes,' said Arthur. 'Me dad's a bit drunk.'

'Don't worry,' she said. 'I didn't understand a word of what he said anyway.' She giggled.

Frances yawned. It was getting late, and most of the guests had started to leave. Margaret was complaining of indigestion, and she was feeling uncomfortable from the baby kicking, so Harold took her home.

Agnes helped to tidy up and then said goodbye. She had agreed to let Arthur take her home.

'It has been a wonderful day,' said Henry as he kissed his mum goodbye. Henry's dad was fast asleep in his chair, snoring.

Frances changed out of her dress and packed her mother's headdress and veil carefully; her hands trembled as she put them away in her bag. All the champagne had made her a little lightheaded. She kissed Mary goodbye and then they left to spend the evening in the pub down the road. Her mouth felt dry and her shoulders tensed; it would be their first night together and she was nervous, despite now being a married couple.

Chapter Thirty-Six

Henry unlocked the door to their room for the night. As Frances was about to walk in, he stopped her.

'Hang on a minute! We need to do this right.' He lifted Frances and placed her in his arms before kicking the door wide open. 'Here we are, Mrs Shepherd!' he declared. He gently placed her down on the edge of the bed and went to lock the door.

'Well, it certainly isn't the Savoy, but it will do,' she said. 'At least it's clean.' It was a large room, sparsely decorated, apart from the large four-poster bed in the middle.

'Have you stayed at the Savoy?' he asked.

'No, but I've seen pictures in magazines.'

Henry closed the curtains and switched on the bedside lamp. He took his place next to her on the bed and held her trembling hand.

'I think the alcohol is starting to wear off,' she said.

'We don't have to do anything if you're not ready.'

'I want to Henry. It's our wedding night.' Frances swallowed. 'My mouth is dry. Would you mind pouring me a glass of water please?'

Henry poured Frances a glass of water from a jug that was on a small table and handed it to her. While she drank, Henry took off his jacket and tie and placed them over a chair. Then he slipped off his shoes.

'Should I take my clothes off too?' Frances asked.

'Only if you want to.' She looks so innocent, he thought. Frances passed him the empty glass and then kicked off her shoes, before leaning forward to take off her stockings.

'Here, let me do that.' Henry grinned and rushed over to her.

'If you wish,' replied Frances.

'I do. You just lie back and relax.'

Frances did just that. Henry leisurely peeled down each of her stockings. Then he lifted her foot to his mouth and kissed the tender part before turning her leg slightly, so her knee fell outwards, leaving her exposed. His eyes hungrily travelled down her body.

'Move up the bed a bit so I can kneel on,' he said.

Frances wriggled up. Henry licked his lips and trailed soft, feathery kisses up the inside of her leg.

'That tickles,' she said.

Henry pushed up her dress so he could see her flat stomach and continued to kiss her, stopping just before he reached her undergarments. Frances shot up and looked down at him. His dark hair between her legs.

'What are you going to do?'

'Do you want me to stop?' he muttered against her flesh,

making her quiver. Frances shook her head. Slowly, he pulled down her silk panties and gulped at the sight of her smooth flesh. 'I want to see you completely naked, Frances,' he said softly.

Henry could feel himself grow hard at the sight of her body, the little tufts of blonde hair between her long, slender legs. She was a goddess. He felt a sense of pride that she was now his wife. He'd longed for this night since the first time he'd laid eyes on her. He desperately wanted to make love to her, but he didn't want to rush and ruin this special moment. It was, after all, her first time. He knew she was nervous, even if she pretended not to be. Her stalwartness was what he admired about her.

He pulled off the rest of his clothes quickly, his maleness springing to life. She reached out and touched him with her delicate fingers. Pleasure seared through him; no longer could he suppress his excitement.

Her heated gaze turned him on even more. He felt so privileged to be her first and, now, her only lover he reassured himself. For a moment, he thought about his previous encounters with women. The other times had been just a quick fumble in the dark, over in minutes – nothing like this.

Henry was unable to speak. He was trying to stay focused. His heart was beating out of his chest. She had no idea the effect she was having on him. She moved her head forward till her mouth was within kissing distance of him. She fluttered her dark eyelashes open and looked up at him. He could feel her warm breath on him. He groaned deeply in response.

'Are you trying to kill me,' he teased.

'Did I do something wrong?' she asked, genuinely concerned.

'No, not at all,' he said, a satisfied grin on his face. 'It's just hard for me to maintain control.'

She smiled at him sweetly, and that was his undoing. He reached down and kissed her mouth. He ran his fingers through her soft hair and held her head. She responded by opening her mouth and touching his tongue with her own. She was everything he had dreamed of and more. He couldn't get enough of her sweet taste. Her little whimpers and cries almost sent him into a frenzy with desire. He thought he would burst from the pressure building inside him.

He gently moved her back down. She was so trusting of him; his heart burst with love for this beautiful creature before him.

'I need you to relax,' he instructed.

She nodded.

He moved his hand between her legs and gently encouraged them to part. She stiffened.

'I won't hurt thee. I would rather die before I hurt thee,' he whispered. 'We can stop at any time, remember that.' He leaned over her and stroked between her legs until she was ready. Then he took himself in his hands and carefully placed himself at her entrance.

'Are you alright?' he asked. He was sweating slightly. His arms trembled as he held his weight off her body. She didn't speak; she just looked at him wide-eyed and nodded. Henry desperately wanted to get this right. Cautiously he eased his way into her just a tiny bit and then a little further. She let out a small cry. 'Did I hurt you?' he asked panicking.

'I'm fine,' replied Frances.

'Are you sure?'

Frances nodded. Henry positioned his body so his face was above hers. His hands rested on either side of her head. A bead of sweat dripped onto her forehead; he quickly wiped it away with his hand before kissing her lips once more.

'I love thee,' he said.

'I love you too,' she replied.

Then he started to move gradually. He didn't want to hurt her, so he slowly pulled himself out and leisurely pushed himself back inside again. Never in his life had he experienced something so soft and exquisite as this before. Her sweet smell, mixed with the scent of their lovemaking, was a potent aphrodisiac, a heady mixture. He moved as gently as he could, but he couldn't hold back any longer. He wrapped her up in his arms and held onto her as he plunged deeper, lost in their peaceful lovemaking. She let out a sweet cry of pleasure, which triggered an animalistic response from him. He wanted to please her, to make this night one she would never forget. She held tightly on to him, and he kissed the side of her face. Panting, he came hard; he thought he was never going to stop. Frances arched her back and bucked her hips, as Henry jerked violently like a man possessed.

Afterwards, Henry held her close and kissed the side of her face. He never wanted to let her go.

'How you feeling?'

'A bit sore, but I feel wonderful,' she replied. 'Although I should probably think about getting home before my parents wake.'

'This has been the happiest day of my life,' he said. 'My heart, body and soul belong to you now, Frances Shepherd. I am your slave for you to do with as you please.'

'Is that so?' she said and positioned her body so she was lying on top.

'Most definitely,' he replied.

'Well, in that case, slave, I demand that you make love to me again.'

'Your wish is my command,' he jested. And as he did so, Henry thought his heart would burst, and he would die from the pain of loving her.

Finding the time to be alone was tricky at times, but as the daylight grew shorter and the temperature cooler, Henry and Frances were inseparable, despite still living apart. They spent most of their time in Henry's bed. Henry had vowed he would find them a home soon but with money being tight and all the uncertainties that came with war, a home would have to wait. For Henry, even though Frances still hadn't told her parents, to call her his wife was an honour. It didn't matter to him that she hadn't told her family because he no longer sought their approval. So long as Frances loved and needed him, that was all that mattered. Their time spent together was perfect. Even though it hadn't seemed possible, they grew closer, and Henry fell in love with Frances more and more with each passing day. When not naked in each other's arms, they would travel to the countryside, go for long walks and watch nature paint the landscape with sepia hues.

One time, while out walking, Henry decided that they should climb to the top of a rocky ridge. It was a steep climb, but it was worth it. When they reached the top, the view was breath-taking; a patchwork of rich autumnal colours could be seen for miles around, russet-reds and browns. The dry, crisp wind whipped their hair about their faces. Henry felt alive.

'Look at the rocks!' cried Frances. 'They look like they've been stacked one on top of the other by giants long ago.' She opened her arms wide and let the wild wind blow over her. 'Let's scratch our initials in one of them so in years to come our grandchildren can see them.'

Henry thought she sparkled in the autumn sunlight. He stood close behind her and wrapped his arms about her waist; together, they breathed in the clean air and watched the sun as it lit up the valley below.

Henry moved Frances' hair to the side so he could kiss her exposed neck. He cupped her breast gently and, with his other hand, he slowly ran it down the front of her dress and settled it between her legs and over her sex. Frances gasped. She turned around and placed her hands around the back of his head. He brought his mouth down to hers, and they kissed.

Henry's eyes darkened as he lowered her down to the ground. He lifted her skirt and groaned as he felt the warmth of the woman he loved. His body entangled with hers, and they moved slowly to begin with, then becoming more restless and urgent. Henry called out her name and collapsed against her; he kissed her cheek and held her body tight.

'My love,' he whispered in her ear.

'I won't be for much longer if we get caught. Now let's get dressed quickly before we give the ramblers the shock of their lives.' Henry laughed and kissed her again.

Chapter Thirty-Seven

'I t's not too far, my love,' said Henry.

'Anywhere away from Sheffield is too far, Henry, if it means I don't get to see you every day.'

Henry pulled her into his arms.

'I will miss you,' said Frances.

'I will miss you too. I wish I didn't have to go. I wish the blasted war had never started. That way, I could look for a better paid job so we could move in together and start our life properly as husband and wife.'

'I hate Hitler!' said Frances.

'You and the rest of the country.' He kissed her cheek and tasted her salty tears. 'Don't cry, my love,' he whispered. 'It won't be forever, you'll see. We beat the Germans before and we can do it again. When I get home, I promise thee on my life, we will never be separated again.'

'But why you?'

'Why any of us? Nobody wanted this war, but we can't sit

back and do nothing. What kind of man would I be if I didn't go? Could you love a coward?' As the train approached the station, a low rumbling sound could be heard in the distance. 'I'm no coward, Frances. I couldn't live with missen if I let others die and did nothing.'

'Well, you better come back to me soon, Henry Shepherd, or else...'

'Or else what? Not even the devil himself could keep me from thee.' He placed his lips against hers and breathed in her sweet scent. 'Oh, Frances, my sweet Frances,' he murmured against her mouth. He moved his hand up through her hair and cradled her head, then kissed her and drew her closer to his body, his tongue wrapped around hers. Nothing existed in that moment for Henry other than the warmth of his wife's body and the feel of her touch. 'I don't want to leave you,' he whispered. He felt her cold tears against his cheeks. Frances clung to him. As the train drew closer, the sound grew louder and more distinct, the rhythmic chugging and the screech of metal on metal. A hiss of steam escaped as the train slowed to a crawl. The whistle blew and the platform filled with people.

'I've got to go. I love thee,' he said.

'I love you too.'

Henry jumped onto the train and waited at the door until the conductor blew his whistle for the final time and it pulled away. His heart felt as if it had splintered into a thousand fragments as he looked at Frances standing on the platform, waving, tears streaming down her face.

The train was overcrowded with other lads his age, some of whom only had a brown paper bag to carry their belongings. Henry carried his battered suitcase and went in search of a seat.

'Goodbye, Sheffield!' Henry heard someone shout.

'Goodbye, Betty!' shouted another.

'Goodbye, Hare and Hound!' shouted a third and everyone cheered.

Henry watched as Sheffield slowly faded from view.

On arrival at Leeds, they were herded together into small groups, each one of them looking lost and bewildered. Then they were shown to their barracks and given something to eat. However, Henry's stay in Leeds was short-lived because, shortly after his arrival, they announced his regiment would be travelling to Scarborough.

It was dark when he arrived at Scarborough. Army trucks were waiting to drive them to their next destination. By the time Henry and the others had arrived at the camp, they were exhausted. He spent his first night in the stables along with other squaddies, sleeping on canvas bags filled with straw, because all the rooms in the huts were full. He longed to be back home and in bed with Frances. He wondered what she was doing. Writing her a quick letter, he informed her that he would not be staying in Leeds and that he had moved to the coast. He joked about being close the sea and hoped they could visit together when the war was over. He tried telling her how much she meant to him. He just hoped Frances would forgive his spelling mistakes.

After a restless night, the bugler woke them early. A roll call was taken, and then they were each told to wash and shave, which he did with cold water in the open air. After the ordeal, his face was covered in bits of paper – shaving in these conditions wasn't easy! With breakfast over, Henry's life in the army officially began.

The next day, he lined up with the other recruits. Each were handed a knife, fork and spoon and they marched to the dining hall. Afterwards, he was allocated a hut. The hut was a simple structure made from timber and corrugated iron sheets. The space inside was bare apart from essentials and the air was thick with the smell of damp wood and sweat. The lighting was dim, with a few bare lightbulbs hanging from the ceiling and only a meagre amount of natural light seeping through. Henry felt lucky to have the bottom bunk. After his first day of training, his bones ached from continual rifle drills and the physical exercise. Every muscle screamed at him when he moved, his head ached and he felt nauseous. Every day following, he was hurried from pillar to post, never having a minute until lights out. He was exhausted and homesick.

Being away from Frances at Christmas had been hardest. They had been exchanging letters, but it wasn't enough. She'd sprayed each one with perfume, and Henry had fallen asleep each night, comforted by her scent. Most of his evenings he polished his brass buttons and shoes to take his mind off home.

'You coming, Shepherd?' shouted his friend Ernest. 'You've worn the ink off those letters. Give it a rest!' Henry had been introduced to Ernest only recently but they'd hit it off instantly. He was older than Henry; never married. Henry thought Ernest fancied himself as a bit of a lady's man.

On a few occasions, Ernest persuaded Henry to go to the

village dances. Ernest was keen to sow his oats before they travelled to Europe and the uniform caused quite a stir with the local girls. Ernest would flirt outrageously, but Henry didn't feel comfortable, much to the disappointment of the girls in the room. He felt as though he was betraying Frances.

Henry was given his first leave in January. Every moment spent with Frances was precious because he didn't know if it would be his last; at any moment, he would have to go to Europe.

His last visit was early March. Henry stepped down from the train and scanned the crowd for the face that had stolen his heart. Standing on the rain-soaked platform in the cold, waving, was Frances. He ran over to her and scooped her up in his arms. She felt so good. He showered her with kisses, never wanting to stop.

They caught the tram to Frances' house and the first thing Henry did was take a hot bath. Frances lathered soap in his hair and massaged his scalp. After he had washed, they climbed naked into Frances' bed together. They knew they wouldn't be disturbed because her parents would be out all day.

Frances' father worked around the clock with his colleagues on new research, looking at treatments for infections and pain relief. Her mother worked with the Women's Voluntary Services and was often tied up with different jobs during the day – Frances and Henry had the house to themselves.

'I've missed thee,' whispered Henry against her mouth. He cradled her in his arms.

'And I you,' she said.

He moved to position his body between her thighs. Frances wrapped her legs around him and welcomed him as he made love to her as if nothing else mattered, only their need for each other – like there would be no tomorrow. Henry wanted to bury himself deep inside her forever. He sank further into a state of bliss. Frances whimpered as her body became one with Henry's.

The rest of his leave they spent going to the pictures or taking long wintry walks in the park. Each day was precious; their love growing more profound and making each other complete.

'How can I leave you?' he said as he kissed her mouth, the tip of her nose and then her eyes.

'Don't go! We could run away!'

'Oh aye, and what if we got caught? I could go to prison.'

'I love you, Henry,' cried Frances. Tears spilt from her eyes.

'Let me look at you.' He ran his hand over her cheeks and cupped her head. 'You have nothing to worry about. I've told you my compass will bring me back to you,' he joked.

'That ridiculous compass.'

'That 'ridiculous compass' is my lucky charm. When I go overseas, I'll rely on it to bring me home.'

'Well, I don't care what it takes; you don't get to leave me, Henry Shepherd. We took vows, remember? You promised to grow old with me.'

'How can I forget.'

He kissed her lips and held her tight. It broke his heart to leave her again; her beautiful face was red with tears as he waved her goodbye.

Henry arrived at his parents' home, feeling empty. He'd just left his heart with his wife. He went to his room to pack his bag and sank down onto the bed, his shoulders shaking. He buried his head in his hands. God, he was scared. Scared of what would happen, scared he would never come home, scared he would never see Frances again. He hadn't noticed the tears falling. He wiped his face and took a deep breath, then reached into his pocket for his compass. 'Please, God,' he whispered, 'if you can hear me. I don't ask for much. But it would be a cruel joke if thee took me away now. I've got so much to live for. I pray you will allow me to grow old with Frances.' He kissed his compass and ran his fingers through his hair, glancing around at his small and meaningless bedroom.

Composing himself, Henry went down to the kitchen and seated himself at the table with his parents one last time.

'I got a letter from our Arthur,' said his mum, her voice wavering with emotion.

'Oh aye. What did he have to say for his sen?' asked Henry.

'Well, you know our Arthur,' said his dad.

'He's been chuffing playing cards and winning money off some of the other men. He says he's doing alreight. His regiment has moved to Scotland now.' His mum was trying hard to hold back her tears as she spoke. Henry reached forward and held her hand. 'He said there was talk of them travelling to Norway on the HMS Sheffield.'

'Right, Mum, Dad. I need to get going now if I'm to catch me train.'

'So soon?' said his mum. 'But you've only just got here.' He stood and picked up his bag. Mary walked with him to the front door with George following. Henry wrapped his arms around his mum and squeezed her tight.

'I'm not going to cry,' said Mary, but she could no longer hold back her tears. 'Oh, Henry love. It seems only two minutes ago you were running through this door crying because you'd grazed your knee or because Arthur or Harold had done something. Where has the time gone?' She wiped her eyes, but the tears kept on coming.

'I love thee, Mum,' he said and kissed the top of her head.

'I love thee more than words can say. You'll always be my little boy and I will pray every night until you come home again. I won't rest till you do. Don't do anything stupid, does tha hear?'

Henry nodded.

'Bye, Dad,' said Henry.

'Bye, son. Take care of thissen.'

Henry left them standing on the doorstep. En route to the tram stop, he passed the rag and bone man with his horse and cart. He breathed in the bitter air and sighed. Even though it wasn't much to look at, he was going to miss his home. It had been hard for him to say goodbye to his mum and dad, but he promised he would write, and he was good at keeping his promises.

*

Henry travelled back to his unit with a knitted balaclava and gloves from his mum. In a pocket, close to his heart, he placed a photograph of Frances she had given him, and a locket of her hair stored in his old compass.

After weeks of travelling about the country, Henry caught a packed train to Plymouth, wearing his full kit and carrying his kit bag with spare clothes and equipment. There hadn't been a seat, so he was forced to sit on the floor. He wrote a letter to Frances telling her that he was on his way to France.

Chapter Thirty-Eight

Frances tried to store his smell, touch, every detail to memory. She waited in the same spot for some time after their final kiss goodbye. Even when the clouds could no longer hold in the rain, Frances waited. She knew he wasn't coming back, but she couldn't force her legs to move. They had made a deal, after his first visit home, that Frances wouldn't go to the station with him – it had been too hard on them both. But while Frances was standing in the pouring rain, she regretted that decision. A strange feeling in her stomach was telling her that she should have gone with him.

'Are you alright, love?' came a woman's voice.

Frances turned her head.

'You'll catch your death standing out here. Do you need me to fetch someone for you?'

Frances shook her head.

'Well, if you're sure.' The lady walked away, but she kept on looking back over her shoulder at Frances.

After Henry had left, she avoided reading the newspapers, ever since learning from his most recent letter that he was sailing to France. But it was virtually impossible to avoid the news, especially when the topic on everyone's lips was the war. Most people she spoke to knew someone who had a loved one overseas. Frances was no exception.

It had been a long, dark and cold winter. To some, it felt like there wasn't a war going on at all. People had even started to call it the 'phoney war' as most of the action appeared to be happening on home soil, with Britain getting ready for a German attack. All that had happened had been the introduction of petrol rationing in September. Food rationing was to follow, first bacon and butter. Although sugar was available, Frances' mother had to register for it at the corner shop. The only other sign that there was a war was the regular blasting of the air-raid sirens when everyone rushed to the closest shelter with their gas mask in hand causing fear and panic.

Frances had kept herself busy volunteering with the city's Air Raid Precautions ambulance service, at ambulance stations often consisting of commandeered commercial garages. Agnes, Harriette and Alice had also volunteered. Although officially not old enough to help, Frances' father knew someone on the council. They were all issued with a steel helmet and an armband with the words 'First Aid'. They had to report for duty at their nearest first aid post three or four evenings a week. Because they all lived close to one another, they some-times found themselves working their shifts together. It was fun in the beginning, before the war got serious.

'Now, ladies, you need to turn the wireless down,' said Miss Turner, their chief warden. 'You won't hear the bell go with that racket.' She looked at Harriette who was trying to learn a new dance step with Agnes. There wasn't a lot of space to move around because of all the garage apparatus, gas masks and first aid equipment.

'Yes, Miss Turner,' replied Harriette sweetly.

A soon as Miss Turner had left, Harriette turned it up again.

'That racket!' She spun Agnes around. 'Artie Shaw is not a racket! He's a dream.'

'You'll get us into trouble,' said Frances.

'Frances! Stop acting like an old maid. Nothing has happened around here in weeks. Come and join us! We need to be ready for the dance Friday night,' said Harriette.

'I won't be going,' said Frances.

'Why ever not?'

'She doesn't have to go if she doesn't want to,' said Agnes.

'Well, I'm going and I'm going to dance with every boy there,' said Harriette.

'They won't know what's hit them,' mumbled Alice. Frances laughed.

About a month after Henry's last visit, Frances began to feel sick and tired all the time and she had trouble keeping her food down. Her mother thought it was the new rationing meals that were making her ill. She didn't think much of Frances' sickness as everyone was looking pale; there was a war on.

Still feeling nauseous and tired, she decided to pay a visit to Henry's parents. It wasn't unusual for her to go during the day. She'd found that being close to the things Henry had touched and the people he loved and who loved him, helped with her heartache and always made her feel better.

When she arrived that morning, Mary and Edna were tirelessly sorting through the salvage materials they had collected for the war effort, ready to take to the local church. Nothing got thrown away: old dusters, clothes, even old meat bones became valuable resources. Frances offered to help, but the smell of rubbish made her gag, and she went running to the yard to be sick. When she returned, Mary had made her a cup of tea, and Edna had a big smile on her face.

'How long has it been going on?' asked Mary.

'I haven't been feeling myself for weeks.'

'Any other symptoms?' asked Edna. Both women were watching her intently.

'Not really, only...' Frances paused and sipped her tea.

'Go on!' encouraged Mary.

'I can't quite understand it. I think I might be dying.' Frances wiped a tear from the corner of her eye. 'I'm sick all the time, but instead of losing weight, I'm gaining it.'

Mary and Edna started laughing.

'It's not funny; I'm serious,' sighed Frances.

'I know it's not, love,' replied Edna. She came and put her arm around her shoulders. 'You're not dying. You're with child.'

Frances looked from Edna to Mary and back to Edna again, finally shaking her head.

'I'm not? Am I?' Her mouth fell open. 'How do you... how can I be?'

'You don't need me to tell you about the birds and the bees, do you?' joked Edna.

'No! I know how. What I mean is how? We... you know.' She blushed. Frances paused for a moment as realisation dawned. 'Oh, my goodness, this can't be happening.' She dropped her head into her hands. 'How could we have been so stupid?'

'It's a bit of a shock to begin with, but you'll get used to it,' said Mary. 'You'll have to; there's no going back now.'

Frances' shoulders shook and tears began to stream down her face.

'There, there,' said Edna rubbing her arm. 'It's going to be alright.'

'My parents don't even know I'm married,' she sobbed. 'I've been such a fool!'

'Well, you're gunna have to come clean now; you're gunna need lots of support. Of course, you'll have us, but we can't be with you all the time,' said Mary. She handed her a clean hanky.

'I'm going to have to write and tell Henry... Henry! What's he going to make of this?' Frances blew her nose.

'He's going to be chuffed to bits,' said Mary.

'But he won't be here,' said Frances.

'Look, don't go worrying about anything now,' said Edna. 'You've got months before it arrives. First things first, you need to go home and tell your parents.'

Frances took a deep breath and wiped her eyes.

'I know,' she said, nodding. 'But it's not going to be easy.'

'Nothing ever is,' said Mary.

'But on the bright side, Mary, there's gunna be another little un.' Edna chuckled and Mary joined in. 'Your house will be full again.'

'Thank you, Frances,' said Mary. 'You've made my day.'

Frances ran her hand over her stomach. 'I can't believe it's real.'

'It's wonderful news,' said Edna. 'Just wonderful. Something to look forward to during these miserable times.'

When Frances got home, she wrote a letter to Henry.

My darling Henry,

I pray that you are safe. It must be dreadful for you being miles away from home. I miss you terribly. Please write to let me know you're well. I need to know you are safe – because I have some news. I hope you're sitting down when you read this.

I'm pregnant. We're going to have a baby! I know this will be a shock – it was to me at first, but now that it's sunk in, I'm so happy. I can't wait. Your mum is over the moon, and I hope you will be too. I realise the timing isn't great, what with you being overseas, and we haven't got our own home yet, but we can't think about all that now. We will just have to get by.

I can't wait to see you again. I count the days till you are next home.

I don't want you to worry about me. I will be fine. I plan on telling my parents soon. Please don't think that I haven't tried to tell them, I have, but the timing has never been right. It has been so hectic here. I have Edna and your parents to help me – and hopefully mine too, so I won't be going through this on my own. I love you, Henry. Come back to me soon.

Yours forever

Frances

x

Chapter Thirty-Nine

The news came that British troops had failed to prevent the occupation of Norway by the Germans. Agnes was deeply concerned about Arthur; their relationship had blossomed after Frances' wedding, when he had first offered to walk her home. Agnes had assured Frances that he was not as scary as he looked and that he had been quite attentive on their way to Agnes' house. Much to everyone's surprise, Arthur and Agnes had met up a few times after that. Agnes claimed that Arthur was the perfect gentleman and Henry told Frances that Arthur was smitten. Now Agnes was upset because she hadn't received a letter from Arthur since he went overseas. Frances tried to comfort her, but it was no use. Agnes, along with the rest of the country, felt more and more downhearted as the days went by.

When Churchill became Prime Minister, the country

celebrated, and Frances witnessed the nation's spirits lifted once more.

It was on one of these happier days that Frances and her friends decided to attend a dance in a West Yorkshire village. Close to the town were four large army camps; Harriette thought it would be fun to go because it would be full of soldiers. Frances wasn't keen on going because her dresses were getting tighter around the middle, but she agreed to go for Harriette and to take her mind off Henry. For the first few months of the year Harriette had kept on pestering Frances for Thomas' address overseas, but, eventually, she gave up, realising there were more men out there in uniform eager to write to her.

They decided to get dressed at Frances' house. Following instructions from a magazine, they applied liquid make-up to their legs they had bought from a chemist because stockings were in short supply. Then they took it in turns to draw a seam down the back of each other's legs with a pen – no one had been able to buy anything new in a while.

It was a bright spring day.

'Thank goodness the clouds have stayed away,' said Alice as they waited for the bus. 'I would hate to be caught in the rain before we even get there.'

'I know, can you imagine?' said Agnes.

They caught the bus to the barracks and entered the mess hall. Bunting decorated the room and at the front was a small band. It was full of military personnel and quite a few Canadian airmen.

When they entered the hall, they received wolf-whistles, causing Alice to almost combust with embarrassment, nearly tripping.

'Would you look at all those men in uniform!' gushed Harriette.

'Harriette, you had better watch yourself,' warned Alice. 'These men look like they could eat us alive!'

'Nonsense,' replied Harriette. 'You need to live a little. Don't you know there's a war on!'

She sashayed towards the edge of the dancefloor to make herself more visible but, to her disappointment, it was Frances who the men lined up to dance with first, then Agnes. Unperturbed, Harriet walked over to a cute guy and asked him to dance. Alice did all she could to avoid eye contact with everyone until a big burly Scot walked over and lifted her off her feet.

'My name's Hamish,' he said. 'But everyone calls me Jock.' He grabbed her hand and, not paying any heed to her protests, moved her around the room to the music as though she were a feather.

The first dance was a slow foxtrot, followed by a more energetic American swing. Frances' feet barely touched the ground. The face of her dance partner kept on changing as each soldier eagerly took turns, twirling her around the hall.

Starting to feel dizzy, she excused herself and left the dancefloor. She had to keep reminding herself that she was pregnant; luckily, it wasn't noticeable. Frances moved to stand close to the entrance to cool down. From where she was standing, she had a clear view of the dancefloor. She watched her friends having a good time; it felt good to be away from Sheffield. She only wished Henry was here dancing with her instead.

She was about to sit down when a man in uniform approached her.

'Care for a beer?' he asked. He held two bottles in his hands.

'Yes, please.' She smiled and took one from him, sure that one beer wouldn't hurt the baby.

'I'm afraid it's not cold.'

'Oh, I don't mind. I'm so thirsty,' she said, taking a sip.

'Smoke?'

'No, thank you.'

'Do you mind if I do?' he asked.

'No, go ahead. Where in America are you from?'

'I'm not; I'm Canadian.' He blew out smoke and sniggered.

'Sorry,' replied Frances, blushing.

'That's OK; I forgive you. You're not the first. Cheers!' He clinked the neck of his bottle with hers. He had a nice smile. He was tall and handsome, and she just adored his accent, even if she had mistaken him for an American. 'I've been waiting my turn to dance with you,' he confessed. He held her gaze. Frances looked away. 'You do know you are the prettiest girl in the room,' he said, smiling and swigging his beer.

'That's sweet of you to say,' replied Frances. 'But I think you are far too kind.'

'I don't think so. Just look at all those envious stares I'm getting just talking to you.' He pointed his bottle at some of the other men in the room.

'Well, you should know, I'm married.'

'Jeez, just my luck. Your husband is a lucky fella. But I don't see no ring.' He lifted her left hand to his face and kissed her fingers. Frances quickly pulled it away. 'Sorry, I didn't mean to offend.'

'You didn't. It's just... never mind.' She glanced around the room and sipped her drink.

'I take it your husband isn't here.' She shook her head. 'So, where's the harm? His loss is my gain.'

'I don't think he would see it like that; besides, I don't even know your name,' she said.

'Where are my manners? My name is William, but my friends call me Billy. What's yours?'

'Frances.'

'Frances,' he repeated melodiously. 'I like it, but I think I'll call you Franny.'

'Will you now,' a soft chuckle escaped from her lips.

'Nice to meet you, Franny.' He held out his hand and beamed a playful smile. Frances couldn't resist and, as she placed her hand in his, he quickly seized his advantage and pulled Frances into his arms. Placing his hands tight around her waist, he said: 'How about that dance now?'

'Seeing as you asked so nicely,' she teased. 'I suppose one dance won't hurt.'

They danced together for most of the evening. At the end of the night, he walked with her to the bus stop. Agnes walked on ahead. Harriette was kissing some Canadian airman, and Alice was exchanging addresses with Hamish.

'I know you're married,' said William. 'And I know you'll probably say no, but will you write to me? I don't have a sweetheart back home, but if I did, I would want it to be you.'

'I don't think my husband would approve,' said Frances.

'I'm sure he wouldn't. Gosh, if you were my wife, I would go crazy! But it would sure make me happy,' he said. 'Please say you will. We're heading to Europe next week. Knowing I had someone as beautiful as you to write to would sure boost my morale. I would be the envy of my platoon.'

'I...'

'Look, let me give you my address. You can sleep on it; that way it will be a nice surprise if you do.'

'I'm sorry. I must go now. My bus will be here soon. We need to get home before dark.'

'Let me just scribble down my address.' He pulled out a piece of paper and called to one of his friends for a pencil. 'Here.' He passed it to her. 'Can I kiss you goodnight?'

'I think that's taking it a step too far,' protested Frances.

'Can't blame a man for trying,' he said. 'A kiss on the cheek then?' Frances rolled her eyes and offered him her cheek. As she turned her face towards him, he leaned in and cheekily stole a kiss from her lips.

'William!' She slapped his face and pushed at his chest. 'I'm married!'

'It was just a tiny kiss. I couldn't resist. I'm sorry,' he said rubbing his face. 'I have been dying to do that from the moment you walked into the hall tonight. The slap was worth it. You've captured my heart, Frances. I will never forget you. I will pray every night that you'll write to me.'

Frances walked over to Agnes and Alice and waved goodnight to William. The bus arrived; Harriette made it just in time.

'Who was that you were talking with, Frances?' asked Harriette, still waving to her new friend.

'No one,' replied Frances.

'He didn't look like no one – he was divine!' Harriette giggled. 'You were with him most of the night.'

Agnes glanced at Frances. Frances felt bad that she still

hadn't told Harriette and Alice about her marriage to Henry.

'Enough about me. Who was the boy whose face you were eating?' asked Frances. Everyone laughed.

'His name is Joseph, and I think I'm in love,' she gushed.

'And you, Alice? What was your friend's name?' asked Agnes.

'Hamish,' replied Alice, blushing.

'Looks like we all had a good night,' said Harriette, grinning. 'Let's make a deal to do it again.'

Chapter Forty

S pring was slowly blossoming into summer. Frances had not heard from Henry in a while, and she was beginning to fear the worst – reports of chaos and confusion swept in from the shores of France as retreating troops attempted to make their way home from Dunkirk. Thousands were stranded, many had died on the ravaged beaches and some had been taken prisoner.

It was an anxious time. Frances hoped and prayed as news came that tiny boats had crossed the English Channel to haul the soldiers from the shore and ferry them to the larger ships at sea.

It was after Frances had returned from a trip to the cinema, she sat in the garden, the sun warming her face, and wrote to Henry.

My darling Henry,

Why haven't you replied to my last letter? I must know that you are safe and that you are happy about the baby. I am growing fatter by the day. You won't recognise me the next time we meet. Your mum has knitted us lots of beautiful things already. I wish you were here. I miss you so much. I talk to our baby all the time. I have told her all about you. Talking to her is like being close to you. I say her, I'm not sure really. I think it will be a girl. I was thinking Hannah for a name. What do you think? I love you, Henry. Come back to me. I miss you with all my heart.

Yours forever

Frances

x

Frances prayed the letter would find him and that he would reply soon.

It was a time of waiting for all of Britain. The government tried to keep morale high by keeping everyone busy. But then came the German bombers, droning across the skies, and with them, the terrifying dogfights over England. These seemed to be never ending. The Luftwaffe bombed and obliterated many factories, airfields and harbours.

It was almost coming up to a year since Frances first kissed Henry. She couldn't believe she had managed to keep her marriage from her parents for so long. It was not like she planned it that way. Now it just seemed irrelevant. Soon, they would guess for themselves because her belly was growing bigger by the day – it was becoming impossible to hide it from anyone, least of all her parents. Not that she saw much of them these days. They were always preoccupied with other matters.

London was the first city to be blitzed. Frances' mother was beside herself with worry over friends and family. As a conscientious objector, Robert claimed he was morally opposed to the war, and, after appearing before a tribunal, he was given a non-combat job back in London. He was still there at the time of the bombings.

'I'm sure Robert will be fine, Mother,' said Frances. 'He has a knack of landing on his feet.'

'What do you know?' snapped her mother. She dropped her teacup onto its saucer, almost breaking it. Frances jumped.

'I don't, I was just saying—'

'Well don't; you know nothing about it.'

'I know what it's like to worry about someone you love.'

'You mean *that* boy, well, you should thank your blessings.'

'My blessings? How can you be so cruel?'

'I wasn't, I only—'

Frances stood up. 'Look at me!' she cried. 'Take a good look at me, Mother! Not Thomas! Not Robert, not Father. Me!'

Her mother stared at her. Frances smoothed down her dress over her belly. Her mother's face paled; then she turned away.

'I have to go.'

'Where are you going?' asked Frances. 'We need to talk.'

'What is there to say?'

'I don't know,' replied Frances. Tears pooled in her eyes. Her mother walked towards the door.

'I'm your daughter!' blurted Frances.

Her mother turned her head slightly. 'You are a foolish girl,' she said.

'Mother! Please!'

'This is just history repeating itself. For years I have watched you, a silly little girl with romantic notions. A cruel reminder of the youth I once had. It pains me to see you make the same mistakes as I did. Now you've ruined your life. For what? Love? You could have had it all, Frances, but now you've gone and thrown it all away on a penniless nobody.'

'Henry is not a nobody!'

'Be that as it may, he will never give you the life you deserve.' She turned and walked away. Frances started to cry.

When her father came home and saw her tear-stained face, he rushed to her side.

'What's happened, Frances?' he asked. 'Why are you crying?' He placed his hand on her shoulder.

'I'm so sorry, Father.'

'For what, my dear girl? You can tell me.' Frances covered her face with her hands and took a deep breath, composing herself.

'I've done a terrible thing. I lied to you.' She paused, steadying herself. 'Henry and I got married in secret.'

'Married?'

'Yes. I wanted to tell you; you have to believe me.'

'I don't know what to say.'

'That's not all... I'm carrying Henry's child.'

'You're pregnant? I need to sit down.'

Frances looked at him, her eyes full of tears. Her father didn't speak for a second or two.

'How could I have been so blind? Does he know?'

'I've written to him, but he hasn't replied.'

'Does your mother know?' Frances nodded.

Edward shook his head. 'After all we have done for you. Well, I must say, I thought I'd brought you up better than this, Frances. At least you had the decency to get married before you... When did you get married?' he said, beginning to pace the room. 'I always dreamed of walking you down the aisle. You've broken my heart, Frances. I don't know who you are anymore!'

'I'm still your daughter,' she wept.

'To say I'm disappointed is an understatement. Why, Frances? Why?'

'Because I love him.'

'Love, you don't know what it is to love someone.' He dropped his gaze to the floor and shook his head. 'I cannot look at you. You're not my little girl anymore.'

'Please Father, don't say that. I still love you, but I also love Henry and we wanted to be together... I'm sorry.'

He lifted his head to look at her. 'You are still so young. I thought you would go places, do wonderful things with your life. My heart breaks, Frances.'

'I'm sorry.'

'What good is sorry now? The damage is already done. You are ruined!'

Frances sucked in her breath; her bottom lip quivered.

'I knew something wasn't right, but I've been too busy to notice what has been going on under my nose... How are you going to get by?'

'I don't know. We didn't plan this.' She blew her nose on her handkerchief.

'Marriage is difficult at the best of times, but to marry when there is a war on, and to marry someone who doesn't have two pennies to rub together. How could you?' He ran his fingers through his hair and sighed heavily. He walked over to his doctor's bag and pulled out a leaflet. 'Here, I think you should read this,' he said and placed it in front of her. 'How could you embarrass me like this, Frances? How could you lie and keep everything a secret for so long?'

'I really am sorry.'

'I need time to think things through. Tell your mother I will be in my study if she needs me.' He strode away leaving Frances all alone.

She dropped her head into her hands and wept.

Chapter Forty-One

The Germans showed no sign of quitting. London had taken a terrible beating. Frances watched the newsreels showing the aftermath of carnage and devastation left behind by the attacks; not even Buckingham Palace was immune. She left the cinema with Agnes in shock.

'What if it happens here?' asked Agnes.

'Let's just pray it doesn't,' replied Frances. She put her hand on a nearby railing to steady herself; the world had started to spin a little faster, making her feel queasy.

'Are you feeling alright?' asked Agnes. 'You've gone awfully pale.'

'I'm... I...' Frances put her hand to her mouth to try to stop it, but it was too late. She quickly turned her head to the side and vomited on the pavement.

'My goodness, Frances!' Agnes stroked her back.

Frances straightened herself and used a handkerchief to wipe her mouth. 'I feel better now.'

'Nevertheless, you should be taking it easy in your condition. You had me worried there for a moment. Maybe you should let your father examine you when you get home.'

'He's still not speaking to me. I can't blame him. I must be a huge disappointment to everyone. I look at myself in the mirror some days and wonder what happened. I had such high hopes for my life, Agnes.'

'Well, I'm glad you've finally told everyone. I hate keeping secrets. Promise me you'll tell him you've been feeling unwell.'

'I'll speak with him when I get home,' she said.

'Promise?'

'Promise, now let's go. I'm on duty tonight.'

'That's another thing. You shouldn't be working anymore,' said Agnes. She put her arm on her friend's to steady her.

'I'm fine. I have ages before the baby is due,' said Frances.

'I've got something for you!' said Harriette. 'It arrived this morning.' She was waving an envelope around in the air.

'What is it?' asked Frances.

'A letter addressed to you. I haven't opened it, but I am curious as to its contents.'

'For me?'

Harriette handed it to Frances, who looked at the letter and then placed it in her back pocket.

'Aren't you going to open it?'

'Not right now,' she replied. 'Who is it from anyway?'

'Well,' Harriette hooked her arm through Frances' and they started to walk towards the base. 'You remember the Canadian I met? It turns out he is good friends with the guy you were dancing with that night. Apparently, he hasn't stopped going on about you, and when he found out I was exchanging letters with his friend, he asked if he could have my address so that he could write to you! Isn't that romantic?'

'Harriette, have you forgotten I'm with Henry, and I am now carrying his child?'

'No—'

'Good, because I wouldn't want you thinking I was going to reply to him.'

'Suit yourself, I won't mention it again but, just so you know, Joe said he would come and visit the next time he's in the North, and he might have mentioned bringing his friend.' Harriette screwed up her face apologetically.

'Urgh! Harriette!'

'Look, if they come, I'll say you're ill. Besides, when he sees the size of your belly, he'll probably run a mile.'

'I can't talk about this right now; we need to get going.' Frances picked up the pace and marched down the hill.

'Frances, wait for me!'

When they got to the station, Frances and Harriette checked the car tyres and radiator, as they did every night. The ambulances had been converted from large saloon cars with the backs cut off and a canvas covering the back, which could be rolled up. It was their job to make sure the back was clean, ready for the next casualties. Frances couldn't drive, so it was up to Harriette to drive them to the scene if there was an emergency.

'Right, I'm hungry,' said Harriette. 'Fancy a sandwich? My mother packed me some.'

'Yes please,' said Frances.

They were sitting eating their sandwiches when the sirens went off. Frances dreaded that sound. Planes roared overhead, but luckily there were no bombs. Instead, they were called out to attend to a man who had fractured his skull. He had been erecting scaffolding in the city and lost his footing. Harriette jumped into the driver's seat, and they drove into town. Frances tried to hide her revulsion at the blood that pooled around the man's head. A few men helped them to put the man onto a stretcher and they drove him to the hospital, but sadly he died before he reached the operating table. Frances wasn't sure if it was because she was tired or pregnant, but she burst into tears. She could never get used to the sight of blood. She hadn't slept for weeks after seeing her first dead body, yet Harriette appeared to take it all in her stride. Every time Frances was called to help an injured person, her thoughts turned to Henry. What if he was injured somewhere in Europe?

When she got home, she tore the letter in two and dropped it in the bin. It had been a horrendously long night; sirens had gone off intermittently. All she wanted to do was crawl into her bed and sleep. Her back ached, and she was having cramps in her belly. By her calculations, she wasn't due for another month but, still, she thought she should take it easy for the next few days. It would be Christmas in almost two weeks – her second without Henry. Frances placed her hand over her stomach and looked at the moon. Somewhere she hoped that Henry was looking at the moon too and thinking about her. Just then, the baby kicked. Frances started to cry both tears of joy and sadness.

Chapter Forty-Two

The next day, Frances was feeling a little melancholy, so she decided to call on Mary and George. She wanted to give everyone their Christmas presents. It wasn't much; she'd spent most of her money on a teddy bear for May, Margaret and Harold's daughter. She'd bought Edna something, and a little gift for Frank's baby too.

Harold was still working in the factory, making parts for big guns and tanks. He was worried, like most men who hadn't been called up yet, that he would receive that dreaded letter soon. Back in spring, they had finally received keys to a new cooperation house; it was perfect for their little family. Frances had helped them move in. She'd met Margaret's delightful parents for the first time. Margaret's mother had packed some sandwiches and Mary had brought flasks of tea. It turned out to be such a lovely day. Frances enjoyed being with her new family, especially baby May.

When she arrived at Mary's, Edna was sitting at the kitchen table. Mary made everyone a cup of tea, and they chatted about how Christmas wouldn't be special on rations.

'You're blossoming now, Frances,' said Edna.

'I feel like a pregnant heifer,' moaned Frances.

'Well, you don't look like one,' said Mary. 'How's things with thee mother?'

'We don't talk much. She's not ignoring me anymore, so that's a good thing,' pouted Frances.

'Well, this will cheer thee up. You know missus that lives round corner?' said Mary.

'Who?' asked Edna.

'You know, young lass, red hair, nose bent like a fisherman's hook,' said Mary.

'You mean Ethel? Aye, go on!' Edna leaned forward and rested her head on her hands.

'She's only coming home with double rations from the butcher. Ada, who lives over the back, told me she's knocking him off, while her husband's overseas.'

'Dirty mare,' tutted Edna. 'Gives a whole new meaning to the word "a good stuffing".' Frances and Mary sniggered. 'Let's hope his sausage is worth it!'

'Oh, Edna, you've got a filthy mind!' chuckled Mary.

Frances stayed a couple of hours. They listened to the wireless while Mary taught Frances how to knit. Edna joked there were more holes in Frances' knitting than a colander. Nobody mentioned Henry, even though he was on everyone's mind. Instead, they preferred to remain positive and focus on his and Frances' baby.

Frances' father was on his way out to see patients. When he saw Frances, he stopped.

'Have you eaten today?' he asked, concern etched across his face. 'You're awfully pale.'

'I did.' Her parents were no longer giving her the silent treatment; they still had a long way to go, but at least they were speaking to her again. Frances was sure that in time they'd forgive her.

'Mind that you get some rest. You are going to need all your strength. Remember, you're eating for two now.' Frances nodded.

'I will, Father.'

'Have you heard from Henry?'

'No.' Frances was extremely worried. She distracted herself by focusing on the baby and preparing for its arrival. But it was no use, she still felt restless, and the slightest thing would upset or anger her. Countless times she'd had to restrain herself from speaking her mind around people.

'I'm sure there is a perfectly good explanation for it. You mustn't worry. Stress is not good for you or the baby. Take it easy. I'll see you later.'

Chapter Forty-Three

I t was the first evening in a long time that Frances and her mother had been alone together. The atmosphere was still slightly tense. Frances was trying to put Mary's teaching to good use and was knitting Henry a Christmas present, but it was a disaster.

Frances was swathed in a wool blanket, trying to keep warm as the temperature had dropped. It had been a mild December, but the evenings were chilly. Her mother was writing a reply to Thomas. In his last letter, Thomas had talked about his adventures in Africa; he was excited that he was putting his medical training to good use and had described the most thrilling part of his time overseas as sailing down the Nile into Sudan and seeing the wonders of Egypt.

The drama show *It's That Man Again* played in the background on the wireless, and they both listened silently, lost in their thoughts.

As Frances dropped yet another stitch, she sighed and thought of Henry. She closed her eyes and pictured his face, his smile, trying to remember the sound of his voice. It was getting harder as the months went by.

It was a cold, clear, moonlit night. Frances should have been at a big dance that was taking place in the city, but her father advised her against it. The cramps in her stomach were getting stronger and happening more frequently, so her father instructed her to rest. He said he'd check on her when he came home.

'Would you like a cup of hot cocoa, Frances?'

'That would be lovely, Mother. Thank you.'

Just has her mother had left the room, the shrieking wail of the air-raid siren invaded the living space. Frances' body trembled; a cold tingling sensation ran up her arms and down her spine. Her mother came running back.

'Quick, Frances!' shouted her mother. 'Get to the shelter!' Frances wrapped the blanket tightly around her body and bent forward to collect her knitting. The house shook, and plaster dust fell onto the floor. 'Hurry, Frances!'

She quickly followed her mother outside. Looking towards the centre of town, she could see black shapes set against the night sky. Thudding and blood-chilling whistling sounds could be heard. Frances became suddenly still, mesmerised by a huge red-and-orange glow over the city. Fires burned. The air smelled of gas. Bombers circled above. There were explosions after explosions. Frances shook her head in disbelief.

'Frances!' Frances turned to follow her mother but, at that moment, she felt something wet and warm between her legs and she froze once more. Her mother ran and grabbed her hand.

'My waters! I think my waters have broken.'

Once inside the shelter, Frances' mother helped her on to one of the beds. It was a well-stocked shelter. Her father had paid an electrician to install power. There were bunk beds and plenty of warm blankets.

'You can't have the baby now, Frances! Your father isn't here, and it's too dangerous to call for a midwife,' flapped her mother.

The ground shook, sending Frances' mother tumbling forward. She grabbed hold of the edge of the bed to steady herself.

'Are you alright?'

'Yes, I'm fine.'

Frances groaned. 'I think it's happening, Mother, whether we like it or not.'

'But it can't; I don't know what to do,' she said, her voice shaky. She sat next to Frances on the bed and held her hand.

'You've given birth before; you know more than I do,' panted Frances.

'I wish your father were here,' she cried.

'As do I, but he's not, so you're going to have to help me,' groaned Frances.

'Right, I can do this... we can do this,' said her mother nervously. Frances squeezed her mother's hand as she screamed. Her forehead glistened with perspiration. 'Right, let's get you out of this dress.'

Dressed only in her slip, Frances paced the small space.

'It's getting worse,' she cried.

'Maybe you should sit again.'

'I can't. It hurts too much.' Her breathing was laboured. Stabbing pains shot across her lower back like waves of tightening pressure. She felt like she was dying. Whistles from bombs drowned out her screams. Her mother smoothed her hair out of her face and used an old rag to wipe her forehead. The pain was relentless.

Eventually she decided it was time to lie on her back and lift her knees.

'I'm going to have to run to the house for clean towels and fresh water,' said her mother. Frances squeezed her hand.

'No, don't leave me!' she cried. She screamed again. 'It's coming!'

Frances' mother lifted her slip to look.

'I don't think so. Not yet. Just breathe slowly. You can do this, Frances!'

'I can't,' she shrieked. 'It hurts!'

'I know, but it won't be long now,' encouraged her mother. 'I will be as quick as I can.' She kissed Frances on the cheek and ran to the house.

Frances let out a piercing cry. She gripped the blanket in her fists as hard as she could and arched her back.

'Mother!' she cried. 'God, help me!' Her body was on fire; sweat dripped between her breasts; it was as though someone was slicing her open. She started to pant heavily, then collapsed back onto the bed.

'I'm here, Frances.' Her mother came rushing in, her arms full of towels, and she was holding a jug of water.

'I can't do this!' cried Frances. 'I'm scared.'

'Don't be. You can do this. You're strong, Frances. You can do anything. Just keep taking deep breaths.' Her mother held her hand and started to sing. Frances recognised the song instantly. It was one she used to sing to Frances when she was a little girl – 'Baby Face.' Frances started to cry.

'I'm so sorry, Mother,' she said.

'For what?'

'For lying to you.'

'Don't be. You followed your heart. I'm sorry I didn't listen to you. I'm the one who should be sorry. I feel ashamed.'

Frances screamed. Her mother wiped her brow with a damp cloth.

'I don't want to bring this baby up on my own,' said Frances. Her breathing grew heavy.

'You will never be on your own. You have your father and me. You have nothing to fear.'

Frances screamed again. Her mother examined her again. 'I can see the baby's head,' she shouted with joy. 'I think you need to start pushing. On the next contraction, push!'

'But I don't have the strength,' moaned Frances.

'Yes you do, now come on! You can do this!'

'I don't! Henry, I need Henry!' she cried.

'You can do this, Frances, now push as hard as you can!' ordered her mother. Frances screamed and pushed as though her life depended on it. Her face contorted with pain, sweat and tears.

'That's it, Frances, it's coming!' said her mother. 'One more push!'

Frances felt as though she was about to rip in two and then she felt the head as it emerged from her body.

'It's here; it's here!' cried her mother.

Next, she felt something warm and wet slither from her.

'It's a boy, Frances. It's a boy! You did it!' Her mother burst into tears. She cut the umbilical cord and wrapped the baby in a towel, then passed him to Frances. 'Isn't he beautiful.'

Frances blinked and then stared at her baby – how small he was! A smile spread across her face as she looked down at him. 'He's perfect,' she cried.

Her mother wrapped her arms around her and kissed her forehead.

'I wish Henry were here to see his son,' she sobbed. 'I miss him so much.'

'I know, Frances, but you have to stay strong; you're a mother now.' She kissed Frances' forehead again. 'You did it, my brave girl.'

The pain stopped briefly, then Frances screamed again as she parted with the placenta. Her mother wrapped it up in old newspapers to dispose of later.

'You need to rest now. I'll clean him up while you get some sleep. You're going to need all your energy.'

'But...'

'Don't worry. I'm here. You sleep.'

Her mother helped her to lie down and placed a blanket over her. Frances thought she would never sleep from the adrenaline high she'd just been on, but she did.

She woke to the sound of her baby crying.

'I'm sorry, Frances, but I think he's hungry.'

'Give him to me,' she said and held out her arms. Frances

put him to her breast and was relieved that he latched on quickly. Her heart filled with love for this tiny human in her arms.

'What are you going to call him?' asked her mother. 'He will need to be registered so you'll have to give him a name soon.'

'I don't know. I was hoping to discuss names with Henry.' At the mention of his name, a tear trickled down her cheek. 'Will I ever see him again?'

'I don't know. I hope so.'

'Why hasn't he written? I can't help but think the worst.' Frances sighed. 'What if he's lying dead in a ditch somewhere?'

'You can't think like that. You must try to stay positive. Believe it or not, I know what you're going through. Remember, I've already lived through one war. But you have a baby now who needs you. Wherever Henry is, you have to believe he's fine. Otherwise, you'll drive yourself mad thinking the worst.'

'Has the bombing stopped?' asked Frances. 'Why isn't Father home?'

'No, it's still going. I don't think there will be much left when it's over. I'm worried about your father too.'

'I'm sure he's safe in a shelter somewhere.' Frances looked at her mother, noticing her dishevelled hair and crumpled clothes. 'Thank you. I couldn't have done it without you.'

'Thank you, Frances. You have given me a beautiful grandson.' She paused and fiddled with the hem of her blouse. 'I really am sorry for the way I've been acting. I know you think I favoured Robert over you, but it wasn't like that. I felt sorry for him. He's damaged and I thought I could help him. I suppose, if I'm being truthful, I resented you, your youth, your innocence. You reminded me of all the things I've lost and can never get back.' She gazed at Frances. 'It's not that I didn't like Henry; I did. I suppose I just wanted a better life for you away from here. Can you forgive me?' Tears began to pool in her eyes.

'Of course,' said Frances. Her mother placed her arms around her shoulders, careful not to disturb the baby. They both wept. It had been a long and arduous night, and it wasn't over yet.

Chapter Forty-Four

Frances' father had to walk home as the roads were impassable. He had witnessed a scene of catastrophic proportions, like something from Dante's Inferno. The damage endured by the city had rendered it unrecognisable. Bombs had flattened streets of terraced houses. Hospitals, schools, shops, churches and cinemas had all suffered irrevocable damage. Steel skeletons jutted from the earth. Mountains of bricks left over from the crushed buildings cluttered the streets. Dust filled the air. Gas mains flamed.

Firemen, air-raid wardens and police all tried to keep everyone back from the most dangerous sections, where buildings looked likely to collapse, or an unexploded bomb might go off. Water was being taken from the river because the water mains had burst. Bodies were slowly pulled from the wreckage as parts of the city continued to glow red. The rail lines were blocked, and trams and buses were burned out.

When the sirens had sounded, some people waited it out in the cinema, unaware of the damage outside. They sang songs to lift spirits. Others had spent the night in the dance halls, emerging in the morning still in their dance dresses and shoes as they walked among the debris through this once familiar city – now an obliterated mess.

Frances' father wiped away his tears and opened the front door to the house.

'Oh, Edward! You're home!' Frances' mother rushed towards him and wrapped her arms about his dust-covered waist. He looked a shadow of himself. 'I've been so worried about you. What a horrendous night!' she sobbed, wiping away her tears of relief.

He dropped his bag in the hall and put his arms around her. He closed his eyes, and she rested her head on his shoulder. 'There, there, it's over now.' He stroked her hair. 'How are you and Frances? Any damage to the house?'

She pulled away from him. Tears stained her face. 'She's had the baby, Edward; you're a grandfather!'

His eyes widened and he ran his hand over his chin. 'Are they both doing well?'

She held his hand and pulled him through to the lounge. 'Come! Come and see for yourself! He's so beautiful!'

Frances was sitting up in an armchair feeding the baby. She hadn't bathed or changed her clothes. She could barely keep her eyes open.

'Frances! Your father is home!' said her mother. Frances placed a blanket over herself.

'How are you, my dear?' Her father kneeled before her; his eyes sparkled with tears.

'I'm tired.' She yawned. 'He hasn't stopped feeding.'

'That is to be expected. I'm so sorry I wasn't here.'

'That's alright, Father. Mother was magnificent.' Frances gazed at her mother.

'I'm so glad you had each other,' he replied, relieved that they seemed to have finally put their differences behind them. 'When he has finished feeding, your mother and I can watch him while you go and get cleaned up. You need to eat and get some rest. I'll send for a midwife, but I'm not sure one will be able to get through anytime soon.'

'Is it that bad?' asked Frances.

'It is awful, absolute carnage. After fighting in the Somme, I never thought I would see such devastation again.' Frances reached forward and held his hand.

'I'm sorry you had to witness it, Father,' said Frances.

'It's those poor families I feel sorry for. The ones that have lost everything.' He patted her hand. 'So, unfortunately, I can't stay long. I need to get back out there to help with the wounded.' He turned to his wife. 'So many people have lost their homes, and with winter, they are going to need our help more than anything.'

'Of course, I'll do my bit, but my daughter needs me right now. When she's settled, I'll go and help but, first, who's for a cup of tea?'

After Frances had washed and changed, she wrote Henry another letter:

My dearest Henry,

Where are you? My heart is broken in two. I miss you so much; please come back to me. We have a son. I can hardly believe it myself.

He came into the world during a night of bombing. We are alright but Father says the city is destroyed. I was so scared. The war has suddenly become more real. I guess after all this it really won't matter who you are or where you come from. Mother and I have patched up our differences. I think she would welcome you into the family now, Henry, if only you would come home!

She was wonderful. I couldn't have delivered our son without her. He's beautiful, Henry, so tiny and perfect. I love him so much. I wish you were here with us now. I need you. I don't think I can do this on my own. There's so much I want to tell you. I walk past the Botanical Gardens and picture us there together, holding hands. Me laughing at your terrible jokes. I love you. I pray every night for your safe return. You need to return to me Henry. You have so much to live for.

Now and forever yours, Frances

x

The city had only just recovered the bodies of seventy people from Marples Hotel when the bombs dropped again two nights later. This time, the steelworks took most of the damage. When it was deemed safe again, Frances wrapped the baby up warm and braved the cold. She travelled to see Mary and George, to show them their grandson and to check on them after the bombings. The day after that, she went with her mother to help in one of the soup kitchens. She and her mother had collected as many blankets as they could carry on the pram, together with many other things they thought desperate families might need.

The days that followed were awful. People walked around

in shock, thousands of homes having been completely oblit-erated. Water had to be brought round in a tanker. But despite all the damage, people still wanted to celebrate Christmas. Hitler had taken so much already; he wasn't going to cheat the children out of Christmas too.

It was a sombre occasion for Frances and her family, what with Henry and Thomas away, but they forced themselves to be merry. Frances and her mother collected the decorations from the loft and tried to make the home look festive. Her father had brought home a small tree; it looked pretty with the fairy lights on. While they listened to carols on the wire-less, they made Christmas pudding – not in the traditional sense, but they did their best given the ingredients they had. Frances' mother had saved their rations; however, as a Christmas bonus, the Minister of Food had doubled the tea and sugar rations. When Frances was younger, Edna had shown her how to make jam tarts so, as a special treat, she made some herself.

On Christmas Eve, they went as a family to watch a pantomime at the Lyceum. It made a nice change to sit in the warmth of the gold and crimson interior and listen to the excited chatter of children and the orchestra tuning up.

Although still missing Henry and Thomas, Frances was kept busy with the baby. She gazed out of her window at the stars that littered and brightened the clear night sky. There had been no sirens in a while, making it a peaceful Christmas.

Not long after Christmas, while Frances and her mother were cleaning the house, there was a knock on the door. As soon as she saw Mary and George standing outside in the cold, shivering, she knew it was bad news. After months of anguish, they had finally received a telegram: Henry was 'missing, presumed killed'. Mary could barely bring herself to say the words. She was pale like she hadn't slept. George had to put his arm around her to steady her.

'It's not true!' cried Frances. 'It's a lie! He's not dead!' She looked at the sad faces of Mary and George. 'What? Why are you looking at me like that? He's alright, you'll see. It says so right there.' She pointed to the telegram. 'Presumed, see?' She tried to force a smile, but the façade cracked. 'He promised he would come back to me!' Her throat tightened and she gasped for air. Slowly she sank to her knees, the telegram screwed up in her hands. 'He promised,' she cried. Her mother rushed to her side. Mary held George's hand and they watched as Frances crumbled before their eyes. She couldn't breathe; her body grew numb. A wave of nausea hit her and she rushed to the bathroom and was violently sick. Catching her reflection in the mirror, she smashed it with her fists and broke the glass. 'You made a vow to me, Henry Shepherd!' she screamed, not caring who heard her. 'You said that blasted compass would always lead you home! Well, if you can hear me, you'd better come home now! We have a son! I need you!' Her hand bled as she sank to the floor and wept uncontrollably.

As she sobbed, strong arms lifted her up. Her father carried her from the bathroom and tucked her up in bed. He bandaged her hand and gave her something to calm her.

❦

'She should sleep now,' he told the others, after leaving her to rest. They were seated together in the drawing room around the hearth.

Mary took the baby from Frances' mother and held him close to her heart. She wiped the tears from her eyes. 'It's heart breaking. My poor Henry – I can't believe he's gone. If only I could swap places with him. He's never going to know he's a dad. I never thought I would witness another war. Didn't we suffer enough the first-time round?'

'We lost so much back then. My brother, God rest his soul, never came home,' said Clarissa. She used her handkerchief to dab away the tears. 'I never wanted Frances to suffer the same pain. I cannot begin to imagine how you must be feeling. I don't sleep at night worrying about Thomas.'

'I've had better days,' replied Mary. 'He looks so much like our Henry, George,' cried Mary. She kissed the baby's head.

'Aye, that he does.' George kissed his head too. Frances' father pulled out the cork of a half-empty bottle of port and poured everyone a glass.

'I'm afraid there's more bad news,' said George. Nobody spoke. It was deathly silent apart from the baby cooing in Mary's arms. 'Edna's identity card has been found in the rubble on Bessermer road, down t'cliffe. We believed she was heading home from visiting Frank, on the night of the second attack, but she didn't make it in time.'

'No! Not Edna!' cried Frances' mother. 'Oh, Edward, poor Edna.'

Edward went to comfort her as she quietly wept.

'I don't think we should tell Frances just yet,' said Edward. 'I think she's had enough of a shock for one day already.'

Mary and George stayed most of the afternoon. Mary helped Frances' mother rustle up something to eat. While they ate, George told stories about Henry's childhood, and they all reminisced about Edna.

'She was a wonderful woman,' sighed Mary.

'Aye, that she were,' said George. 'So, what she gunna call this young un?' asked George. It was his turn to nurse the baby.

'She doesn't know yet,' replied her mother. She was on her second glass of port and was feeling a little tipsy. 'She was waiting for Henry but... but now.' She burst into tears. Mary put a hand on her shoulder.

'I have always liked the name Harry,' said Frances' father. 'If Frances had turned out to be a boy, I would have called her Harry.'

'Isn't it also a nickname for Henry?' asked Clarissa between sobs.

'Yes, Harry's a nice name,' agreed Mary, finishing the last of her port.

'I think we should be getting off now,' she said. 'George, hand the baby back. Give Frances our love when she wakes and tell her to call on us anytime. We love having the two of them over.'

'Well, you must come to see us again too,' replied Edward.

'We wouldn't want to impose,' said Mary.

'Nonsense, it will be nice for Frances and the baby to have you here. Besides, we're family now,' said Edward.

Mary looked at George. 'Aye that we are,' she said. 'We'll be seeing you then.'

$$\text{\textit{\&}}$$

Frances' mother gently knocked on the door. 'Are you awake,' she whispered. 'The baby needs feeding. When you've finished, I'll take him downstairs again; you need your rest.'

As Frances held her son to her breast, a sense of hopelessness swept over her.

'What will I do without him Mother? He was... is my world. Everywhere I look, I'm reminded of our time together. I see his face and hear his voice. He can't be gone; he can't leave me! How can I go on without him?' She let the tears fall freely down her cheeks.

'I don't know, darling,' replied her mother. 'I wish I could take all your pain away. I hate to see you suffer like this. But you must stay strong; you need to, if not for yourself, for your child. He needs you, now more than ever. You can't give up. You have to keep living; we all do. Life goes on.'

Chapter Forty-Five

Many a time, Henry wrote to Frances, but each letter ended up scrunched up and thrown away. All his letters began the same: *I miss you. I think about you every second of every day. I pray you are well. Please don't worry.* But he couldn't bring himself to send them; he just couldn't do it. He couldn't lie and say everything was good when it wasn't. After he was captured, he lost all hope of ever seeing her again. He was lost and alone. A heavy cloud gripped his heart and he couldn't seem to shake the darkness that hovered over him.

When the ground was hard with ice and snow, and his fingers were blue with frostbite, Henry thought he was going to die. Starving and frozen to the bone, he had even grown a beard to keep warm. A loaf of bread had to be shared between ten men because parcels from the Red Cross hadn't arrived. It was just when he had almost given up hope that, one frosty morning, a Polish soldier, transferred from another camp, entered the hut, looking emaciated. Henry offered him his blanket and some of his bread.

'I think you need this more than me,' said Henry.

'Thank you,' replied the soldier gratefully.

'I'm Henry. Welcome to hell.' The soldier laughed.

'This will be paradise compared to the hell I've left behind.'

'Why's that?' asked Henry.

'I don't wish to talk about it. Another time, maybe.'

After many weeks as a prisoner, Henry had managed to pick up the odd word or phrase in German from listening to the guards, but he couldn't speak a word of Polish. However, that didn't matter because the Polish soldier spoke perfect English, even though he had a hard time understanding Henry's accent. They hit it off from the outset and kept up each other's morale by playing cards together way into the night.

'So, how long you been here? How did you end up in this shithole?' asked Oskar, one evening.

'I've lost count of the weeks. My last day as a free man was at Dunkirk. I never made it to the beach because all bridges across the river had been blown up by the Germans. It was a scary time; I hid in the cellar of a building until morning with some other men from my battalion. After the last of the rescue boats had left the harbour, the Germans rounded up the British troops who hadn't managed to flee to Dover. I was one of them. The Germans took thousands of French soldiers captive too. We were exhausted and shell shocked, and the bastards took advantage. I survived on two sugar lumps and some potato mixture a day. Me and the other men had to march through France, Belgium and

Holland, and then we were placed in trucks and taken to Germany. From there, we walked, barely standing, to the train station, and were loaded into cattle carts and taken to a prisoner of war camp in Poland. But although we were hungry and tired, I regarded myself as one of the lucky ones. As the British evacuated Dunkirk, the SS executed some British regiments who'd surrendered in northern France.'

Oskar spat on the ground. 'Those bastards.'

'That's exactly what they are. We were moved from place to place and forced to work in fields or help build houses, all the time with Nazi guards watching our every move. Sometimes they denied us food and medical treatment and forced us to drink ditch water. Before this, I was in good physical shape – now look at me.'

After months of misery, starvation and exhaustion, Henry had lost weight and hope. His spirit broke after watching men die and then having to bury them in ditches along the roadside; his friend Ernest had been one of them. He fought hard to stay alive; only the thought of Frances kept him going. The Germans took everything, but he managed to hide his compass. The photograph of Frances had fallen out. The Germans found it and they sneered at him and forced him to stand in front of them while the officers made rude and sexual remarks about his wife, before they tore up her picture.

'And what about you? What's your story?'

'Me? I'm lucky to be alive. We were in total disbelief for weeks. Never did we think we would lose our homes. When we tried to defend our land, my father was placed against a wall outside our house and shot. My mother pleaded for his life. I hid, like a baby, in the cellar. I should have done more.'

He rubbed his eyes and blinked back tears. 'So many people I grew up with died trying to defend their homes from the invasion. Some bravely fought the German tanks on horseback. Can you believe it?'

'I'm so sorry for your loss. It must have been dreadful,' said Henry.

'It will haunt me for the rest of my life.'

'That's why we need to win this bloody war! They can't get away with what they've done,' said Henry as they chatted in the dark of their hut. The candle had burned down to just a flicker; the moon peeped in through a small window – their cold breath hung in the air, forming a halo of mist around their heads. 'I need to get out of here and get home to Frances, my wife. She's my life. You understand?'

'I understand, my friend, but how do you propose we do it? Barbed wire surrounds the camp,' replied Oskar.

'I don't know,' sighed Henry.

'You know what happened to the others they found trying to escape; they shot them point-blank.'

'I know, but death has to be better than this. I need to try. I just can't sit back and do nothing,' said Henry.

After a night of heavy snowfall, Henry decided he was going to attempt an escape. Although he knew his actions were reckless, he felt compelled to try, even if it meant failure. Uncertain whether the dangers outside the walls were greater than captivity, he knew that not attempting to escape would leave him with unbearable regret. Oskar agreed to go with him willingly, despite Henry's warnings. It was late and all the other prisoners were in bed. He waited until the guards were changing duty, and he and Oskar ran. They didn't have a plan.

'Hurry!' said Henry, his cold breath leading the way. 'We don't have long before they'll notice us missing!'

Oskar ran behind him, but it was difficult running through deep snow. They reached the barbed wire and fought their way through, risking lacerations. Henry's arm was bleeding, having sliced it on its razor-sharp edges. Suddenly, floodlights lit up the night sky and sirens tore through the winter silence.

'They're on to us!' shouted Oskar. They only made it as far as the woods before the Germans quickly recaptured them, their footprints having given them away all too easily. They only escaped execution because the usual officer in charge wasn't there. Instead, as punishment, the German soldiers took away their boots and blankets. They vowed to try again when the weather was milder and during the next movement of the camp.

Chapter Forty-Six

It was early spring when Henry discovered that he and Oskar would be marching again. The officers called out their numbers, and they were told they would go to a new camp to work. Henry thought that it would be a perfect opportunity to attempt a second escape, while they still had the strength.

'Do you have any idea where we are?' asked Henry as they marched.

'Some. I have visited these areas before the war. I think we're not far from the mountains. I'm trying to make a mental map of which direction we need to travel.'

'Good, because I'm relying on your knowledge to get us out alive.'

They marched for two days before they stopped in a village not far from the border with Czechoslovakia. The town was in ruins. Most of the buildings were already destroyed by the Germans when they had invaded before the war.

Henry and Oskar deliberately stayed at the back of the line. Henry's heart quickened as he took out his compass from his pocket and gave it a kiss. 'Come on,' he whispered to it. 'Help me find my way home.' He looked to the heavens and took a deep breath to steady his nerves.

When the German officers weren't looking, they seized their chance and made a run for it. As he ran, Henry's legs almost gave out. He followed Oskar through long grass until they found an abandoned barn. Panting heavily and gasping for air, sweat dripped down his face, his whole body trembled with adrenaline. They froze when they heard dogs barking and German voices approaching. Quickly, they climbed inside an empty container, which looked like it had been used to store grain, there they tried to remain still and silent even as rats crawled over their bodies and their insides trembled with fear. They hid in the container until nightfall. When it was deemed safe, they left the barn and began their long trek through more fields.

'We're not too far from the mountains,' said Oskar. 'If we make it out alive, you owe me.'

'What's tha mean 'if' we make it?' said Henry.

'When we make it out,' said Oskar. 'And when the war is over, we will have a drink together and I will finally get a chance to beat you at cards.'

'Are you still going on about losing?'

'Yes,' replied Oskar. Henry laughed.

'You're on, but I wouldn't go getting your hopes up; nothing can part a Yorkshireman from his money.'

'We will see my friend.' Oskar grinned.

They survived by eating whatever they could salvage. Tired and hungry, they made it through the hills barely alive. Along the way, there were several close calls with German troops travelling through; they had to take cover in the woods until it was safe to continue. If it hadn't been for Oskar's knowledge of the area, Henry would surely have perished.

Before they left the mountains, they stumbled across an empty church. The roof had collapsed. Burnt pieces of wood that once protected it from the elements lay crisscrossed along the aisle. The smashed alter stood empty, its gold crucifixes looted. Bullet holes adorned the walls where images of Christ and the Virgin Mary had once been. They walked on a carpet of dry blood and leaves.

Henry and Oskar searched for any food left over from its previous occupants, but it was empty. Heading outside and around the back, Henry discovered a stone well. He called to Oskar and started to pull up the bucket from the shaft. As he did, he heard a rustling coming from nearby trees. He quickly crouched down behind the well, but it was too late.

'Podnieście ręce do gory!' shouted a middle-aged man brandishing a rifle. He looked like a farmer. 'Podnieście ręce do góry!' he shouted again. He fired a shot at the well.

'I am unarmed!' shouted Henry. 'Don't shoot!'

'Wyjść!' shouted the man.

'Nie strzelaj!' shouted Oskar. 'Don't shoot!'

The man turned his gun and pointed it at Oskar.

Nie strzelaj!' repeated Oskar. He lifted his hands high above his head. 'Przychodzimy w pokoju. Chcemy po prostu pić wodę, a potem będziemy w drodze.'

'What are you saying?' shouted Henry from behind the well.

'I'm just telling him that we come in peace and that we will go when we have had a drink of water.'

'Is he buying it?' asked Henry.

'I don't know,' shouted Oskar.

Two other men with guns appeared, each wearing a uniform. Oskar recognised them as Polish resistance.

'Who are you?' shouted one of the men. 'Why are you here?'

'We have escaped from a prisoner of war camp. My friend here is trying to get back to England. Can you help us?'

'Come out!' the other man shouted to Henry. Henry hesitated.

'It's safe, Henry,' said Oskar. 'You can come out now.'

Henry slowly crept out from behind the well, his hands in the air.

'Ey up,' said Henry.

'Follow us!' ordered one of the men.

They walked Henry and Oskar through the woods to a small clearing. There they saw about twenty or thirty more people dressed in the same uniform. They had guns and a few vehicles. Some of them were sitting around an open fire. Henry smelt something delicious roasting. His stomach growled, and saliva pooled in his mouth.

'Sit,' ordered one of the men. Henry and Oskar found space around the fire. Henry couldn't take his eyes off what looked like rabbit.

'Are you hungry?' asked a woman in broken English. Henry nodded. She cut off a small piece of the animal's flesh and handed it to them. 'How far have you travelled?' she asked.

'I don't know,' said Henry almost choking on the meat. He hadn't chewed food in a while.

'We've been walking for days,' replied Oskar.

'Where are you hoping to get to?' she asked, offering them some water.

'Home,' said Henry.

'Come with me!' ordered one of the men from earlier. Henry and Oskar jumped up and followed him to a small cabin.

Henry was startled by what he saw inside. A family comprising of an older woman, possibly the grandmother, a young man, and two small girls, were huddled in a corner clutching their possessions. They looked half-starved and frightened. Henry noted the Star of David sewn on their clothes.

The man pointed to two empty chairs and signalled to them to sit; then he walked out of the cabin. Henry nodded to the family and smiled. Nervously, they acknowledged him.

A rotund middle-aged man appeared. He scraped a wooden chair across the stone floor and sat down next to them.

'Cześć, my name is Piotr. My comrades tell me you are escaped prisoners. You did well to make it this far.' He spoke slowly and deliberately.

'That is correct,' said Oskar.

'It is not safe for you here,' he said.

'That's why we need your help,' said Oskar.

'What is it you think we can do for you, my friend?'

'I know all the good work that you do,' replied Oskar, glancing at the family. 'I know you can help us obtain papers so we can cross the border.'

Piotr rubbed his chin, his eyes sharp and focused; he seemed to be thinking. Then he looked at Henry.

'Why should we help you?' he asked.

'Because I need to get home to my wife,' replied Henry.

'We all have wives we want to get home to; we all have families. That man there' – he pointed to the young man in the corner – 'has been separated from his wife since all this began. She's probably dead. What makes you so special?'

'If you need me to beg, I will,' said Henry. He slid off his chair and fell to his knees.

'Get up!' Piotr bellowed. 'You don't need to beg. Get up!' Henry sat back in his chair. 'I need to think about it some more. It is dangerous.' He left the two of them sitting there and walked outside. As they waited for him to return, Henry's palms grew sweaty. He unbuttoned his shirt a little because he was struggling to breathe. As the minutes passed Henry felt his chance to return home slip further away from him.

'What's keeping him, Oskar?' said Henry.

'Don't worry,' replied Oskar patting Henry's knee. 'All will be well.'

It seemed an eternity before Piotr finally returned.

'As it so happens, you're in luck. We got this family out of the ghetto yesterday, and we have organised safe passage for them, as well as a few more families that are due to join us tonight, God willing. In a few days, we will attempt to leave here. We should have your papers ready by then.'

'Thank you,' said Henry, and shook his hand.

'Don't thank me yet. Things can go wrong. We have people all over who are tracking the movement of the German army, but we have a long way to travel. The plan is to drive to Yugoslavia, then take a ship to France, but things can change. It is a long trip. We can only travel at night, so it will take many days. If you reach France, you will be taken to one of the underground movement's stations there; after that, well, I am not sure. If you get caught, we will all die.'

'I understand,' said Henry.

Piotr nodded. 'Good. Now eat some food. You need to build up your strength. You are in for a tough ride.' He stood up and left the room.

Henry released a heavy sigh of relief. 'I can't believe it is happening, Oskar,' he said. 'We're going to England!'

'You, not me,' said Oskar.

'What? What do you mean?'

'I'm going to stay here and help the resistance. Look at those people.' He jutted his chin to the family. 'I can't leave my country knowing what is happening.'

'I understand,' said Henry. 'I will miss you though, pal.'

'And I you, my friend. I will travel with you to Yugoslavia, and then I will say goodbye.'

'But...'

'It is for the best.' Henry reached forward and hugged him.

'When this is all over, you must come to Sheffield. I can find you work. It can be a new start for you,' said Henry.

'I would like that,' said Oskar. 'I can finally meet your Frances and see what all the fuss is about,' he joked.

'I will give you my parents' address. My mum makes a blinding Yorkshire pudding,' grinned Henry.

'What is Yorkshire pudding?' asked Oskar.

'You haven't lived my friend till you have tasted one.'

'In that case, I will see you when the war is over.'

Henry held out his hand and Oskar shook it. 'Deal!' said Henry.

Chapter Forty-Seven

Harry was christened during April. It had snowed the first few months of the year, so it had been too cold to hold a celebration then. Arthur was home on leave, so that was a delightful surprise for everyone, especially Agnes. Although pleased for her friend, Frances couldn't help feeling resentful at seeing them happy together. Mary and George had waited until Arthur was next home before telling him about Henry. As expected, Arthur didn't take the news well. He exploded into a violent rage when Mary sat him down and told him. They both wept, after which, Arthur stayed in his room for most of his first day home.

The biggest surprise of all was when Frances' father turned up with Thomas the day before the christening. He hadn't told anyone that he was collecting him from the station. Frances and her mother were in the kitchen trying out a disgusting new recipe for rose-flavoured potatoes, when in he walked.

'Are you feeling well, Father?' asked Frances. 'Has the war ended? You're smiling like you've just struck gold,' she joked.

He rushed over to her and took her hand. 'Right, you stand here, and Clarissa, I want you to stand next to her,' he said excitedly.

'What's going on, Edward?'

'You'll see,' he said, laughing. 'You'll see. You can come in now!'

Thomas appeared in the doorway. Frances and her mother screamed and ran over to him. Edward raised his arms and clapped like a sea lion. Tears filled Thomas's eyes as he walked over to his family and hugged them all.

'Oh, Thomas!' gasped his mother. 'Oh, my darling boy! Let me look at you!'

It was the happiest day for the family since Harry had been born.

Thomas's arm and leg had been damaged after being hit by shrapnel, but he was fine. His ship had come under heavy fire in the Mediterranean. Although he was injured, he was alive, and it was a most joyous occasion to have him home, even if it was only until he had recuperated.

'Where is he then?' asked Thomas smiling.

'He's asleep upstairs. Come on.' Frances held out her hand. 'Let's meet your nephew.'

On the day of the christening, Frances momentarily allowed herself to forget about the war and to enjoy Harry's special day, despite wishing Henry could be there to see their families together. Robert had travelled from London for the occasion. Frances was pleased to see him. He had lost weight, but he was doing well, all things considered.

After the christening, everyone went back to Frances' house for food. Mary had saved her rations to bake a small cake and, while they celebrated a new life, they remembered the ones they had lost.

Chapter Forty-Eight

T he people of Sheffield were busy piecing the broken parts of their lives together and putting the blitz behind them as best they could. George had joined the Home Guard, and Edward did some shifts as an air-raid warden. Life seemed to be moving on.

Harry was flourishing; he was looking more like Henry every day, which created mixed emotions for Frances. Of course, she adored him, but looking at him kept her wounds raw and prevented her from healing.

Not long after the christening, Harriette received a visit from Joe, her Canadian airman. There was a dance, with a big American band, taking place in town. Agnes and Arthur were going, and Harriette and Joe. Alice telephoned Frances and begged her to go, claiming she needed a dance partner as most of the men would be absent.

'I just don't feel like it,' protested Frances.

'That's the point! You haven't been out in ages. I think

we could all do with cheering up,' said Alice. 'I know I do. My grandmother died yesterday.'

'Sorry to hear that. Are you alright?'

'I'm fine. You know my grandmother – she was as old as the hills. She had a good life. Many a time I thought she'd passed already in her sleep; I'd have to stick my finger under her nose to check if she was still breathing. Sometimes she'd peel open one eye and catch me doing it. It always made me jump,' said Alice. Frances giggled.

'What about Harry?'

'I'll look after him,' called her mother.

Frances glared at her.

'Sorry,' her mother whispered.

'See. You have no excuse,' said Alice. 'Your mother can watch Harry, and I bet you have a dozen dresses in your wardrobe you could wear. We could all do with forgetting about the war for a while.'

'Alright, I'll go,' Frances said reluctantly.

'Excellent. I'll pop over to yours, and we can jump on the tram together. See you then.'

'See you then,' repeated Frances, and they both hung up.

Thomas wasn't feeling up to going, preferring to stay home and write to his sweetheart Gladys, a nurse he'd met overseas. She'd tended to his wounds and nursed him back to health. They had grown close while he recuperated in hospital.

When it was time to go, she kissed Harry goodnight. He beamed at her, showing his first tooth coming through. Frances thought her heart would burst from the love she felt for him. Alice couldn't resist picking him up and kissing him too.

The dance hall was full despite there being a war on. Frances and Alice looked around the room for the others. There were lots of couples dancing, mostly girls with girls, but there were also quite a few men in uniform.

Frances spotted Agnes and Arthur close to the bar and waved. Agnes came rushing over and hugged her friends.

'Guess what?' said Agnes, grinning from ear to ear. Frances looked at her blankly. 'Arthur has asked me to marry him, and I said yes!' she squealed. 'Of course, we plan on waiting until the war is over.'

'That's wonderful news,' said Frances. 'Congratulations!' She grabbed her friend and kissed her cheek.

'Yes, congratulations, Agnes,' said Alice.

'Ow do, Frances,' said Arthur as he approached and kissed her cheek.

'Congratulations,' said Frances. 'You and Agnes make a wonderful couple.'

'Thanks, I can't believe she said yes.'

'Do you ladies want a beer? The fella behind the bar owes me a couple of favours.'

'Yes please,' replied Frances. Alice nodded.

Harriette came running over, waving her hands; a man in uniform followed behind her.

'Joe, come here,' she said. 'These are my friends. This is Agnes.' Agnes smiled. 'This is Alice.' Alice blushed. 'And this is—'

'Franny,' came a male voice. Frances turned her head. 'I remember you.'

Frances turned beetroot. William, looking as dashing as

the last time she saw him, stepped forward and held out his hand but she didn't take it.

'Yes, this is Frances,' said Harriette.

Frances glared at her.

'How are you, Franny?' asked William. He was standing next to her, watching her. He smiled, but it didn't quite reach his eyes. 'You look well.'

'Hardly,' she scoffed. 'How are you?'

'You'd know if you had bothered to reply to my letters.'

Frances looked away, pushing her hair behind her ear. 'Yes, well. I never told you I would reply. You knew I was married.'

'Will you dance with me?' he asked.

'I promised Alice I would be her dance partner tonight.' She glanced at Alice. William followed her gaze.

'You don't mind if I dance with Franny now, do you?' Frances waved her hand under her chin and shook her head behind his back.

'I...I...' Alice spluttered and blushed.

'See, she doesn't mind. That's settled then. Just you and me honey.' He grabbed her hand and walked her towards the dancefloor.

'I am not your honey,' she snapped.

'No?' he laughed. 'Well, you sure is sweet.'

Frances huffed.

He pulled her into his arms just as the band began playing 'Little Brown Jug'. Frances quickly forgot her annoyance and danced. They danced together for the next song and the one after that too. For the first time in what seemed like forever, Frances felt like her old self again.

They left the dancefloor laughing and panting. She placed her hand over her heart and fanned her face.

'Let me get you a drink,' said William. He walked away and left Frances talking to Alice.

'I'm so sorry Alice,' said Frances. 'I'll make it up to you, I promise. I just need to catch my breath.'

William returned carrying three beers. He handed them out and took a long gulp from his.

'You were amazing!' he said to Frances. He leaned in closer to her. She could feel the heat from his breath close to her skin.

'You weren't so bad yourself,' she said. Alice coughed. 'Oh, Alice. I'm sorry,' she said, remembering herself. 'William, would you mind dancing with Alice, please? I need to cool off a little.'

'Sure thing.' He put his beer down on the table and offered Alice his hand.

'I'm fine,' Alice protested.

'I insist,' winked William.

Frances watched them dance. She had tried to forget William by not answering any of his letters, but he was proving too difficult to ignore. As she watched on, she was glad he was here. He was kind and attentive, just like Henry. Henry – a shiver ran down her spine. She hadn't thought about Henry all evening. She wrung her hands, as guilt coursed through her veins. 'Poor Henry, what am I thinking, allowing another man to flirt with me?' she chastised herself quietly. 'From now on, I won't give William any more encouragement.'

When the dance was over, Frances grabbed Alice's hand and dashed for the exit.

'Whoa! Hang on a minute,' William shouted after her. 'Where's the fire?'

'William,' said Frances. 'I need to get home. It's been lovely, thank you, but—'

'That's it? You were just going to leave without saying goodbye?' He put his hand on her shoulder and Alice stepped to the side. 'I thought we were friends.'

'We are, but that's all we are. I'm sorry. I need to leave,' she repeated.

'I don't understand.' He reached for her hand, but she placed it behind her back.

'What is there to understand? I'm married. I have a baby. What did you think would happen?' she snapped.

'I thought... when Harriette told me about your husband, I thought that maybe...' He dropped his gaze then lifted his eyes to meet hers.

'Maybe what? That I would just forget him and jump into bed with you?'

'No! Not my bed, but I thought you would at least give me a chance,' he pleaded.

'I'm sorry,' she whispered. 'I can't.' She turned to leave but William grabbed her again to stop her. 'Let go of me!'

'What's going on 'ere?' said Arthur. He ran towards them and put his hand on William's arm. 'Get your hands off her pal or else I'll knock thee through that glass.' He pointed with his head towards one of the windows.

'We're just talking,' replied William, losing his patience.

'Conversation is over,' said Arthur.

'Frances, please,' begged William.

'I need to go. I'm sorry.'

'Just five minutes of your time, that's all I ask and if you don't want to see me after that. I'll go.'

'Piss off, Yank!' warned Arthur. 'That's my brother's wife.'

'Look, mate, you're starting to get on my nerves – and I'm Canadian.' William took a step closer to Arthur. 'Can you leave us alone? Or I swear...'

Arthur scowled. 'Or what?' he asked. 'And I don't care where you come from, you'll be going home in a box if you put so much as another finger on her.'

Agnes put her arm through his.

'Come on, Arthur!' said Agnes. 'Just leave them to it.' She managed to drag him away.

'I'm watching you, pal,' said Arthur as he walked towards the door. He scowled at Frances and shook his head.

William took Frances by the hand and led her outside. Frances shivered so William put his jacket around her shoulders.

'Thank you,' she said. He took a packet of cigarettes out of his trouser pocket and offered her one. She shook her head. He placed one between his lips and lit it. He inhaled deeply and slowly puffed out the smoke; it lingered in the air between them. Frances waited for him to speak.

'Beautiful night, ain't it,' he said, looking at the stars.

Frances didn't speak.

'Look, I'm just gonna give it to you straight. I like you.' Frances opened her mouth to speak. 'No, let me finish. I know you still love your husband. I would be kidding myself if I thought you didn't, but in time I hope you can learn to love me too. When this war is over, Frances, I want to be with you. It's a gamble, I know – you hardly know me, but I think I'm worth the risk.' He turned to look at her, his eyes earnest. A second or two passed; Frances gazed at him, incredulous.

'Go ahead, you can speak now,' he said.

'I'm speechless! That's a lot to take in,' she said.

'Just say you'll think about it. I'm here for the next few days; then I fly back to Europe. Just say I have a chance.'

'I can't promise you anything, William. You know that. I love my husband and I always will.'

'I'm not asking you to stop loving him, but he's gone. I'm only asking you to make room in your heart for me too.' He threw his cigarette on the ground and cupped her face in his hands. His eyes implored her. 'Just sleep on it.' William leaned forward and his lips brushed hers delicately. Frances closed her eyes. 'Night, Frances,' he whispered. Frances' eyes flashed open. 'If you want me to kiss you, you're gonna have to meet me tomorrow,' he said.

'These look wonderful,' said Frances, twirling in the middle of Mary's front room. 'They are just like the ones Katharine Hepburn wears. I love them!' She walked over and hugged Mary.

'I'm glad you like them,' said Mary. 'I've never made trousers for a woman before.'

'Well, you've done a marvellous job,' said Frances. 'I can't wait to show them off.'

'They look good on you,' said Mary. 'You've soon got your figure back.'

'Thanks,' said Frances.

'I think this little un has grown some more,' said George, bouncing Harry on his knee.

'That's because he doesn't stop eating,' said Frances.

'It's good for babies to have an appetite,' said Mary, ruffling Harry's hair. It was thick and dark like Henry's. 'Look at those chubby little legs; I could just eat him up.' She squeezed his thighs. 'He looks more like Henry every day.' Mary's eyes were teary.

'He's a happy little chappy too,' said George. 'Aren't you?' he said to Harry. Harry gurgled.

'Has George told you about having to be a fire watcher?' said Mary. Frances shook her head. 'Aye him and some other blokes have to be ready to protect houses and factories if there's another attack.'

'Talk about shutting chuffing stable door after horse 'as bolted,' said George.

'Have you seen much of Harold and Margaret?' asked Frances.

'Yes, he's alreight. They were round other day. It's her I worry about; she's looking reight pasty. Harold's working double shifts and May's not been sleeping so she's keeping her up all night. She's a little varmint, that one. Margaret has her hands full there.'

George nodded. 'Aye, I wonder who she takes after.' He looked at Frances and winked. 'We've got some of the boys' old toys in t' basement. I'll go and fetch them. Here, Mary, you hold Harry a second.'

Frances went up the stairs to Henry's room. She sat on his bed and picked up his comb, which was sitting on a small table, and ran it through her fingers. She placed the comb down and ran her hand over his pillow. Would

she ever get to know what happened to him. If he was
dead, did he die alone? Her eyes started to sting. Trying
to free her mind of that image, she quickly changed
back into her dress and put her new trousers in a paper
bag.

When she came back into the main room, Harry was on
the floor, banging some lead soldiers on a tin. Mary was in
the kitchen.

'Are you staying for some tea?' asked Mary.

'If there's enough,' replied Frances.

'There's always enough,' said George.

Frances sat in one of the armchairs and watched George
play with Harry. George was trying to line all the soldiers up,
and Harry kept on knocking them down.

'By gum, he can shift. Look at him crawl. I've got some
boiled spice; can he have one?' he asked, his blue eyes
twinkling.

'No! You daft sod! Do you want him to choke?' said
Mary.

'I'm only kidding,' said George. He pulled out a box from
his pocket and took a pinch of brown powder and sucked it
up his nostrils. Frances watched. 'Snuff,' he replied to her
confused expression.

The front door opened and in walked Arthur.

'What's she doin' 'ere?' he said, staring at Frances. Frances
raised her eyebrows.

'What's got into thee?' asked George.

'Ask her,' said Arthur. George looked at Frances.

'What's gone on?' he asked.

'I don't know what he's talking about.' She lowered her
eyes. Mary entered, wiping her hands on a tea towel.

'What's goin' on?' She folded her arms under her large bosom.

'She...' he said pointing.

'Oi, who's she? Cat's mother?' retorted Mary. Arthur mumbled something under his breath.

'Frances were with some fella t'other night. Our Henry is... God knows, and she's... Frances... is off gallivanting with some other bloke.'

'Is this true?' asked Mary. Frances slowly raised her head.

'I wasn't *gallivanting*,' replied Frances. 'We danced, and that's all.'

'And are you going to see him again?' Mary scowled.

'I don't think that's any of our business, Mary love,' said George.

'While she's still married to my son it is,' Mary replied, her voice slightly raised.

'I don't know,' replied Frances, somewhat sheepishly. 'If I do, it will only be as friends. I love Henry; you know I do.' Frances shot Arthur a look. Arthur smirked.

'Well, we'll say no more on the matter for now,' huffed Mary. 'Reight, who's hungry?' Both George and Arthur put up their hands. Frances remained still and quiet, smarting about being put on the spot by Arthur. She knew he had every right to be upset, but he didn't have the right to embarrass her like that in front of Mary and George.

A loud banging on the door jolted her from her thoughts. Male voices could be heard shouting.

'Who the chuffin' 'ell is that?' said Mary.

'I'll go,' said Arthur. He stomped to the front door; his fists clenched. When he opened it, he gave a loud gasp. Two military police officers stood at the door.

'Arthur Shepherd?' they asked in unison. Arthur turned to run, but they grabbed his arms. Mary came rushing to the door, Frances and George followed.

'What's going on?' she shouted. 'Get your hands off my son!'

'Your son, madam, has been a naughty boy,' said one of the officers. 'I'm afraid he's been here when he shouldn't have.' Mary glared at Arthur; her mouth screwed up.

'Right, sunshine,' said the police officer to Arthur. 'Put your hands behind your back, you lazy sod; you're coming with us.' They pushed him up against the door and hand-cuffed him. Arthur stopped struggling.

'Sorry, Mum,' he grunted. 'Get Frances to tell Agnes I'm sorry and I'll write to her first chance I get.' Mary nodded and watched as the two officers walked him to a waiting army truck.

Chapter Forty-Nine

'I'm thinking of growing a few vegetables. What do you think?' asked Frances' mother, who was reading a gardening book in her armchair.

'You, get your hands dirty?' sniggered Frances.

'I don't see why not!' she tutted.

'I'll believe it when I see it.' Frances had Harry pinned on a blanket on the floor, changing his nappy. It was a struggle to keep him still.

'Are you meeting that William today?' asked Frances' mother.

'Yes. We're going to the pictures,' mumbled Frances. She held a nappy pin between her teeth.

'You're seeing an awful lot of him.'

'Not really. Besides, he's heading back overseas tomorrow, so I don't know when – or if – I'll see him again. There, all done.' She picked up Harry and blew a raspberry on his belly, causing him to chuckle.

'You must be fond of him.'

'We're just friends,' said Frances, tickling her son.

'Does he know you're "just" friends?' added her mother. 'He's clearly fond of you.' She lifted her eyes from her book and looked at Frances. Frances placed Harry in his crib.

'Mary doesn't approve,' said Frances.

'Can you blame her? I'm not sure I do either.'

Frances shook her head and sighed.

'Has he said what his intentions are?' asked her mother raising one eyebrow.

'Not really,' replied Frances.

'No?' pushed her mother. Frances walked over to the window and gazed out at the garden at a robin perched on the fence.

'Well, if you must know...' She glanced over her shoulder at her mother before turning her attention back to the bird. 'He did ask me to move to Canada with him when the war is over, but I think he was only joking. Besides, that's a long way off.'

'Is that something you want?'

'Honestly, I don't know. I'm afraid, Mother.' She turned fully around. 'Henry has been gone a long time, and although I don't want to admit it, I don't think he's ever coming back.' Her eyes were watery. 'So, I need to think about what is best for Harry and me and our futures. Of course, I don't want to accept that I may never see Henry again, but I don't want to bring Harry up by myself.' She tilted her head back to stop the tears from falling. 'Besides, I've always wanted to travel to America,' she said, her smile faint.

'Yes, but Canada isn't America.'

'I know that.' She stiffened. 'But it's closer than we are.'

'What about your friends?'

'Joe has asked Harriette to marry him, and she's said yes. She's thrilled to be moving to Canada with him after they're married.'

'What about Mary and George; they'd never see Harry again.'

Frances sighed. 'I know. Look, it probably won't happen and, like I said, the war is still raging on, anything can happen between now and lord knows when, but I would be a fool not to consider it. William is a wonderful man; he's caring, and he loves me.'

'Yes, but do you love him?'

'I don't think I will ever love again, not the way I loved... love Henry; he was... is my everything. But I have to keep moving forward because if I stop, I know I will crumble and that will be the end of me.' She dropped Harry's dirty nappy into a bucket. 'And I could grow to love William.'

'That's not the same,' replied her mother.

'I will only ever truly love one man. Henry is the love of my life. William understands that.'

'Well, he's a better man than most.' Her mother closed her book, stretched out her arms and yawned. 'Are you going to let him meet Harry?'

'I haven't thought about it. Like I said, it's early days. Right, I need to soak Harry's nappies, and then I need to change; he'll be here soon.' She headed for the door and then stopped. 'I forgot to tell you; Alice is driving a bus these days.'

'What, little Alice? I'd like to see that,' laughed her mother.

'She started two days ago. She said that some of the older

men are dour, and don't give her the time of day, but the rest have been nice. There are a lot of women driving the trams and buses in town.'

'Yes, times are changing,' added her mother.

'Indeed,' said Frances.

Later that evening, William held Frances' hand as they walked together to her front door.

'Thank you, William...'

'You know you really should call me Billy; only my mum calls me William and, well, it doesn't feel right coming from your lips, especially when I'm about to do this...'

'Do what?'

'This.' He placed his hands on either side of her face and brought his lips to hers. Gently, he caressed her face as he explored her mouth. He kissed her softly to begin with, but then his kiss became more urgent. Frances gripped his collar in her fists and pulled his mouth closer to hers. Her heart beat faster and faster as his hands leisurely travelled from her face to her waist, and he ground his body into hers.

Frances became lost in the moment. It had been a long time since she had been held like this. Although it was William kissing her, she pictured Henry's face. William's breath and the warmth of his skin made her forget that Henry was gone for a moment. Their tongues flickered and danced. William groaned, making Frances gasp.

The neighbour's cat knocked the lid off the bin, causing it to clatter to the ground. Frances jumped, and the moment was lost. Breathing heavily, she swallowed and bit her bottom lip. William ran his fingers through his hair.

'That was some goodnight kiss. Remind me to go to war more often,' he joked.

Frances didn't respond. She placed her fingers to her lips and looked at William. She suddenly felt uneasy. Her mouth went dry and she felt sick.

'What's wrong?' asked William. He reached for her hand. She put her hands in her pockets.

'Nothing,' she lied. 'I'm just tired.' Secretly, she wanted to run to the bathroom and wash any trace of William from her. She felt bad because William was a nice man – he deserved better.

'Well, goodnight then. Make sure to write to me this time,' he teased.

'I will,' she said.

'Good.' He leaned forward to kiss her again, but she turned her head only offering him her cheek.

'Goodnight Wil... Billy. Take care of yourself over there.'

'Don't worry, I will. Now that I have you waiting for me.'

Frances put her hand on the door handle and waited for him to walk away before she opened the door. She waved one last time to him; then she entered the house. Closing the door behind her, she slid down to the floor.

'Forgive me, Henry,' she cried.

Chapter Fifty

Hiding out in Yugoslavia, waiting for calmer weather, Henry was feeling weary after so many days spent looking at the endless blue water. To pass the time, he played cards and dominoes with a Jewish man called Roman, who had paid for his family to sail to America. His family had escaped Warsaw, thanks to the underground movement.

'Do you know anyone in America?' asked Henry. They had been playing three card brag for the past half an hour.

'I have a cousin,' replied Roman. 'I have his address. He's not expecting us though. I didn't have time to write and tell him of my plans.'

'It must have been hard for you,' said Henry.

'Before Hitler came to power, communities were mixed. We had a good life. Of course, we knew what was happening in Germany – Jewish people being treated like vermin, but we didn't think the demonisation of Jews would happen in Poland. But then the Germans attacked, and it wasn't long before our people were ordered into ghettos. It was degrading.' He wiped a tear from his eye. 'Before the war, I was a college professor. We lived in a beautiful house in Warsaw; we had our house taken from us,' he said bitterly. 'My family and I were stripped of everything.'

'I'm so sorry,' said Henry.

'In the beginning, life appeared normal, but then, six weeks later, the camp was sealed, and food became harder to come by. Some of us risked our lives to smuggle supplies inside the ghetto. It was becoming harder to avoid death. We heard stories of children being smuggled out, and then families. When rumours spread about people from the ghetto disappearing and being sent to camps. I knew I had to get my family out somehow.'

Henry looked at Roman's family as they slept peacefully, unable to imagine the horrors they had witnessed. 'I wish you luck on your onward journey,' he said. Roman nodded his thanks.

'And you? What's your story?' asked Roman, placing down a flush.

'I win again,' said Henry, placing down a run. He collected the broken cigarettes from the table.

Roman mumbled something in Polish.

'My story is nothing compared to yours. I just need to get back to my wife.'

'What do you keep in your hand?'

'What, this?' Henry held up his compass.

Roman nodded.

'It's my lucky charm.'

'Well, I hope it brings you luck on your onward journey, my friend.'

After days at sea, Henry watched as the sun began its descent over the harbour, casting a golden glow on the pastel colours of the pretty little fishing houses. They had to wait on the small vessel until it turned dark, after which they all quietly came ashore. Henry shook hands with Roman.

'Good luck, my friend,' said Roman, and he slapped Henry on the back.

'You too,' replied Henry. The two parted ways. Henry was told to climb in the back of a truck, and Roman and his family were ushered into a small fishing shack to await their next boat.

Henry was given some bread and water and, having eaten, he fell asleep against some wooden crates, only disturbed later by the sound of a cockerel crowing. The truck stopped, propelling him forwards. He was instructed to get out and wait in some bushes; then it drove away.

Henry waited in the heat for what seemed like an hour. Every rustling noise made him jump. He sat on the dry, dusty ground and tried to get a look at his surroundings. From the bushes, he could see endless fields and country lanes.

Just as he was beginning to think no one was coming, he heard a motorcycle approaching. A young man stopped abruptly and looked around. Henry watched and waited as the young man climbed off his bike.

'You can come out now!' said the young man. Henry

cautiously made his approach. 'My name is Marcel. Hurry, jump on!' Henry did as he was told. 'You'll be staying with my family for a few days until we can arrange for you to safely leave France.'

They arrived at a white stone farmhouse, with blue shutters at the windows. It was surrounded by golden wheat fields and a few scattered green trees. Chickens foraged about the yard. Marcel and Henry climbed off the bike, and Henry followed Marcel into the house.

'Let me introduce you to my family,' he said. He only looked about fifteen, but he was full of confidence. 'This is my maman,' he said. He walked around a large wooden kitchen table and kissed the woman on her cheek. She was sitting at the table, shelling peas.

'Bonjour,' replied the woman. She didn't look that old, but her black hair was streaked with grey.

'How do,' nodded Henry.

'My père is in the village; he'll be back later,' said Marcel. He turned to his mum. 'Où est Anaïs?'

His mum shrugged.

He turned his attention back to Henry. 'My sister is around somewhere. Come! You can have a wash in the yard and I'll give you some clean clothes.'

'Thank you,' said Henry. Henry looked down at his dirty clothes. He hadn't bathed in weeks; he had grown used to his smell, but now he felt embarrassed. He was sure that something was living in his beard.

In the yard, he stripped down to his pants. Marcel pulled the handle on the water pump until the wooden barrel was full. He handed Henry a bar of soap, who proceeded to wash his top half.

'I will fetch you a towel and some clothes,' said Marcel. He ran back into the house and came out carrying a small bundle. 'I'll leave the towel and clothes on this bench over here,' shouted Marcel.

'Thank you,' replied Henry.

Marcel walked back inside, giving Henry some privacy.

The pump stood under the shade of an old tree. Henry dipped his head into the cold water and rubbed soap in his hair and then rinsed the suds off. He applied more soap to his chest and then looked around to see if anyone was watching; when he was happy no one was there, he took off his pants, then continued to clean the rest of his body.

When he had finished, Henry jogged over to the bench. He jumped back and quickly covered his privates when he noticed a young woman, about the same age as Frances, sitting on the bench, smiling at him.

'Hello,' she said. Her eyes assessed his wet body.

'Hello,' said Henry. 'You must be Marcel's sister. My name is Henry.'

'My name is Anaïs.' She stood up and walked towards him, holding out her hand.

'I'm afraid my hands are full,' joked Henry. 'It's nice to meet you, Anaïs. Would you mind passing me that towel?' He nodded with his head towards the bench. 'It's getting a little chilly.'

Anaïs looked over her shoulder at the towel. 'What are you going to do for me?' she smirked. She had an attractive smile, dark brown hair and brown eyes. He couldn't help noticing her fuller, voluptuous figure.

'You have me at a slight disadvantage, Anaïs,' said Henry. 'Maybe when I'm dressed, we can talk favours.'

'Anaïs!' shouted Marcel. 'Maman wants you! Leave Henry alone and go and help in the kitchen.'

'Vas-t'en, Marcel, tu m'embarrasse,' She flushed red and groaned. 'Vous êtes tellement ennuyeux!'

'Arrête de flirter et vas-t'en!' Ignore her flirting, Henry,' said Marcel.

'Je te déteste!' she shouted and stormed off.

'Nice to meet you, Anaïs,' said Henry.

Later that day, Henry felt a million times better. He had clean clothes, his beard was gone and his belly was full. He relaxed with Marcel on the long grass and enjoyed the warm summer's evening. It was so peaceful. Henry watched the swallows swoop and listened to the lulling sound of the crickets.

'My brother's clothes fit you well,' said Marcel.

'Your brother?' asked Henry. 'Where is he now?'

'Dead,' said Marcel sombrely. 'He went to fight and never returned.'

'I'm sorry to hear that.'

'Do you have any brothers?'

'I have two, both older than me.'

'Do you get along?'

'Not always, but we get along better now we're older,' said Henry. He plucked a tall blade of grass and ran it through his fingers.

'I miss my brother,' said Marcel. Henry looked at him.

'I miss mine too,' he said.

'Hopefully, you will see yours again,' said Marcel.

'Hopefully.'

'All I have left is a stupid sister.' Marcel hugged his knees.

'I'm sure she's not that bad,' laughed Henry.

'No, she is worse. Do you have a sister?'

'No, but I have a wife,' said Henry. He looked at the heavens; stars had started to sprinkle the clear night sky.

'A wife? My sister will be jealous. I think she fancies you,' said Marcel. 'What is your wife like?'

A dreamy expression spread across Henry's face. 'What is she like?' he repeated. 'Her eyes would shame them stars.' He pointed to the sky and then ran his hand through his hair. 'Her lips... God, her lips.' Henry groaned.

'So, she is very beautiful,' said Marcel.

'She's more than that. Her smile would warm the coldest heart. When she laughs, you can't help but laugh too. When she's angry or confused, a tiny crease appears above her nose – and her kisses, oh, how I miss her kisses. They are sweeter than the summer fruits we ate earlier. And she has spirit – she doesn't think it, but she's brave.'

'You must love her a lot.'

'I love her more than life itself,' sighed Henry.

'Then we must get you home,' said Marcel.

The next day Henry did what he could to help Marcel and his father on the farm. He pretended he hadn't noticed Anaïs watching him from afar. It was a long, back-breaking day. The sun scorched the land, and Henry's shirt clung to him as he sweated. But his hard work was rewarded with a sumptuous dinner cooked by Anaïs and her maman. Marcel's father poured him a couple of glasses of homemade wine, and they spent a merry evening together, chatting about life before the war and what life had in store for them all after. Anaïs looked longingly at him all evening, earning her a few scornful stares from her père.

Henry slept soundly for the first time in months; it was so peaceful on the farm. He dreamed of Frances, of touching her soft skin. Dreamily, he stretched out his fingers as though feeling her naked breast and was rewarded with warm, tender flesh beneath his hand. It took him a second or two to realise he was no longer dreaming. Henry opened his eyes and jumped out of bed. Lying naked beneath the sheets was Anaïs.

'Jesus fucking Christ! What are you doing?'

'I thought you could do with some company,' purred Anaïs, her lips slightly parted, her eyes devouring his naked body. Henry grabbed a blanket to conceal himself.

'I am a married man, Anaïs. You're an attractive woman, but I love my wife.'

'But she's not here. I am,' she said.

'She might not be here in the flesh, but she is always here.' He pointed to his head. 'And here.' He rested his hand over his heart.

'So, you do not want me?' A tear trickled down her cheek.

'I never gave you cause to think otherwise. Now please, don't cry, but I think you should leave.'

Anaïs' cheeks reddened; she jumped up out of Henry's bed and ran out of the room. For the remainder of Henry's stay, she avoided him, which suited him fine.

Henry thought he would never leave the farm, not that he minded. If it hadn't been for Frances, Henry could've stayed forever. He loved working outdoors. It was hard work, but it wasn't as dangerous or stifling as working in the factory. It was such an easy way of life. It made him want his own farm all the more. One could quite easily forget there was a war going on.

After a few days, Marcel told him they had received word that a boat would be sailing in a day or two back to England. It was time to leave. On the evening before he was due to go, Anaïs had tried to kiss him once more. He politely refused her advances, and she had run off weeping again.

Before Henry left for what he hoped would be his final journey before sailing to England, he said goodbye to his host family and thanked them for looking after him so well. Anaïs watched from her bedroom window.

Marcel shook his hand and wished him luck. His mother had packed Henry some bread, cheese and wine. Henry was sad to be saying goodbye, but not to be leaving. He couldn't wait to get going.

Henry climbed into the back of Marcel's father's truck. They covered him with fruit crates and empty bags used for wheat. He just hoped he would make the trip in one piece. This part of the journey would be the hardest one as the further north they travelled, the riskier it got – the Germans were everywhere. Henry prayed he'd run into British soldiers first.

Chapter Fifty-One

The drive was a bumpy one. The truck was old, and the roads were damaged from the war. Henry's body ached from being crouched down so long.

As night fell, Marcel's father drove through a small war-ravaged village. He pulled up behind an abandoned school and gestured to Henry to get out. He tried to explain that someone would come for him, but his English was not good. Henry thanked him and took shelter in the school. Not long after, Henry found himself in the back of a bigger truck, filled with French soldiers.

He must have fallen asleep because he felt someone poke him with their foot. Henry jolted awake.

'Your stop!' shouted one of the soldiers.

Jumping down from the truck, Henry could feel the summer breeze stroke his skin and taste the salt in the air from the sea. Tears filled his eyes; he was closer to home than he had been in a very long time.

Henry kept to the shadows and made his way to the harbour. It was a busy historic town. A few of the locals stared as he passed, but nobody really paid him much attention – they were too busy going about their business.

Henry walked a short distance until he reached the shore. The sun was like a heavenly orb shining down on the crystal waters. He gazed at the stunning view, wishing Frances was there to share it with him. He listened as the waves lapped against the sand, wanting to take his shoes off and run in the water. He'd never been in the sea before.

'Hello,' came a voice behind him. Henry froze. Slowly, he turned around. 'I'm Corporal Jones. Someone said they spotted a fucking stupid English bastard heading this way. I believe we've been expecting you. Come, we'd better hurry, lad, or we'll miss the boat, and Christ knows when there will be another one!'

Henry followed him to a large fishing vessel that had apparently been commandeered by a Welsh battalion. They welcomed Henry on board and set sail for Portsmouth.

All the way across the English Channel, Henry ensured endless ribbing about being an Englishman, but he gave as good he got. They played cards and sang songs to pass the time.

When he finally arrived in Portsmouth, he climbed down from the boat before crouching down and touching the ground with his hand. His eyes stung with the onset of tears and a wave of emotion threatened to engulf him. An unrehearsed chorus of gulls swooped in greeting overhead. He pulled out his compass, kissed the glass and looked to the heavens. 'Thank you,' he whispered.

He was taken to a nearby army barracks, where he was allowed to shower, after which he was given a clean uniform and a hearty meal. When he had finished eating, he was taken to the commanding officer's headquarters.

The room was small. The only light came from a round window at the back. The commanding officer, a tall man with greying hair and a ginger moustache, stood behind a table. He wore little round spectacles which kept on slipping to the end of his bulbous nose. On the table lay a large map of Europe with several aerial photographs scattered over it. Two other men in uniform were standing either side of him, listening.

'So, old chap. I bet it feels good to be back in Old Blighty, eh?' said the officer.

'It does that, sir,' agreed Henry.

'Terrible time it must have been. Miserable affair. But you must put it to the back of your mind and move on, old chap. Take a seat.' He pointed to a chair behind Henry. Henry sat down. 'We won't keep you long,' said the officer. 'We just have a couple of questions for you.' He walked to stand in front of the table, crossed his legs one in front of the other and folded his arms. 'Can you tell us what happened?'

'Do you have a cigarette, sir?' asked Henry.

'Of course, here, take the packet,' replied the officer. Henry pulled one out and placed it between his lips before lighting it. He inhaled deeply and breathed the smoke out slowly.

'My battalion tried to hold off the German attack in a village a few miles from Dunkirk. We were being attacked on all sides. We stayed for days, trying to hold back the Germans while thousands of men fled to the beach. The town was just a pile of rubble, charred and bloody corpses.' Henry pinched the bridge of his nose and closed his eyes before continuing. 'When we were ordered to retreat, we couldn't get past the German line. I was one of the lucky ones, sir. Many men didn't make it. I heard that those captured by the SS were machine gunned down. I was fortunate to be captured by regular German troops.'

'I expect it was a dreadful experience,' said the officer.

'If you'll excuse my French, sir, it was a fucking bloodbath, sir.'

The officer pushed his spectacles back up his nose and stroked his moustache.

'Continue,' he said.

'We marched for days; the bastards forced us to drink putrid ditch water and eat rotten food. When we reached the camp, some of the men were interrogated but I wasn't. After they gave us our POW numbers we were put to work.'

'So how did you escape?'

'I met a Polish soldier and we managed to make a run for it,' said Henry. 'The Polish Underground helped us.' Henry yawned. 'Sorry, sir.'

'No need to apologise. You must be exhausted. You can go and get some rest now. But before you go on leave, I would like a full written statement from you. You can read and write, I take it?'

'Oh aye, sir.' Henry stood up. The officer held out his hand and Henry shook it.

'Well done, old chap,' said the officer. 'With men like you, we will win this insufferable war!'

In the morning, he was driven to the station, and there he caught the first train to London with a group of English soldiers.

'What was it like then?' asked a red-haired lad from Newcastle. 'Were the Germans complete bastards? Filthy scum.' He spat on the floor of the train to show his disgust.

Henry told them all about his time as a prisoner and how he had escaped. The soldiers gave him a packet of cigarettes and patted him on the back.

'Well, you're home now,' said a man called Tom. 'Enjoy your freedom while you can; you deserve it!'

Henry waited for the connecting train north. With shaking hands, he lit a cigarette and crouched on the platform while he watched crowds of people pushing and shoving. The clatter of metal wheels on the tracks, steam engines and whistles filled the air. Passengers shouting to one another, luggage carts and porters added to the chaos. Momentarily, Henry missed the quiet of Marcel's farm. It felt strange to be back in England, to not have that fear of being captured hanging over him. He tried to picture Frances' reaction. He couldn't wait to hold her in his arms again. He looked at the clock, only five minutes to go before the train arrived.

'Do you have a smoke?' Henry looked up and saw a man in a uniform smiling down at him.

'Of course,' replied Henry. Henry rose to his full height and pulled out his packet of cigarettes, offering the stranger one.

'Thanks,' said the man and took one. 'I hate to be a pest, but do you have a light too?' Henry passed him his box of matches. 'Great, thanks again. The name's Joe,' said the man and held out his hand.

'Henry.' Henry shook his hand.

'Where you heading to, Henry?' asked Joe.

'Sheffield,' replied Henry.

'Small world, me too. I'm travelling with my friend over there.' He pointed to another man in uniform. 'We've got forty-eight hours on leave. I'm planning on visiting my sweetheart. It's going to be a surprise.' Joe inhaled sharply and then blew the smoke out slowly.

'Oh, aye and is she in Sheffield, your sweetheart?' asked Henry.

'She most certainly is,' said Joe. 'A proper little firecracker.'

'And you, where are you from?'

'Canada. I'm from Vancouver, and my buddy lives close to Toronto.'

'Does your buddy have a sweetheart in Sheffield too,' asked Henry. Henry flicked his cigarette to the ground.

'He's hoping she'll be his sweetheart soon.'

'Is she playing hard to get?' joked Henry.

'It's complicated.'

'Always is,' agreed Henry.

'How's it going?' said Joe's friend, having wandered over to join them. He held out his hand, and Henry shook it.

'Not so bad,' replied Henry.

'Henry here is heading to Sheffield too, Billy,' said Joe.

'Do you want a smoke?' asked Henry.

'That would be great,' said Billy.

'You seen much action?' asked Joe.

'Fair bit. You?'

Joe nodded.

Henry looked at the clock; the train was one minute late.

'Who you got waiting for you in Sheffield?' asked Joe.

'My wife,' replied Henry.

'How long is it since you've seen her?' asked Joe.

'Too long.'

'I bet you can't wait to get home,' said Billy.

Henry nodded in agreement.

'I can't wait to see my girl too. She's not exactly my girl; she's still hung up on her husband, but one day she will be.'

'So she's married then?' asked Henry.

'Sort of,' replied Billy.

Henry exhaled when the train finally pulled into the station.

'At last,' said Henry, smiling.

All three made their way towards the train.

'How can you be 'sort of' married?' asked Henry. He opened one of the doors and climbed up inside the carriage.

'Her husband has been missing in action for over a year,' said Billy. Henry turned quickly to face him; his eyes widened, his mouth slightly open.

'What's her name?' asked Henry.

'Frances,' said Billy. 'But I like to call her Franny.'

'Do you now?' Henry's eyes narrowed; a vein in his neck twitched and his fists clenched at his side.

Billy put his hand on the handle and was about to pull himself up inside the train, but Henry reached out his hand to stop him.

'Hey! What's up?' shouted Billy. Joe was looking over

Billy's shoulder to see what was happening. The train's whistle blew.

'This carriage is full, pal,' said Henry.

'What? What you talking about? There's no one in it,' exclaimed Billy.

'I don't think you heard me right.' Henry put his face close to Billy's. 'This carriage is full.'

'You're nuts!' shouted Billy. 'We need to catch this train!'

'Appen I am, and I think you gents ought never to set foot in Sheffield again, or else you'll find out just how 'nuts' I can be.'

Henry pushed him so he landed back on the platform and then slammed the door shut. He put his head out of the window. 'It's been nice chatting with thee, gents, but if you'll excuse me, I wouldn't mind getting my head down before we arrive in Sheffield. I'll tell Frances you said hello.'

Billy and Joe watched, their mouths agape, as the whistle blew and the train chugged out of the station.

Chapter Fifty-Two

F rances had not been outside in days. Although it was supposed to be summer, the weather had been miserable. She played with Harry on the rug by the fire while her mother did some admin work for the WVS. It was dank and dreary, making the already gloomy city look even grimmer.

The rain showed no sign of stopping but, then, as though listening to Frances' heavy sighs, the clouds dispersed and a rainbow appeared. The sky turned blue, and the sun shone down on the pools of water left behind in the roads by the storm.

'Oh look, a rainbow, Harry!' Frances held Harry up to the window and pointed to the sky.

'Why don't we all go out for a walk,' said Frances' mother. 'We could all do with some fresh air.'

'That's a wonderful idea. I'll get Harry dressed. We can have a walk to the duck pond. Harry loves the ducks.'

Frances and her mother put on their summer coats and placed Harry in his pram. They were about to go outside when the phone rang.

'I'll get it,' said Frances. She ran to the phone and picked up the receiver. 'Hello,' she said.

'Hello, Frances, is this a bad time?' sniffled Harriette.

'No, we were just heading to the park. Is everything alright?' asked Frances. She placed her hand over the receiver and mouthed to her mother to take Harry and go on without her.

'I'll catch you up,' she whispered. Her mother nodded and left her to it.

'It's Charles, Frances,' cried Harriette. 'He's dead!'

'Oh, Harriette, I'm so sorry. Poor Charles. What happened?'

'He was shot in Africa,' blubbered Harriette. Frances didn't know what to say. 'His wound became infected after being shot. It could have all been avoided,' she said, through the tears, 'if he had received treatment back home.'

Frances wiped away a tear. 'How utterly dreadful.'

'I'm going to miss him so much,' said Harriette, blowing her nose.

'We all will. If there is anything I can do, don't hesitate to ask,' said Frances.

'Thank you,' replied Harriette. 'It's just so terrible.'

'I know,' agreed Frances. 'There have been so many deaths. The whole thing is frightful.'

'Absolutely awful,' said Harriette. She'd stopped crying but Frances didn't know what else to say.

'Have you heard from Joe?' she asked.

'Yes, last week.' Her tone brightened. She went on to tell

her about their plans for when the war was over. Frances listened patiently. Her legs ached from standing. She was about to grab a chair to sit down when she heard banging at the door; she tried to ignore it at first but whoever it was sounded determined.

'I'm sorry, Harriette, but someone extremely impatient is hammering on the front door.'

'You go,' said Harriette. 'I'll catch you later.'

'Take care, Harriette. I'll be thinking of you,' replied Frances. There was more banging at the door. 'I'm coming! Hold your horses! Got to dash, bye Harriette.'

Frances replaced the receiver. 'This better be important,' she shouted as she marched to the front of the house and flung open the door. 'I really don't...'

Frances gasped. Her heart stopped beating for a moment; she just stood there, wide-eyed and speechless. Her knees wobbled and she grabbed the door frame to steady herself. She swallowed hard and let go of the air that had expanded her lungs. Standing on the other side of the door was Henry. She had no control over the tears, which streamed down her face. She drew back her shaking hand and slapped him across the cheek.

'Well, hello to you too,' said Henry, rubbing his cheek. Frances' eyes were ablaze with anger. She lifted her hand to slap him again, but Henry caught her wrist mid-air.

Frances tried to tug free. She looked at him, her eyes glittering with tears. She lifted her other arm to strike him in the chest, but again he stopped her. Crying, she collapsed to the floor. Henry fell to his knees, alongside her, still holding her wrists.

'You left me,' she cried.

'It wasn't my fault.' He let go of her hands and wrapped his arms around her and held her as she wept. Henry cupped her face. Frances closed her eyes. 'Look at me,' Henry whispered. Frances sobbed, keeping her eyes tightly shut. Henry pulled her onto his lap and held her close to his chest. He rocked her as she cried. He stroked her hair and ran his hand over her cheek to wipe away her tears. 'I'm so sorry, Frances.' He kissed her forehead, then her eyelids and then the tip of her nose. 'If I could have got home sooner, I would.' She opened her bleary eyes and gazed at him.

'You said you would never leave me. I thought you were dead,' she snivelled, her bottom lip trembled. The tiny crease appeared above her nose. Henry kissed it.

'I'm here now.'

She lifted her hand to touch his cheek. With her index finger, she traced the outline of his face and felt the softness of his lips.

'Is it really you?' Henry nodded.

She turned her body so she was kneeling in front of him. Her head became level with his. She stared longingly into his eyes. Henry brought his mouth closer to hers, close enough to feel the heat of her breath against his skin. He leisurely drew a line with his fingers up her arms.

Frances looked at his mouth and licked her bottom lip. Slowly, she pushed her palms up his chest and over his shoulders, resting her hands on the back of his neck.

'You've been gone so long,' said Frances. 'I thought that I would never see you again. Where have you been all this time?'

'I'll tell you all about it later, first...' He kissed her.

Henry pushed himself up from his knees and lifted

Frances with him, kicking the front door closed. Frances wrapped her legs around his waist. Henry walked, with Frances clinging to him, and he pushed her up against the wall. Soon she was lost, floating away; nothing existed, only their love.

Henry rested his head against her forehead.

'I have crossed mountains to be here,' he whispered. 'I want to hold thee in my arms and never let thee go.'

'I don't want you to let me go either,' she said and kissed his lips. 'I wish we could forget everyone and everything and stay like this forever.'

Henry put his nose to her neck and breathed in her scent.

'I have dreamed of this moment.' He placed delicate kisses up her neck and along her jaw. 'My love,' he murmured against her mouth. He lifted his head, so his eyes locked with hers. 'You are still my love, aren't you?

'Always,' she said and brushed her lips against him. Reluctantly, she pulled away. 'I expect you're hungry. I'll make you something to eat.'

Frances was just finishing making the cups of tea when she heard her mother calling.

'Sorry we took so long, Frances. I got talking to Mrs Redgrave, you know how she loves Harry. If you're making a cup of tea, I'll take one please. What happened to you? I thought you were joining us.'

'Yes, sorry Mother,' she called back. 'Something came up,' she giggled quietly.

'Who's Harry?' he whispered. Frances bit her bottom her lip and took his hand.

'I need to tell you something. Come with me. I did write to you, but clearly you never received my letters.'

'No, we moved around a lot. I did write to you several times, but I never sent them. Sorry.'

'That doesn't matter now. All that matters is you're home.'

She led him by the hand to the lounge.

'I'm bushed,' her mother said as she heard Frances' footsteps approached. 'I think Harry will sleep for hours.'

'Did you get a dog?' asked Henry. Frances shook her head and opened the door.

'Better than that,' she said. 'Much better.'

Frances' mother shot up when she saw Henry.

'Oh, my lord!' she screamed, causing Harry to wake up in his pram and start crying. She put her hand over her heart. 'Henry!'

Henry looked at Frances' mother and then at the baby in the pram.

'Whose is the child?' he asked Frances. He walked over to the pram and stared at the crying infant. Harry put up his arms to be held. Henry looked at Frances, tears pooled her eyes.

'I'll leave you to it,' said Frances' mother, and left the room.

Frances picked up Harry. 'Say hello to your son, Henry.'

For a moment, Henry looked lost for words. He looked at Frances and then back at Harry, then softly stroked Harry's face.

'Can I hold him?' he asked, his voice choked.

Frances passed Harry to Henry. 'Say hello to your daddy, Harry.'

Henry held Harry close to his chest and then the tears flowed uncontrollably. 'I should have been here for you both,' he cried. 'I let you down.'

'You're here now; that's all that matters.' Frances wiped her eyes and put her arms around the two most important people in her life.

'Thank you, he is the best home coming present, Frances,' he said. 'He's perfect.'

'I'm so happy you're home. I love you, Henry.'

Chapter Fifty-Three

Henry played with Harry for hours, and when Harry got hungry, Henry fed him and watched while Frances changed his nappy. When it was time for his bath Henry did that too. Finally, when Harry fell asleep in his arms, Henry refused to put him down; instead, he just watched him sleep, mesmerised by the life he held in his arms – his son. He still couldn't get his head around the fact that he was a dad. Frances eventually insisted that he put him in his crib.

'I can't believe we have a son.' Henry grinned, still staring at him. 'He's so beautiful, just like you. I wish I could have been here. I have missed so much.' He wiped away a tear from the corner of his eye.

'We have our whole lives ahead of us now, you, me and Harry,' said Frances. She pulled him onto her bed. He lay on top of her and they kissed.

'Are you sure he won't wake up?' asked Henry. 'It doesn't feel right, him being in the same room.'

'It's fine, trust me.'

They made love slowly and leisurely, savouring the moment. Afterwards, they lay in each other's arms.

'What was it like in Europe?' asked Frances.

'Hell. I just needed to get home to you. I couldn't bear the thought of leaving this earth without ever seeing you again.' He kissed the top of her head.

'I'm so happy you found your way back to me.' She kissed his chest and rolled on top of him, staring into his blue eyes. 'It's funny how things turn out. I was the one that wanted to see the world,' she joked.

'I will have to return, you know that, right. The war is not over.' Frances put her finger to his lips.

'Shush! We'll think about that tomorrow. You made it back to me, that's all that matters.'

'I told you my compass was lucky.' He grinned.

'You did.' She smiled. 'I think it deserves to be in a display cabinet somewhere.'

'It's never leaving my side.'

'Tell me what happened to you,' she said. Henry switched positions, so he was lying between her legs. Henry's body trembled. He forced the images of what he had been through to the back of his mind.

'Not right now, first I want to make love to my beautiful wife again.'

'Henry, why did you ask me if I was still yours?' asked Frances. Henry was holding Harry up to the tram window as they travelled through the city.

'I can't believe the damage,' said Henry. 'Half of the houses have gone. I told Oskar what a beautiful city it was; it looks nothing like how I left it.'

'Yes, it's terrible. Who is Oskar?' asked Frances.

'My friend. He kept me sane. Without his help, I wouldn't be here with you, and I would have died not knowing I had a son.' Henry kissed Frances' lips and ruffled Harry's hair. Harry pointed to a bus.

'Then he is my friend too,' said Frances, and kissed him back.

'Good, because I've asked him to come to Sheffield when the war is over.'

'Do you think he will?' asked Frances.

'I hope so.'.

'Why did you ask me, if I was still yours?'

Henry turned in his seat, so his body was facing hers. He could tell she was getting impatient.

'It doesn't matter now,' he said, squeezing her knee.

'It was a strange thing to ask.'

'I only asked because so much time has passed. If you thought I was dead... I wouldn't blame you.'

'Blame me for what?'

'You know... if you'd met someone else.'

Frances was silent for a second. Henry watched as she played with her gloves.

'I want to be honest with you, Henry. I don't want to keep any secrets from you, ever,' she said. Henry closed his eyes briefly, then held her hand. She was trembling. 'I've done something terrible.'

'If you're about to tell me about your friendship with the Canadian, then don't waste your time. I already know.'

'How?' Frances looked at him, her mouth slightly open.

'It doesn't matter how? Did you... do you have feelings for him?'

'No! Henry, I swear.' Tears trickled down her cheeks.

'Then I don't care,' he said. Tears filled his eyes too and a wave of relief washed over him. 'We're together now, Frances, and that's all I care about. You, me and our son. Nothing else matters.'

'I love you, Henry Shepherd.' Frances put her arms around his neck and kissed him. Harry sucked on his thumb and watched his parents.

'I love you too, Frances Shepherd. So, tell me, what else has been going on?'

'Where do I begin? Agnes and Arthur are engaged.'

'No!'

'Yes, but when he'll next be home is anyone's bet.'

'Why?'

'Well, the military police came for him. He went AWOL.'

'Nothing changes. Our Arthur's still a reight gormless chuff,' joked Henry.

'It's not funny – poor Agnes. The last thing your mum heard was that he'd been sent to India.'

'He'll hate that. He doesn't like the heat.'

'I was thinking, Henry...'

'About what?'

'How would you feel if I asked my father for a loan so we could buy that small piece of land you talked about?'

Henry turned to look at her. 'Are you serious?'

'I think it's about time we had a home of our own, don't you?' said Frances.

Henry walked in carrying Harry. Mary saw them and collapsed against the Welsh dresser, thinking she was seeing a ghost. She screamed and burst into tears. Frances cried tears of joy as she watched Henry reunited with his family. It was an emotional afternoon. Mary held on tight to her son's hand, afraid he would disappear again. George ran down to the corner shop and bought tankards of beer for everyone to celebrate Henry's return, telling anyone and everyone he came across, whether they were interested or not. The war wasn't over by a long shot, but it no longer mattered because Henry was home where he belonged, and that was all the victory they needed, for now.

Acknowledgments

Thanks to my supportive early readers and to all the people I have had the pleasure to work with during this project. A special thanks to my family for inspiring me to write this book and for never doubting.

About the Author

K French was born and educated in Sheffield. She lives in Hertfordshire with her husband and two children. She has previously lived in Ireland and Australia but still regards the north as her home.

Connect with her at her website or on social media:

http://kfrenchbooks.co.uk

www.instagram.com/kfrench9/

www.facebook.com/teatimereads

Printed in Great Britain
by Amazon

26978596R00219